MW00781406

"This book shifts the focus about the causes of homelessness, moving from individualistic explanations to social and political causes. I am unaware of other books that take this perspective exclusively and thus this book will be of value to a variety of audiences, particularly undergraduates, many of whom are considering broader issues for the first time upon starting their college careers."
—**Catherine Mobley**, *Professor of Sociology, Clemson University*

"Southworth and Brallier approach homelessness with the keen eyes of sociologists who understand that the homeless make choices within constraints of a social structure over which they have little control. The authors' comprehensive treatment of the interplay between structure and agency that generates homelessness sets this book apart from other efforts to illuminate and address this social problem. The Rolling Forward Project epitomizes their thoughtful, feasible, creative, and empowering efforts to reduce homelessness by addressing one structural cause in Myrtle Beach, SC."
—**Roslyn Arlin Mickelson**, *Chancellor's Professor of Sociology, University of North Carolina at Charlotte*

"Southworth and Brallier offer a major advance in scholarship on homelessness through a compelling and insightful investigation of historical trends and policies that exacerbate poverty and constrain housing accessibility. Their extensive dataset and rich analysis expose how changes in US social and political structure over the last half century, including neoliberal economic reforms and the expansion of the non-profit industrial complex, function to increase homelessness over time. Most importantly, their analysis offers tangible pathways for solutions via affordable housing, living wages, access to mental and physical health care, and public transportation. This book shows that homelessness is a choice: a choice made by policy makers who refuse to fund basic public services that would provide a lifeline for the most vulnerable among us."
—**Jaime J. McCauley**, *Associate Professor of Sociology, Coastal Carolina University*

Homelessness in the 21st Century

An accessible and engaging introductory text on homelessness and housing policy, this timely book uses a sociopolitical framework for understanding issues of homelessness in the United States.

The authors, leading sociologists in their field, use data from over 250 interviews and field notes to demonstrate that homelessness is rooted in the structure of our society. They identify and describe the structural barriers faced by people who become homeless, including the lack of affordable housing, the stigmatization and criminalization of homelessness, inadequate access to health care, employment that does not pay a living wage, and difficulty accessing social services. Despite seemingly insurmountable odds, most of the people included in this book believe strongly in the American Dream. This book examines how the belief in the American Dream affects people experiencing homelessness. It also highlights individuals' experiences within the social institutions of the economy, the criminal justice system, and the health care system. Furthermore, this book explores how stereotypes of people experiencing homelessness affect individuals and guide social policy. The authors examine policy changes at the local, state, and national levels that can be made to eradicate homelessness, but argue that there must be a political will to shift the narrative from blaming the victim to supporting the common good.

Expertly combining history, theory, and ethnography, this book is an invaluable resource for those with an interest in housing policy.

Stephanie Southworth, PhD, is an assistant professor of sociology at Coastal Carolina University. Her current research focuses on using applied, community-based research to find structural solutions to social problems. She believes strongly in the value of educating the public about the reasons for social inequalities to reduce stereotypes. Southworth has published over a dozen peer-reviewed articles and book chapters and regularly presents the findings of her studies to community groups and conferences. She is on the Board of Directors of several organizations serving low-income community members. She, along with co-author Sara Brallier, have started several community programs based on the results of their research.

Sara Brallier is a professor of sociology at Coastal Carolina University. She teaches social inequality, sociology of religion, the sociology of aging, the sociology of death and dying, and research methods for the social sciences. Her current research focuses on housing and food insecurity. She has published numerous articles and book chapters and frequently shares her research with community groups and at academic conferences. She uses her research to inform her activism; she serves on the boards of several agencies serving marginalized populations and frequently consults with community groups interested in instigating social change. Her areas of expertise include social inequality, family demography, gerontology, and the scholarship of teaching and learning.

Homelessness in the 21st Century

Living the Impossible American Dream

Stephanie Southworth
and Sara Brallier

Routledge
Taylor & Francis Group

NEW YORK AND LONDON

Designed cover image: Getty Images

First published 2023
by Routledge
4 Park Square, Milton Park, Abingdon, Oxon OX14 4RN

and by Routledge
605 Third Avenue, New York, NY 10158

Routledge is an imprint of the Taylor & Francis Group, an informa business

British Library Cataloguing-in-Publication Data
A catalogue record for this book is available from the British Library

Library of Congress Cataloging-in-Publication Data
Names: Southworth, Stephanie, author. | Brallier, Sara, author.
Title: Homelessness in the 21st century: living the impossible
   American dream/Stephanie Southworth and Sara Brallier.
Other titles: Homelessness in the twenty-first century
Description: Milton Park, Abingdon, Oxon; New York, NY:
   Routledge, 2023. | Includes bibliographical references and
   index. |
Identifiers: LCCN 2022051124 (print) | LCCN 2022051125
   (ebook) | ISBN 9781032351605 (hardback) | ISBN
   9781032351599 (paperback) | ISBN 9781003325581 (ebook)
Subjects: LCSH: Homelessness—United States—History—21st
   century. | Housing policy—United States
Classification: LCC HV4505. S728 2023 (print) | LCC HV4505
   (ebook) | DDC 362.50973—dc23/eng/20221101
LC record available at https://lccn.loc.gov/2022051124
LC ebook record available at https://lccn.loc.gov/2022051125

ISBN: 978-1-032-35160-5 (hbk)
ISBN: 978-1-032-35159-9 (pbk)
ISBN: 978-1-003-32558-1 (ebk)

DOI: 10.4324/9781003325581

Typeset in Bembo
by Apex CoVantage, LLC

Contents

Figures

Tables

Introduction

"I have a job, but it's not enough. I can pay child support for my kids and food. Then I run out of money. I am on the list for housing, but they say it will be two years. What do I do until then?"

Andrew, 43-year-old White male

One morning, Sara burst into Stephanie's office and announced, "I feel like we are the passengers on the SS Minnow who signed up for a three-hour tour and ended up living on Gilligan's Island for years." This statement sums up our journey; we never planned to write a book. We began this research as a project for our students in which they would conduct a needs assessment survey with individuals who were staying in a homeless shelter, and we would hold a fundraiser to meet those needs. We intended for this project to last one semester. Six years and 250 interviews later, here we are.

Before conducting the surveys, we (naively) assumed that the interview participants would need new clothes, food, or other necessities. Students would then create an end-of-the-semester fundraiser to meet that need, and the study would be complete. We began collecting data in the fall semester of 2016. However, it did not take long before we understood that we could do something more meaningful and sustainable than donating food and clothes to a homeless shelter. In fact, in the initial round of surveys, most respondents said they could get many of the material items they needed. Respondents, particularly those staying at Springhouse (the homeless shelter), did not report problems finding clean clothes to wear or personal care items, and most of the respondents said that they ate well. Sentiments such as Amelia's (a 64-year-old Asian female) were represented in many interviews: "I don't have trouble getting anything. They have everything at the shelter. There is plenty of food."

We did hold a fundraiser at the end of that first semester, but when we began analyzing the interviews, we started thinking more broadly about ways in which we could make a real difference for people who are experiencing homelessness in Myrtle Beach, SC. Collecting money for food and clothes would not be enough to help anyone. Trey, a 32-year-old Black male who was staying at Springhouse, told us, "I've never seen such well-dressed homeless in my life." This finding does not necessarily mean that people experiencing homelessness in other places do not need food and clothes, but we did not see this need in Myrtle Beach. Thus, what began as a one-semester project became a study that has changed and evolved over six years and continues as of the writing of this book.

A year into our journey, we realized that most of the people who are homeless, and those who work with them, believe wholeheartedly in the American Dream. The American Dream ideology purports that everyone in the United States can be economically successful if they work hard enough. Yet, over the past six years, almost every story we heard highlighted the structural barriers to becoming housed. We met people who are working hard but see their work do little to help them escape homelessness. We talked to people who became homeless merely because they could not afford their medical bills or who cannot work because they are mentally or physically incapable of working. We spoke to people who have signed up for every subsidized housing list imaginable but who still sleep on concrete or dirt every night. We encountered people who believe so strongly in the American Dream that even as they are arrested for trespassing because they fell asleep, they still see themselves in the future as sleeping in a house with a picket fence.

It did not take long before we started asking ourselves how it is possible for the wealthiest country in the world to be so horrible at housing its citizens. We wondered why people are so eager to blame individuals who are sleeping rough or in shelters for being homeless. We did not see how it could be possible for so many people to be without a home unless there was something else going on. As we investigated the WHY, we found that the type and level of homelessness in the United States today could have been avoided. We saw no other choice but to write this book because the history of homelessness and the stories of the people we meet every day must be told.

Our goals in writing this book are twofold. Our first goal is to provide a detailed history of homelessness in the U.S. and describe how homelessness became an acknowledged, accepted, and stigmatized part of the American landscape. Second, we seek to humanize people experiencing homelessness and provide examples of how social structures and public policy have real-world consequences regarding the ability of low-wage workers, or people who are mentally or physically disabled, to house themselves. It is possible to end episodes of homelessness before they start, but it will take a concerted effort to do so. As we will show in the following chapters, homelessness is not inevitable, nor is homelessness something that should be accepted as a fact in the wealthiest country in the world.

Chapter Outlines

Section One

Homelessness is under-researched and vastly undertheorized. Very few texts address homelessness from a sociopolitical perspective or combine history and policy as a backdrop for discussing the magnitude of homelessness we see in the U.S. today. This book is separated into two sections. In the first section, we describe the history of homelessness in the United States and how federal policy and public perceptions of homelessness have shaped the type and quantity of homelessness in the United States.

In Chapter 1, we ask the questions, 1) How has the characterization of homelessness changed over time? and 2) How did the United States become a place where homelessness is an accepted and normalized part of the fabric of society? We describe the wave of homelessness that accompanied the Industrial Revolution and the Great Depression. We also discuss how societal perceptions of and responses to homelessness have changed from early America through the War on Poverty. By the 1970s, homelessness had shrunk to the point that academics and policymakers thought that the 'problem' had been solved and that homelessness would soon cease.

By the late 1970s, there began to be an ideological shift in policymakers' thinking about the role of government in people's lives, and homelessness began to increase. In Chapter 2, we discuss the change in public policy from an emphasis on the common good to an emphasis on a neoliberal marketplace in which, at least theoretically, consumers could select from various goods and services to best meet their needs without government interference. This chapter discusses the cuts to housing and social welfare programs that intensified during the presidency of Ronald Reagan and have carried through until today. We discuss how neoliberalism affected policy decisions regarding poverty and homelessness, created the non-profit industrial complex, and contributed to the dramatic growth of homelessness in the United States.

Although homelessness itself is not new, the characteristics of the "new homeless" (1980s–the present), and the risk factors for homelessness, are different today than in the past. Chapter 3 outlines several risk factors, specifically the incarceration epidemic, the commodification of space, and the lack of affordable, accessible mental health care, which became more prevalent under the new neoliberal economy. We discuss the history of mental health care and the deinstitutionalization of psychiatric patients from hospitals in the U.S. Although merely institutionalizing people is not efficient and can be cruel, the publicly funded outpatient facilities that should have replaced the closed psychiatric institutions were never fully realized. We then describe the effects of the criminal justice system on homelessness; specifically the ways in which homelessness itself has become criminalized. We outline the effects of anti-homeless policies on individuals' abilities to become and stay housed.

Chapter 4 focuses on the ways in which sociologists and other academics use theory to explain the existence of homelessness. We begin by discussing our use of grounded theory to conduct this research. Grounded theory is an inductive process in which hypotheses come from findings in the study rather than the researcher starting with a hypothesis and trying to understand whether the hypothesis is true. We describe several structural and intersection theories in more detail. We explore how theories such as Marxist theory, Guy Standing's theory of the precariat, Foucault's theory of inequality, Nicholas Pleace's "new orthodoxy," and Anthony Giddens' theory of structuration all contribute to our understanding of the complex interplay between individual actions and ideology with social structure.

Section Two

The second half of this text documents our six-year investigation into the lives and experiences of homeless individuals in Myrtle Beach, South Carolina, and connects those experiences to the broader neoliberal economy. We rely on over 250 interviews with people who are experiencing homelessness, service providers, and city officials, along with field notes from thousands of hours we spent working with and for people who are experiencing homelessness. Although all our interviews were conducted in South Carolina, our participants' problems, hopes, and dreams can be applied to many people across the country—both housed and unhoused. Our research is unique in that this is one of the few studies that ask people who are experiencing homelessness what services and resources they believe would help them secure safe and stable housing. Most of the current literature comes from the perspective of service providers, focuses on the experience of being homeless, or addresses the pathology of individuals.

In Chapter 5, we set the stage for the rest of this book and provide information that is the backdrop for our research in Myrtle Beach, South Carolina. We begin by examining how the extent of homelessness is calculated in the United States. Then we provide a more nuanced analysis of the prevalence of homelessness in Horry County, where Myrtle Beach is located. We conclude this chapter by exploring the primary non-profit agencies responsible for serving the needs of the homeless community in and around Myrtle Beach.

The American Dream ideology is the focus of Chapter 6. This ideology posits that every person, even those born into poverty, can be successful with perseverance, hard work, and determination. Most of the people experiencing homelessness who we interviewed believed in the American Dream and blamed themselves if they could not achieve it. The American Dream ideology is problematic because it ignores the structural conditions that make homelessness a social problem. Working hard will not be enough to reach the Dream if the job does not pay a living wage. Despite seemingly insurmountable odds, most of the individuals we spoke to believed that if they worked hard enough, they would make it.

In Chapter 7, we discuss the relationship between homelessness and health. When we first began this study, we were surprised by the number of people telling us that they felt 'fine,' even though they reported having severe disabilities and chronic illnesses while they were experiencing homelessness. We were not necessarily surprised that people were ill, but we were floored by how nonchalant most individuals we met were about their disabilities. We soon realized that severe mental and physical illnesses are the norm rather than the exception in the homeless community and that being 'nonchalant' is the only option for some individuals who experience homelessness in Myrtle Beach. Sixty percent of the people we interviewed indicated that they had problems with their mental or physical health. Of these sixty percent, only three percent mentioned minor health problems such as colds or coughs, while the other ninety-seven percent reported (often multiple) chronic health conditions. In this chapter, we begin by outlining what previous research has found about the extent of health conditions in the homeless community and describe what we heard from individuals in Myrtle Beach.

In Chapter 8, we describe the stigma associated with being homeless. Homelessness is stigmatized by the public as well as by service providers and government officials. Service providers and city officials use the toxic charity model to support the idea that people must work for what they are given, or they will become dependent. Even people who are experiencing homelessness often stigmatize others who are in the same situation as they are. In a country that promotes the American Dream, in which hard work is thought to lead to success, it is easy to stigmatize people who are perceived as being unsuccessful in the game of life.

In Chapter 9, we describe local, state, and federal policies that target people who are experiencing homelessness. Laws that criminalize behaviors such as sitting or standing in the wrong place, or sleeping in public, criminalize homelessness. We describe how if a person does not have a criminal record before they become homeless, they will likely have a record before they become housed. We also discuss interactions people experiencing homelessness have with the criminal justice system which we have heard and interactions we have witnessed. Most of the people we spoke with have had some interactions with the police. Some of the interactions were positive, although most of the interactions were negative. Some people who are homeless believed that the police or the criminal justice system caused them to become homeless. Others described their difficulties getting back on track after being arrested for minor infractions such as loitering.

Chapter 10 outlines several programs we started using information from our surveys. Although these programs do little to stem the prevalence of homelessness, they have served as a vehicle for us to interact with service providers and government officials. We have used this opportunity to advocate for meaningful change, especially affordable housing and expanding the homeless community's access to physical and mental health care. In 2018, we started a bicycle rideshare program in the men's shelter. We named it Rolling Forward, and started the Rolling Forward Project to help meet the unmet needs of the homeless community in Myrtle Beach. We discuss the evolution and implementation of the Rolling Forward bike-share program and other programs we have created in the community from the needs expressed by people we interviewed.

In each chapter in Section Two, we outline strategies to reduce homelessness. In the Conclusion, we bring together all of these recommendations to highlight how homelessness can be reduced if not eliminated. Throughout this text, we examine policy changes that can be made to eradicate homelessness. These policy changes can be legislated at the local, state, and national levels. Still, there must be a political will to shift the narrative from blaming the victim to supporting the common good. For example, during our study, Horry County (the county where our research is conducted) changed the public bus system—fares were eliminated, routes were revised and expanded, and buses were made easier to access and ride. Using data from before and after the changes were implemented, we saw over a 20 percent (from 52 percent to 30 percent) decrease in the number of homeless individuals who indicated that lack of affordable and reliable transportation was a barrier to their employment and accessing health care and social services.

We argue that we need a fundamental shift in how our society, including the government and service providers, views and responds to homelessness. Policies must shift from trying to "fix" the personal pathologies of people experiencing homelessness to finding structural solutions to a solvable problem, particularly for the newly homeless or people at risk of becoming homeless. This book shows that the extent of homelessness we see today is not inevitable and that, as a society, we should work to provide sustainable solutions before people become homeless rather than trying to 'fix' the individual.

Section 1

Homelessness in America

Chapter 1

How Did We Get Here? A Brief History of Homelessness

"They treat us horribly because we are homeless. We are disrespected and they treat us like garbage. I am looking for two jobs; I want a backup in case the first one doesn't work out."

Shawna, a 32-year-old White woman

Introduction

The current U.S. Department of Housing and Urban Development (HUD) definition of homelessness includes people who are spending the night in a place not meant for housing humans (such as the street, a car, or a shed or other building without running water and electricity). It includes people sleeping in a homeless shelter or who are leaving jail or hospital if they were considered homeless before entering. A person is also categorized as "homeless" if they are staying in a motel paid for by a non-profit organization or government entity, but not if they are staying in a motel room that they paid for themselves.[1] The government's definition of homelessness means that many people are excluded and unable to qualify for help from organizations that receive funding from the federal government.

This narrow definition of who is included in the category of "homeless" in the twenty-first century is an example of how homelessness is a social construct. A social construct is a definition or condition created by people in power. Social constructs can change from one time to the next and from place to place.[2] Although people in power make up social constructs, these constructs have real-world consequences. Since the mid-eighteenth century, the social construct of being "homeless" has been used to ostracize and discriminate against people without a secure place to stay in the United States.

Homelessness is not a new problem, but the current causes and consequences of homelessness are relatively recent. Today, for the first time in American history, homelessness is not caused by a lack of work but by a lack of employment that *pays a living wage* and a lack of affordable housing.

DOI:10.4324/9781003325581-2

In this chapter, we explore the following questions: What does it mean to be "homeless," and how has the public characterization of people who are unhoused changed over time? We know that homelessness is not inevitable, so how did the United States become a place where homelessness, and the stigma associated with it, is an accepted and normalized part of the fabric of society?

To answer these questions, we offer a brief history of homelessness from the eighteenth century to the present. We then explore the evolution of the depiction of people who are without permanent housing, from the "wanderers," "vagabonds," "tramps," and "bums" from the late eighteenth century through the early twentieth century to the more pervasive "new homelessness" that began showing up in the 1980s and continues to the present day. We posit that the difference in the characteristics of people experiencing homelessness today from those of the past is a result of decades of public policy decisions that have created an economy in which even workers with full-time jobs can be at risk of becoming homeless.

Early American Vagabonds

Being without a home is not new. In fact, living in a fixed residence is a relatively recent concept. In the earliest civilizations (hunting and gathering societies), people spent most of their time following their food source, so it would be inefficient for people to reside in permanent structures. The few hunting and gathering societies that remain today are still largely nomadic.[3]

In the eighteenth century, most residents of the United States were farmers, and the concept of "home" meant having a roof over their heads in the place they worked. Most families worked on farms, but even those who sold or traded goods tended to live and work in the same place. There were nomadic Native Americans, but most European residents lived in small towns, seaports, and farms.

During this time, homelessness was not typically viewed as a social problem. Individuals without a home were mainly men traveling for work or the thrill of adventure. These men, commonly seen in small port towns and emerging cities, were characterized as vagrants or beggars. They were more of a nuisance than anything, and there were not enough of them to attract policymakers' attention at the federal level. Most of the people who were houseless were former indentured servants, escaped slaves, runaway servants, or people who were displaced by Native American uprisings or war.

Although "homelessness" was not yet viewed as a social problem, many towns did not welcome the "vagrants." Numerous vagrancy statutes brought from Europe to the colonies made it illegal to loiter or be without work or other productive endeavors. If individuals who entered towns could not show that they had a skill that would be valuable to the community, they were often told to leave. If the vagrants refused to leave, and could not show proof of where they were going, they could be at risk of being branded or beaten.[4]

There were fewer unhoused women than men, but because women could not work in most occupations, being unmarried or widowed increased women's risk of becoming homeless. Churches took the most responsibility for tending to the needs of houseless individuals. The first almshouse opened in New York in 1736. The almshouse, *The House of Correction, Workhouse, and Poorhouse*, included workhouses, an asylum, military barracks, and a jail. Most of the people housed, either voluntarily or involuntarily, at the almshouse were men, but widows and unmarried women, along with their children, were also present.[5]

Vagrancy increased throughout the 1700s and the first part of the 1800s. Still, Southern landowners were more concerned with catching runaway slaves than punishing the mostly White vagabonds, and Northern employers needed the labor that the vagabonds were willing to perform. In places with shipping, mill, and mining economies, such as Rochester, New York, businesses relied on transient workers' labor, so if men had to be without housing to go to places they could work, they were seldom punished.[6]

"Homelessness" as a Social Problem in the Nineteenth Century

In the mid-nineteenth century, the Civil War, the first great depression, and the Industrial Revolution combined in a perfect storm to upend the U.S. economy. Farming machinery replaced countless workers, and wage work began to replace self-employment and farming as the primary means of earning a living. Before the Civil War, fewer than ten percent of Americans lived in cities. As the economy shifted and cities became hubs of manufacturing, people began to leave farms and travel to cities looking for work. It was at this point that "homelessness" was, for the first time, viewed as a social problem.

"Home" now had a new meaning. A person's home was no longer a place to live while they worked on a farm; it was a place where people resided while working for others. Rather than home being a place where one earned income, the rent people were paying on their homes became a drain on their finances. If one was not working, or their pay was insufficient to meet the cost of rent, individuals were forced to travel from city to city looking for work in mills or factories. Although work was frequently available in cities, the migrants typically did not have a home lined up before they began their travels. Once they entered cities, migrants often found that there was not enough available housing to meet the growing demand. The increasing numbers of men moving into cities looking for work, and the lack of adequate housing led to the stereotype of these men as "tramps" or "wayfarers."[7]

In the 1800s, residents of cities could no longer merely tell the tramps to leave; there were just too many of them. New institutions were formed to alleviate some of the problems associated with people who were homeless. Public charities stepped up to organize community members to feed and clothe the tramps, and workhouses were constructed. Across the country, police created tramp rooms in their jails to give the people without shelter a bed for the night and keep them off the streets. In his book "Citizen Hobo," DePastino notes that the "tramp army" of the 1800s was so large that "Nineteenth-century police departments often fed and lodged more people than they arrested. By the 1870s, police stations had replaced poorhouses as the primary public shelter for indigent working-age males."[8]

Almost every major city had some type of lodging for the working poor, whether it was public tenements, boarding houses, or tramp rooms. In some cities, such as the burgeoning New York City, there were entire sections that consisted only of people who did not have a permanent home and were working odd jobs in the informal economy.[9] Many chose not to become housed because the public accommodations were so poor that the migrants would rather live outside and risk being encountered by police than to stay in them.[10]

Although there were a significant number of transient and houseless women, they could not use police stations for shelter in the same way as men. Unlike men, White women were often rendered invisible to the public because of the socially constructed role of the White female as a caregiver, wife, and mother. Women could not be as easily denigrated as lazy because paid work was not considered their societal role at the time. Because the dominant ideology of the time categorized women as "dependent" on men to survive, women were often left with two choices; to become a prostitute or a ward of the charity institutions that were popping up to deal with women. Thus, women were more likely to be given housing assistance from the state than men. When the state did not come through with housing, women were more likely than men to be provided help by private charities.

While women were ignored, men without permanent housing became more stigmatized over time. The young, White, and predominantly Irish tramps that were fast becoming part of America's landscape became more visible after the Civil War as newly built railroads crisscrossed the country, allowing them to travel farther from their homes. Due to their ability to "ride the rails" and travel from place to place, the tramps were more visible, increasing the stigma surrounding people without shelter. This new transient population was stereotyped as "bums" looking for a handout and a free ride.[11]

By the late 1800s, being "homeless" became acknowledged as a unique condition. Along with people who were houseless because they were looking for work or adventure, some people lost their housing due to the physical and mental problems associated with the Civil War, illness, and natural disasters.[12] Unlike today, where a lack of housing is blamed for homelessness, being a tramp was viewed as a way of life that included random employment, migration, and unstable housing.[13] Interestingly, people who were unhoused were typically single White males. There were few minority tramps as they feared discrimination, debt peonage, vagrancy ordinances, and sundown towns (where being seen after dark could lead to imprisonment, beatings, or worse).

Like today, chronic homelessness was reserved for a minority of the poor in the nineteenth century. Despite the stigma surrounding tramping, many men were sporadically employed and housed. They moved in and out of homelessness as they moved in and out of work in factories, odd jobs, and farm labor. As most of the employment opportunities were seasonal, even in factories where they only produced goods during times when there was a demand, the wage workers of the nineteenth century moved around the country following the jobs.[14] In addition to those who were intermittently homeless as they traveled for work, numerous men became homeless due to unsafe working conditions. Every year, thousands of men were forced to take time off work to recover from injuries sustained while they were on the job. It was common for men to lose an eye or a hand while toiling in the fields or factories.

The Wall Street crash of 1873 and the resulting depression created an explosion of homelessness that caused service agencies, the government, and reporters to begin questioning what to do with the tramps.[15] Policymakers and reporters began calling attention to the "tramp army" traversing the country's landscape. Rather than dealing with the tramp problem as an issue of jobs or housing stemming from the economic conditions, policymakers began advocating for widespread arrests of the "bums." Like city officials in many areas today, policymakers believed that if there were harsh consequences for being homeless, people would find a way to house themselves. The tramp army was viewed in such a negative light that several newspapers suggested eliminating the tramps by poisoning their food or drowning them in their jail cells.[16]

In the late 1800s, cities began to open wayfarer's lodges. The stated goal of a wayfarer's lodge was to house the indigent. Still, due to the stereotype of homelessness being a consequence of laziness, the owners of the lodges often attempted to instill a work ethic in their residents. The lodges instituted work requirements to separate the deserving (those willing to work) from the undeserving poor because it was believed that those who worked were worthier of aid than those who were not working. Similar to the toxic charity ideology of today, Americans often criticized charity that did not have strings attached, noting that if people were not made to work, they would expect more charity and become dependent on handouts.[17] Women were often required to sew and men to chop wood or break stones as payment for their beds.[18]

The tramp army was given stereotypes of lazy, shiftless, and savage. The Civil War veterans and new Irish immigrants who formed much of the tramp army were easily stigmatized by housed citizens. People believed that Irish immigrants were somehow less civilized than those who already resided in the U.S. Others blamed the culture of the Civil War, arguing that Civil War veterans had gotten used to camping and living off the land and that they were averse to working.[19]

The increasing economic inequality resulting from the Industrial Revolution did not help the circumstances of the tramps. The 1873 depression had destroyed many businesses while at the same time concentrating wealth in the hands of fewer people. For individuals who lacked access to wealth, the depression meant that although jobs were available, few of them paid workers a living wage. Therein lies the problem: the tramps were needed as workers while at the same time they were reviled as "having their hands out."

The need for workers led to numerous "tramp acts" that incentivized people to work by punishing them if they were not employed. From 1876 through 1890, numerous states created laws that made even minor offenses illegal if they were committed by people who were not employed. These tramp acts required men to accept any work, and the wages they were offered for that work, or risk incarceration. At the same time, charities were being told to stop their outdoor relief as it created "dependency." The tramp acts, and the pressure on charities to stop providing relief to the tramps, were meant to coerce those without jobs to find work. The belief was that without charities to support them, tramps would find jobs to support themselves and not depend on handouts for their survival. Due to the new economic inequality and the influence of those with money, the new capitalist economy was contingent on lower-income folks depending on wage work for survival. The new industrialized America—an America in which, for many citizens, survival meant depending on others for pay—had arrived.

Homelessness 1900–1945

In the 1880s, as tramps were increasingly stigmatized, the term "hobo" began appearing in popular literature. Unlike the shiftless and lazy tramps, writers such as Jack London and Walt Whitman characterized hobos as adventurers seeking relief from the oppressive industrial capitalists and factory work. Although hobos were essentially doing the same thing as tramps, the new term romanticized the perception of some of the wanderers. Hobos were envisioned as a group of men who were 'riding the rails,' free of the oppressive constraints of society.

It was not until the early twentieth century that the term "homeless" became popularized in American culture. Writers began to explore the characteristics of people who were homeless to understand and create typologies for them. In a 1923 book, *The Hobo: The Sociology of the Homeless Man*, Nels Anderson described men who were homeless as being people who were attracted to work in railroads, mines, and harvests, either because of their need for a job or their desire for adventure. He further elaborated on the various types of men without permanent housing. He wrote:

> Almost all 'tramps' are 'homeless men,' but by no means are all homeless men tramps. The homeless man may be an able-bodied workman without a family; he may be a runaway boy, a consumptive temporarily stranded on his way to a health resort, an irresponsible, feeble-minded, or insane man, but unless he is also a professional wanderer, he is not a 'tramp.'[20]

The Great Depression and the New Deal

The Great Depression (1929–1933) of the twentieth century further increased the prevalence of homelessness. Millions of workers were laid off, including over two million construction workers. Unemployment across the country averaged about 25 percent, and in small towns such as Toledo, Ohio, and Lowell, Massachusetts, unemployment was over 80 percent.[21] Because so many people could not pay their rent, evictions skyrocketed. Hoovervilles (shanty towns or makeshift campsites) began popping up near charities and soup kitchens. The Hoovervilles were named after Herbert Hoover, who was the president at the time. Hoovervilles became so prevalent that the federal government was spurred to intervene.

The response to the effects of the Great Depression was a level of federal action never before seen in the United States. The policies, beginning under President Hoover, were a series of acts designed to help ordinary citizens house themselves and lift the economy out of the Depression. The Emergency Relief and Construction Act of 1932 (ERCA) was the first of these acts. This act allowed the Reconstruction Finance Corporation (a federal government corporation) to provide loans to non-government corporations to build low-income housing and create other public works projects. It also provided federal relief loans to states to provide welfare benefits to the poor. This act was the first federal relief paid to states by the federal government.

When President Franklin D. Roosevelt was elected, the end to the Great Depression seemed far off, so he immediately set forth to enact a series of legislative acts, which are referred to as the 'New Deal.' One of the first acts was the National Industry Recovery Act of 1933 which authorized federal funding for slum clearance and the construction of nearly 40,000 housing units.[22] This act and ERCA were important because, for the first time, the federal government supported funding to build housing specifically for low-income and middle-class people rather than sending them to poor houses or allowing them to live in shanty towns because they could not find affordable housing.

Another part of the New Deal was the establishment of the Federal Transient Service (FTS) (1933). This program helped to alleviate much of the homeless problem by setting up shelters around the country to house homeless men, women, and children. The FTS also provided food, job training, help with rent, and vouchers for rooms in boarding houses. Two years later, funding for the FTS expired, and shelters began expunging over 400,000 residents.[23] Without shelter, people who were homeless began constructing shanty towns, tents, or house-like structures created with wood, cardboard, or other materials they scavenged. Most of the time, the police quickly found them and destroyed their newly constructed shelters. Police excavated the shanty towns and corralled people who were homeless into larger "skid row" areas of cities where the authorities could better monitor them.

The Housing Act of 1934 created the Federal Housing Administration (FHA). The FHA provided federal backing for loans so that more people could buy homes. Mortgage companies could provide low-interest home loans to people with less risk. For the first time, working-class people could own their homes by making a low down payment and paying the mortgage over thirty years rather than the five or ten years previously required by mortgage companies. This act allowed more people to purchase homes and spurred the construction industry into action. Soon, suburban neighborhoods were growing around most major cities and caused a mass migration of working- and middle-class families out of cities.[24] This act was the catalyst for what was soon to become known as the American Dream.

In 1935, Congress signed the 1935 Social Security Act. This act included pensions for the elderly and Aid to Families with Dependent Children (AFDC), which authorized federal funding for assistance for individuals (primarily women) with dependent children. Further authorizations of AFDC expanded who was eligible for the program.

The Housing Act of 1937 targeted low-income people living in tenements. This act created public housing units in which tenants only paid 20 percent of their income (This was eventually raised to 30 percent.) and created the U.S. Housing Authority which is responsible for what we consider public housing today. The act got many people off the streets. However, public housing had serious problems (increased segregation, subpar construction, and its opponents called it communist).[25]

In addition to providing work in construction and social safety nets for the poor, Roosevelt also signed many acts meant to spur job creation and help banks and other industries recover. Roosevelt's policies were not unanimously applauded. There were cries of social safety nets being communist, and the economic rebound was slow. Despite the backlash, Roosevelt's policies were beginning to show results. Slowly more people became housed, and many were put back to work. Many of Roosevelt's policies, such as Social Security and FHA loans, continue to be part of the American way of life.

World War II

World War II became an economic engine that put the nation to work. The number of people experiencing homelessness shrank drastically during WWII as most able-bodied men joined the military. Men unable to enlist in the military were often employed in factories manufacturing supplies for the war. Those still experiencing homelessness were typically White males over fifty years old who had significant mental or physical health problems. Many of these individuals resided in cheap hotels, flophouses, or single-room occupancy hotels (SROs) in urban America's poorest neighborhoods and skid row areas.[26] Ironically, the people living in SROs and rooming houses during this period would be considered "housed" under HUD's current definition of homelessness. This observation underscores the difficulty in defining and studying homelessness throughout U.S. history.

The Aftermath of World War II

After WWII ended, soldiers came home to find a severe housing shortage. It was more imperative than ever that the federal government step in and do something about the housing problem. In 1949, Congress passed the Housing Act of 1949. This act authorized cities to clear their slums and replace them with public housing. Under this act, almost 800,000 units of public housing were created, but rather than replacing all the slums across cities with one- and two-family housing units, high-rise public housing complexes were created. These complexes served to concentrate poverty in smaller areas in cities, causing new problems.[27]

The 1949 Housing Act created segregated cities, but it also provided avenues for working- and middle-class White families to own homes. The act expanded the FHA and its ability to offer loans to returning GIs, resulting in a dramatic increase in the movement of people and resources out of cities and into the new suburban communities.[28] In contrast to the benefits Whites and the middle classes gained, the new housing programs caused problems for racial and ethnic minorities and residents of low-income public housing projects. Many neighborhoods were redlined, meaning that people (mostly minorities) who lived in the redlined neighborhoods could not get loans to move out of or invest in those neighborhoods. If this did not work to keep minorities from getting home loans, restrictive neighborhood covenants ensured that minorities could not move into White suburban communities.

The policies of the FHA during the 1940s created a new society: one in which being White meant living in a single-family home in the suburbs, and being a minority meant living in public housing or low-income inner-city neighborhoods, regardless of their income. When White people who could afford to leave moved to the suburbs, they took their tax dollars with them. Without tax dollars to support schools and infrastructure, these areas declined quickly.

Federal Policy's Effect on Homelessness

By the 1950s, skid rows contained a much different demographic than the wandering beggars of previous decades. Skid row residents were typically older men who were still feeling the psychological effects of recent wars and had no family to shelter them. The Housing Act of 1954 once again increased the prevalence of homelessness. This act called for more urban renewal and the destruction of most of the pay-by-the-night or -week lodging houses for the poor. Across the country, housing and rental costs were escalating, and low-income citizens (particularly those who were not White) were left with few housing options that they could afford. The lack of affordable housing caused a significant increase in the number of people who became homeless.

In contrast to previous decades, many people who were homeless in the mid-twentieth century were not beggars. Most were not "tramps" or "hobos" riding the rails looking for their next adventure. A sizable number of this group had spent much of their lives working, and many of them were still working, despite being without a home. Often, those who were unemployed received a pension or other aid from the government (public assistance, veteran's benefits, or Social Security). Their income, however, was insufficient to pay for the rising cost of housing. Another difference from previous cohorts of people without a home was that this group was largely sedentary. Mostly, they no longer traveled throughout the country for work and typically stayed where they were when they lost their housing.

The stereotype of the undeserving poor lingered, however. The skid row inhabitants were typecast as alcoholic bums who were dependent on the government. News stories portrayed people experiencing homelessness as drunkards who were too lazy to get a job. Even academic studies often reinforced the stereotype of the homeless, bum, by focusing on the personal pathologies of skid row residents. Scant attention was paid to an economy that created increasing numbers of homeless men and women.

Public responses to homelessness during this time contributed to the stereotypes. Police across the country concentrated on cleaning up skid row areas, demolishing places where people slept, and arresting the residents. As more skid rows were "cleaned up" and arrests increased, individuals experiencing homelessness began to stick to places where they thought they would be safe from police harassment. Searching for areas out of sight, they often became isolated and lost much of their social capital. As with housed citizens, people experiencing homelessness often depend on social networks for information and resource sharing. Knowing where services are and how to access those resources can become more challenging without access to information provided through their weak ties.

"Weak ties" refer to relationships that are beneficial for sharing information and resources. For example, if a person is experiencing homelessness, their weak ties may include individuals they trust to look after their possessions while they go to work or to find a place to eat. Weak ties are also important for resource sharing. A person may use weak ties to find where to go for food or shelter. Without these ties, a person can become socially and physically isolated. The result is often a lengthening of a person's time without a home. As Julian, a 48-year-old Black man who had been living in the woods for four months, told us, "You need to learn to be homeless."

The War on Poverty

The structural problems after World War II led to a targeted effort by the federal government and many state governments to get people off the street. President Johnson's War on Poverty expanded access to social programs such as food stamps, Title I, and Medicare. The expansion of social safety nets again reduced the number of people who were homeless. The programs enacted during Johnson's tenure intended to create new housing options that people could afford without the overt discrimination that had been present previously.

In 1965, President Johnson signed the Housing and Urban Renewal Act of 1965. This act expanded federal housing programs and allocated more funding for rent supplements for disabled, elderly, or low-income people. The Department of Housing and Urban Development (HUD) was also created in 1965 to provide government-backed insurance for home loans and funding for the creation of new housing. To compensate for some of the discrimination in lending of prior decades, the Fair Housing Act was passed. This act prohibited discrimination in lending and housing access based on race, disability, or family status.

In 1974, President Gerald Ford's administration passed the Housing and Community Development Act of 1974. This act combined several urban development programs into the broader Community Development Block Grant (CDBG) program. It allocates funding to states and communities for affordable housing, anti-poverty programs, and other community development activities. This legislation also formed the Housing Choice Voucher program, which gives rental subsidies to low-income individuals to use for housing. The vouchers essentially pay the landlord the remaining rent after the low-income tenant pays thirty percent of their income. This program is commonly referred to as the Section 8 program today. At least theoretically, in this program, families with vouchers can choose safe and affordable housing. Today, over two million U.S. households use the Housing Choice program. By 1980, the programs implemented in the years following World War II had significantly reduced the number of people who were homeless in America.

Conclusion

Over two centuries homelessness morphed from a way of life, to a nuisance, to a social problem; finally, with various social programs, it became something that could potentially be solved. The War on Poverty appeared to be working to reduce homelessness. By the 1970s, as more people benefitted from social safety nets, the reduction in homelessness was so pronounced that scholars began predicting an end to homelessness.[29] If our text had stopped here, we would have argued that the United States had successfully eliminated most homelessness. There would have been a happy ending.

Unfortunately, this is only the beginning. After the 1970s, it did not take long for homelessness to skyrocket again. In the early 1980s, across the country, people began seeing more homeless men, women, and children in their cities, towns, and rural areas. At first, the visibility of the new homeless took communities by surprise, but it did not take long before homelessness once again became a normalized part of the social landscape. So why then did homelessness increase so much in the early 1980s, and why haven't we been able to control it since then? The following two chapters discuss how public policy decisions created the "new homeless" we see today.

Notes

1 United States Interagency Council on Homelessness. (2018). *Key federal terms of housing among youth.* www.usich.gov/resources/uploads/asset_library/Federal-Definitions-of-Youth-Homelessness.pdf.
2 Berger, P., & Luckman, T. (1966). *The social construction of reality.* Penguin Books.
3 Fortier, J. (2009). *Kings of the forest: The cultural resilience of Himalayan hunter-gatherers.* University of Hawai'i Press. www.jstor.org/stable/j.ctt6wqr2c.
4 DePastino, T. (2005). *Citizen hobo: How a century of homelessness shaped America.* University of Chicago Press. https://doi.org/10.7208/chicago/9780226143804.001.0001.
5 NYC Department of Records & Information Services. (2015). *National archives almshouse ledgers.* www.archives.nyc/almshouse.
6 DePastino, T. (2005). *Citizen hobo: How a century of homelessness shaped America.* University of Chicago Press. https://doi.org/10.7208/chicago/9780226143804.001.0001.
7 National Academies of Sciences, Engineering, and Medicine. (2018). *Permanent supportive housing: Evaluating the evidence for improving health outcomes among people experiencing chronic homelessness.* The National Academies Press. https://doi.org/10.17226/25133.

8 DePastino, T. (2005). *Citizen hobo: How a century of homelessness shaped America*. University of Chicago Press. https://doi.org/10.7208/chicago/9780226143804. 001.0001.

9 Ibid.

10 Kusmer, K. (2001). *Down & out, on the road: The homeless in American history*. Oxford University Press. https://doi.org/10.1086/ahr/110.1.124-a.

11 Ibid.

12 Ibid.

13 DePastino, T. (2005). *Citizen hobo: How a century of homelessness shaped America*. University of Chicago Press. https://doi.org/10.7208/chicago/9780226143804. 001.0001.

14 Ibid.

15 Ibid.

16 Ibid.

17 See Chapter 7 for a discussion of how the toxic charity ideology is used in some Myrtle Beach nonprofits.

18 Ibid.

19 DePastino, T. (2005). *Citizen hobo: How a century of homelessness shaped America*. University of Chicago Press. https://doi.org/10.7208/chicago/9780226143804. 001.0001.

20 Anderson, N. (1923). *The hobo: The sociology of the homeless man*. University of Chicago Press.

21 H: History. (2009). *New deal*. www.history.com/topics/great-depression/new-deal.

22 National Academies of Sciences, Engineering, and Medicine. (2018). *Permanent supportive housing: Evaluating the evidence for improving health outcomes among people experiencing chronic homelessness*. The National Academies Press. https://doi. org/10.17226/25133.

23 Weiser, K. (2019). Hooverville of the great depression. *Legends of America*. www. legendsofamerica.com/20th-hoovervilles/.

24 Heathcott, J. (2012). The strange career of public housing: Policy, planning, and the American metropolis in the twentieth century. *Journal of the American Planning Association*, 78(4), 360–375. https://doi.org/10.1080/01944363.2012.740296.

25 Ibid.

26 Rossi, P. H. (1990). The old homeless and the new homelessness in historical perspective. *The American Psychologist*, 45(8), 954–959. https://doi.org/10.1037// 0003-066x.45.8.954.

27 The high-rise public housing projects concentrated poverty in areas without resources, often in areas of cities that were near jobs. This concentration, along with the new suburbs, created an unprecedented level of racial and economic segregation in American cities.

28 These benefits mostly went to White veterans. The impact of these benefits will be discussed in more detail in Chapter 2.

29 Rossi, P. H. (1990). The old homeless and the new homelessness in historical perspective. *The American Psychologist*, 45(8), 954–959.

Neoliberal Ideology and Homelessness

"I go here, I go there. No one understands that I can pay for housing. I just can't pay that much. I need to be able to put gas in my car and eat."

Jared, a 40-year-old White male

Introduction

Social problems, such as homelessness, do not occur in isolation and can be mitigated with good policy decisions. The magnitude of homelessness we see today was not inevitable. As we discussed in Chapter 1, in the late 1970s, homelessness had almost disappeared from the social landscape in the United States. In his 1976 book about the history of housing, Anthony Jackson wrote, "The housing industry trades on the knowledge that no Western country can politically afford to have its citizens sleep in the streets."[1] The belief that wealthy countries should be able to house all their citizens was one of the guiding forces of social policy from the Roosevelt administration (1933–1945) through the Johnson administration (1963–1969). The government-backed housing programs, and the social safety nets implemented and maintained during these years, reduced poverty and were a key mechanism for keeping people housed.

In the late twentieth century, however, there was an ideological shift in policymakers' thinking about the role of government in people's lives. Politicians began to advocate for smaller government. The focus of public policy conversations and political platforms shifted from the common good (policies to help everyone) to a more individualistic (neoliberal) perspective. Neoliberalism is an ideology based on the assumption that a free market is an efficient market and that government involvement in the lives of citizens is detrimental to the economy.

Neoliberals expect that their policies will produce an economy in which hard work is rewarded and everyone has the chance to succeed. This expectation does not mean that success is possible for everyone, however.

DOI:10.4324/9781003325581-3

Neoliberals assert that just as everyone has an equal chance to succeed, they also have an equal opportunity to fail. There is an assumption that it is the individual's personal responsibility to compete for economic survival. If a person is poor or becomes poor, neoliberals point to the individual's deficiencies in human capital, motivation, and discipline. This mindset does not consider the individual's ascribed statuses or structural obstacles to success.

When it becomes necessary for the government to intercede to support the economy, neoliberals look for ways to increase the productivity of, or competition between, businesses. In theory, businesses that are more productive and competitive can pay workers higher wages, and employees will be better able to support themselves. To increase competition, the government may lower tax rates for corporations, deregulate industries, or privatize public services. Over the last four decades, wealthy individuals and corporations have benefitted from neoliberal policies—often at the expense of lower-income citizens. Neoliberals assert that tax cuts and bailouts will trickle down benefits from the wealthy to lower-income citizens in the form of more jobs and higher wages; however, this has not been true in practice.

Regardless of market conditions, in a neoliberal economy, there will still be people who cannot work or for whom working does not pay a livable wage. The neoliberal response is to address these needs by shifting the burden of care from the state (the federal and state governments) to non-profit and for-profit organizations in the economy's private sector. Neoliberal social welfare policies treat social service agencies as a part of an economy of profit seekers who compete for customers. Theoretically, those who serve their clients best will stay in business, while the inefficient businesses will be forced to close.

In this chapter, we discuss the shift in federal policy from focusing on the common good to emphasizing personal responsibility and free-market economics from the Ronald Reagan presidency through the present. This ideological shift resulted in a reduction of social safety nets and the creation of a non-profit industrial complex that has institutionalized homelessness.

Setting the Stage for a Neoliberal Shift

President Roosevelt's 1944 State of the Union address to the United States outlined a Second Bill of Rights. He described an economy in which every citizen would have the right to a safe and "decent" place to live, the right to a good public education, and work that paid enough for food, clothing, and recreation.[2] The Second Bill of Rights never became a law. However, for several decades after Roosevelt's address, both Republican and Democratic administrations passed policies that (for the most part) aligned with Roosevelt's sentiments. Although some policies were more successful than others, the presidents following Roosevelt (Truman [1945–1953], Eisenhower [1953–1961], Kennedy [1961–1963], Johnson [1963–1969], Nixon

[1969–1974], Ford [1974–1977], and Carter [1977–1981]) invested in government programs that provided social safety nets for the poor and middle classes. These administrations acknowledged poverty as a social problem and sought structural solutions to alleviate it.

From Roosevelt's administration through the end of President Carter's term, the minimum wage grew, as did investments in the country's roads, housing, and infrastructure. Social Security and welfare benefits increased, and bills were passed that expanded civil rights for women, individuals with disabilities, and racial and ethnic minorities. Although these administrations did not eliminate poverty, and we are not applauding all of the programs they put forth, progress was being made in reducing the risk factors for homelessness. In fact, by the 1970s, homelessness had shrunk to a point where some scholars believed that it would soon disappear.

This, however, was the calm before the storm. The stage was being set for an explosion of homelessness across the country. One of the main factors in the coming explosion was the loss of affordable housing. In the 1960s and 1970s, city officials across the country began to tear down skid rows and low-income housing to "clean up" their cities. Most razed housing was not replaced. Along with the loss of affordable housing, in the 1970s, there were oil shortages, high unemployment rates, and high interest rates. As the U.S. economy started to stall, even people in the middle class began to struggle.

Ronald Reagan's Administration

Ronald Reagan's presidential platform promoted neoliberal solutions to America's problems. Reagan believed that the federal government should be less influential in citizens' lives, and he set out to dismantle many of the social programs that his predecessors had enacted. Reagan's philosophy (at least where it applied to social programs) was exemplified in his inaugural address, where he stated, "Government is not a solution to our problem. Government is our problem."[3] He believed that many of society's social troubles could be solved if the federal government would stand back and let the free market regulate the economy.

When Reagan assumed the presidency in 1981, the U.S. was about a year into an economic recession. Despite the economic suffering many Americans faced, Reagan's first major legislation cut federal funding for programs that were primarily used by the working poor. The Omnibus Reconciliation Acts of 1981 and 1982 reduced federal funding for the federal school lunch and school milk programs, Aid to Families with Dependent Children (AFDC), food stamps, Supplemental Social Security (SSI), and psychiatric care. Additionally, rather than give states money for specific programs, the funding was allocated as block grants for states to decide how to spend it.[4]

The new requirements mandated that eligibility for AFDC benefits be reassessed every four months.[5] Many low-income people move in and out of poverty, so this provision meant that over 400,000 welfare recipients lost all their benefits, and almost 300,000 recipients saw their benefits reduced. By 1988, the average welfare recipient received 35 percent less than they would have received eight years earlier.[6] There were also funding reductions for health care, childcare subsidies, and low-income housing programs. Between 1981 and 1989, the budget for HUD went from 32.2 billion to 6.9 billion dollars (a 78 percent reduction).

The Section 8 Housing Program, which provides housing support for many of the lowest-income Americans, was cut in half.[7] Funding for public housing was one of the key provisions of the Housing Act of 1937 (and subsequent reauthorizations of the act). This policy worked so well at housing low-income Americans that by 1970, there were more rental units available for low-income households than people to live in them. The cuts to Section 8 Housing increased homelessness because, even though there was available housing, without subsidies, many families could no longer afford their rent.

In 1984, Congress did not authorize any funding for new public housing units, and since then, fewer than 7,400 units have been funded each year, far fewer than what has been needed.[8] Reagan justified much of this belt-tightening by characterizing the poor as "welfare queens" out to scam the government out of taxpayers' dollars.[9] This mischaracterization of people receiving welfare is still prevalent today, even though welfare fraud is low. In fact, the Supplemental Nutrition Assistance Program (SNAP), which helps provide food to low-income families, is one of the most efficient federal programs.[10]

Reagan characterized people who were homeless in an even harsher light. His philosophy was exhibited in a 1984 interview on the television show *Good Morning America*. Despite the surge in homelessness after his election, Reagan was either so indifferent to or so uninformed about the skyrocketing number of people who were newly homeless that he told the host, "People who are sleeping on the grates—the homeless—are homeless, you might say, by choice."[11]

Reagan's administration cut government funding for non-profit organizations while simultaneously expecting the same non-profits to take over much of the responsibility of supporting low-income individuals. Between 1982 and 1984, government funding to non-profit organizations was cut by 26 billion dollars.[12] Government-sponsored worker training programs were also defunded. For example, the Reagan administration eliminated funding for the programs falling under the 1973 Comprehensive Employment and Training Act (CETA). CETA gave government-sponsored jobs to people who could not find work, and its elimination meant firing almost all the program's 300,000 employees.

CETA was replaced with the Job Training Partnership Act of 1982 (JTPA). Rather than training workers directly and providing them with jobs paid for by the federal government as was done under CETA, money would now be allocated to states. Theoretically, states would create training programs that prepared people to work in the private sector. However, from the start JTPA was criticized for inequitable funding between states, and race and gender discrimination.[13]

Replacing CETA with the JTPA is an example of the shift in the allocation of resources from the federal government to the states. Previously, the federal government mostly gave money directly to organizations and individuals. Under Reagan, a reduced level of block grant funding was allocated to states to apportion however they chose. For example, in 1981, the Reagan administration repealed the Mental Health Services Act. This act, passed by President Carter's administration, awarded money to community health centers that served clients who had mental illness. When the funding was rerouted as state block grants, many states decided to cut the amount of money they gave to community health centers, using the grants elsewhere to offset the reduced revenue stream caused by the economic recession.[14]

The Non-Profit Industrial Complex

The shift in government funding being allocated to states and organizations instead of to individuals helped to create a non-profit industrial complex that has only grown since Reagan's administration. Similar to how the military-industrial complex perpetuates itself by creating a self-feeding loop between the military, the government, and for-profit firms, the non-profit industrial complex links government and private funders to the non-profit organizations they support.

To receive funding, the organization must prove it is providing the services they advertise. The organization "shows" how many people they help by keeping records. These records are sent to the non-profit's funders as proof of the non-profit's success so that more money will be allocated to the organization. The non-profit must keep a steady stream of clients because if they do not, there will be no "results" to show the funders, and they will lose their revenue stream. If the organization were a total success and eliminated the need for their services, they would have no evidence to support their requests for money.

Although many agencies assert that their goal is to end homelessness, the reinforcing feedback loop contributes to the perpetuation of homelessness. Without funding, the organization would be forced to go out of business. Thus, it is in the non-profit's best interest to show that they are helping just enough people to continue the funding loop to keep receiving money. In contrast, if the government were to fund people directly, it would be in the government's best interest to eliminate homelessness so that tax dollars could be spent elsewhere.

Consequences

During the Reagan era, housing morphed from a right to a privilege, and, as in previous generations' wayfarers' lodges, some people were declared deserving of aid while others were not. When Reagan took office, 29.3 million people were living below the poverty line. By 1985, there were 34 million. Many of the newly impoverished remained poor while working full-time. Another consequence of Reagan's policies can also be seen in the proliferation of homelessness. A perfect storm of fewer safety nets, inflation, skyrocketing housing costs, high interest rates, Vietnam war veterans with few resources for psychiatric care, deindustrialization, and the razing of skid row areas quickly created a crisis.[15] In Reagan's first two years in office, homelessness doubled from 250,000 to over 500,000 people.[16, 17]

Because Reagan advocated for less government intervention, people often associate his administration with a reduction in government spending. The reality is the opposite. During Reagan's eight years in office, government spending increased so much that it reshaped the American economy. While Reagan's administration was cutting and reallocating funding for social programs, it was simultaneously increasing funding elsewhere. Military spending skyrocketed during the Iran-Iraq war, as did funding for foreign aid to fight communism. The federal government also funded the banking industry after the 1981–1982 economic recession. Although Reagan aimed to cut government outlays, all the extra military and corporate welfare expenditures resulted in the highest government spending since World War II. When Reagan assumed the presidency, the national debt was 738 billion dollars. By the time he left office, the debt had ballooned to 2.1 trillion dollars.[18] The United States, previously a creditor nation, became a debtor nation, and within the U.S., social inequality soared.[19]

Fixing the New Problem: The McKinney-Vento Act

During Reagan's first term, wealthy people enjoyed unprecedented prosperity, but homelessness doubled. This increase forced the Reagan administration to acknowledge how the funding cuts and reallocations contributed to homelessness. In response, Congress passed the Stewart B. McKinney Homeless Assistance Act of 1987 (Later renamed the McKinney-Vento Homeless Assistance Act).[20]

The McKinney-Vento Act contributed to the non-profit industrial complex by shifting the responsibility for services from the federal government to states and non-profit agencies. Rather than increasing welfare and housing programs at the federal level, the McKinney-Vento Act provided competitive grant funding to private and non-profit agencies. This act was the first legislation that provided federal funding for emergency homeless shelters and job training for people who experience homelessness. The initial federal government investment was 350 million dollars to fund supportive housing and emergency shelters.[21]

After the McKinney-Vento Act was passed, non-profit organizations began popping up nationwide. The act created thousands of non-profit jobs, all dependent on a steady stream of homeless "clients." In what Teresa Gowan calls "one of the greatest volunteer mobilizations of the century," thousands of students, church members, and other citizens volunteered in these non-profit organizations. Homeless shelters proliferated.[22] Rather than preventing homelessness, the McKinney-Vento Act served to institutionalize it.

The McKinney-Vento Act has been reauthorized every year since 1987 and continues to be the primary means of funding organizations serving people who are homeless. This money is not for everybody, however. The funding allocated under the McKinney-Vento Act can only be used for programs targeting individuals defined as homeless by the federal government.[23]

In sum, Reagan's policies did not cumulate in the great American Dream being achievable for all, but instead fostered a growing level of inequality. Reagan's neoliberal marketplace of goods and services shifted the burden of survival of the poor from the federal government to individual organizations and created a non-profit industrial complex that has become institutionalized. The increase in homelessness during Reagan's term did not change his mind about why people became homeless. Shortly before he left office, Reagan told ABC News, "They make it their own choice by staying out there . . . there are plenty of shelters for them to go to."[24] Reagan did not acknowledge that 'plenty of shelters' were not needed before he took office. The ideology that all one must do to succeed is to "pull yourself up by your bootstraps" was part of the new neoliberal agenda that has continued to drive social policy for the last forty years.[25]

Bill Clinton's Administration

George H.W. Bush's administration is often referred to as Reagan's third term. In alignment with the goals of the Reagan administration, President Bush continued passing policies that benefitted wealthy individuals and corporations while cutting benefits for the poor. It was not until President Bill Clinton was elected that any significant alterations were made to Reagan's agenda.

During Clinton's presidential campaign, he promised to govern for the common good. Once in office, however, most of his reforms focused on further reducing the role of government. To do this, Clinton enacted a new series of cost-cutting reforms focusing on balancing the federal budget by cutting federal expenditures on social safety nets and reducing the number of people the federal government employed.

Clinton's philosophy of governing is exemplified by the National Performance Review (NPR), an interagency task force created as part of Clinton's "Reinventing Government" initiative. One of the first recommendations of NPR was to eliminate 255,000 federal jobs. This was accomplished by authorizing government agencies to give financial incentives to employees to quit, loosening government regulations, and reducing the employees to enforce those regulations. By the time Clinton left office, 377,000 positions had been eliminated from the federal workforce.[26]

The Emergence of the Continuum of Care

The Clinton administration further institutionalized the non-profit industrial complex with HUD's "Continuum of Care" (CoC) approach for coordinating grant funding under the McKinney-Vento Act. Federal funding is allocated to CoCs in each municipality to coordinate a continuum of private and non-profit organizations to provide services for people experiencing homelessness. In theory, the goal of each CoC is to reduce the fragmented, often disconnected, delivery of social services that were common in the past. The CoCs provide support for people who have substance or alcohol use disorders or who are mentally ill while experiencing homelessness.

The CoC model is how resources are distributed today. Although the model gives guidelines on how to facilitate meeting the needs of people who experience homelessness, it does not address the structural causes of homelessness. Instead, the CoC model uses a band-aid approach to house people after they become homeless rather than blocking the emergence of homelessness before it occurs. This strategy goes back to the notion that assistance should only be offered to those "deserving" of care. The CoC framework requires people who are homeless to earn their way into permanent housing by transitioning from the street to a shelter and then from the shelter to transitional housing before they are eligible for an actual housing subsidy. Rather than chopping wood or sewing, as they did in previous generations' wayfarer's lodges, the person must prove they are worthy of aid by working their way up the CoC with case managers monitoring them at every step.[27]

Although this model can work well, it is typically underfunded. Federal funding is available for agencies that apply for it if they meet the stringent criteria, but the actual grants are seldom sufficient for the need. Most importantly, the housing subsidies initially included in these programs' funding never materialized. As in previous administrations, voters and politicians surmised that the dependent poor would not work hard to find a way out of subsidized housing and would become complacent, relying on the government for survival.

Welfare Reform

The notion of the "dependent" and undeserving poor can also be exhibited in Clinton's welfare reform. As a presidential candidate, Clinton vowed to "end welfare as we know it." Once he was elected, his administration set out to do just that. As part of the Personal Responsibility and Work Opportunity Reconciliation Act (PRWOA), Clinton replaced AFDC, which had been in place to support low-income families since 1935, with Temporary Aid to Needy Families (TANF), the primary social safety net for the extremely poor today.

TANF aims to ensure that no one freeloads and that benefits are "earned." TANF requires recipients to show that they are working or looking for work to ensure that the government is not merely issuing "handouts" to people who are unworthy of aid. TANF has time limits on how long a person is eligible to receive financial support from the government. The assumption is that poor parents will only work if they are forced to take fiscal responsibility for their children. From this perspective, mothers are no longer viewed as the caretakers of their children who should be supported. They are now considered able-bodied workers who should be in the workforce rather than *sitting around* collecting welfare.[28] TANF funding is given as block grants to states to spend on those whom each state deems eligible for aid, and it allows for the contracting of private organizations to complete the intakes of applicants.[29] Eligibility for TANF, and the funding available, can vary from state to state. For example, the maximum TANF benefit for a family of three in South Carolina is $286.00 per month, while in West Virginia, it is $542.00 per month.[30] In both cases, the subsidies are insufficient to support a family.

Due to the time limits on how long a person can receive TANF benefits (five years), and the other restrictions, TANF cut the number of welfare recipients in half. Although policymakers cheered, the reduction was not because fewer people were in poverty. In fact, the opposite was true. The time limit reduced the number of people receiving subsidies, but the low-wage work that former recipients often found typically did not result in upward mobility. The policymakers were correct that fewer people were using TANF, but poverty levels increased.

Culture of Compliance

Today, TANF is still the primary method for allocating social welfare benefits. The time limits and criteria for eligibility mean that only 23 percent of families below the poverty line receive TANF assistance. In contrast, in 1979, over two-thirds of families who were poor received some level of federal assistance.[31] The lack of financial support, and a nationwide dearth of affordable housing, mean that low-income families today have an increased risk of becoming homeless compared to prior generations.

The stringent eligibility requirements for TANF benefits and rules are designed to shape the recipients' compliance using negative sanctions. Even if the caseworker does not hold ill will for an individual the way TANF is structured stigmatizes recipients. Regardless of how much effort the person puts forth into supporting themselves, asking for help represents a moral failing in the eyes of government officials. Welfare recipients are responsible for proving that they are not abusing the system and that there "really" is a need. Recipients are subjugated to endless forms and paperwork, training, and workshops, and there are accelerating levels of sanctions for those who are unable to comply.[32]

To limit welfare caseloads, caseworkers often use strategies such as locking the doors of mandatory workshops so that anyone late is marked as non-compliant, or scheduling appointments early in the morning so that recipients can *prove* they will be able to get to work on time. These policies may sound 'normal,' but for many TANF recipients who rely on public transportation, compliance can be difficult regardless of how much effort they put forth.[33]

States can decide how much cash assistance they give to individuals with a maximum of five years in a lifetime. Some states have limits for cash transfers as low as one month per year. The lack of funding often pushes individuals to the street or into homeless shelters. In many states, becoming homeless will reduce or eliminate any cash transfers a person is allowed. The rationale for the reduction in benefits is that people are irresponsible with the money they are given, or that "they will use the money to buy drugs."[34]

The George W. Bush Administration

In 2002, the Bush administration brought the United States Interagency Council on Homelessness (USICH) back to life. The USICH, comprising 19 governmental agencies coordinating the federal response to homelessness, had been funded initially under the McKinney-Vento Act, but was not authorized from 1994–2000. In 2002, the USICH spearheaded the Chronic Homelessness Initiative. Chronically homeless individuals comprise about ten percent of the homeless population but consume almost half of the services provided (shelter days, emergency rooms, jails, and social services).[35] This initiative focused on ending chronic homelessness in ten years using a Housing First approach. The premise of Housing First is that if you provide housing for people who are chronically homeless without preconditions, they can work on their physical and mental health, sobriety, and re-entry into the workforce.

Housing First provides private landlords federal subsidies for housing people. In theory, this strategy simultaneously gets people off the streets while saving the government money. Housing First continues to be the primary strategy for dealing with chronic homelessness. However, because it is a profit-seeking strategy, there is little investment in finding structural solutions to homelessness.[36]

The Barack Obama Administration

The commitment to end homelessness continued under the Obama administration. In 2009, Obama signed the Homeless Emergency Assistance and Rapid Transition to Housing (HEARTH) Act. This act mandated that the USICH create a comprehensive plan to reduce homelessness.[37] In 2010, the USICH released the nation's first comprehensive strategy to prevent and end homelessness, titled *Opening Doors: The Federal Strategic Plan to Prevent and End Homelessness*. The plan established four key goals: (1) Prevent and end veteran homelessness in 5 years; (2) End chronic homelessness in 7 years; (3) Prevent and end homelessness for families, youth, and children in 10 years; and (4) Find strategies to end all homelessness.[38]

In the strategic plan, the UCISH mostly stayed within the neoliberal framework of prior administrations. However, the plan was advertised as an approach that considered more of the systemic predictors of homelessness rather than the pathology of individuals. The plan called for the federal government to work with private and non-profit organizations, as well as states and local governments, to implement solutions. This plan focused on evidence-based best practices for eliminating homelessness. It increased funding for HUD-VASH (housing vouchers for veterans) and combined a Housing First approach with the acknowledgment that nothing can be accomplished unless health, education, income support, and housing are also factored into the equation. Funding for Housing First went from 59 percent of HUD's grant funding in 2009 to 73 percent in 2016.[39] From 2010–2016, family homelessness decreased by 23 percent, chronic homelessness decreased by 27 percent, and veteran homelessness decreased by 47 percent. These were the first significant decreases in four decades.

The Donald Trump Administration

The Trump administration explicitly purported neoliberal approaches while simultaneously ignoring homelessness. In a tweet, which was how Trump typically relayed information, he stated, "The homeless situation in Los Angeles, San Francisco, and many other democratic party run cities through the nation is a state and local problem, not a federal one . . ."[40] Trump generally ignored the subject of homelessness or threatened to either reduce funding for homelessness or increase arrests of people experiencing homelessness.[41]

Trump's disdain for people who are homeless, along with a global pandemic, put homeless policy on the back burner for much of his four years in office. In 2020, the National Low-Income Housing Coalition (NLIHC) and the National Alliance to End Homelessness (NAEH) began sounding the alarm when Trump nominated Robert Marbut to head the USICH. These agencies asserted that Marbut's programs were based on outdated ideas and that he rejected evidence-based policies. Marbut did not support permanent supportive housing; instead, he wanted people experiencing homelessness to earn their right to beds in shelters.[42] He opposed programs that "enabled" homelessness (such as programs providing free meals) and endorsed the criminalization of homelessness.[43] By the end of Trump's term, over 30,000 more people were homeless in the U.S. than before his presidency, and far fewer people were living in government-subsidized housing.[44]

Joe Biden's Administration

Shortly after Joe Biden's inauguration, he removed Marbut as director of the USICH. Congress, via the CARES Act of 2020, and the American Rescue Plan Act of 2021, authorized billions of new dollars for programs for people experiencing housing insecurity. The American Rescue Plan invested five billion dollars into developing affordable housing, rental assistance for tenants, supportive services, and non-congregate shelter units to get people off the streets.[45] Thus, at least theoretically, the number of people placed in permanent housing should continue on an upward trajectory.[46] As of the writing of this book, CARES Act funding is dwindling, and housing prices are skyrocketing. Time will tell what the Biden administration will do.

Neoliberalism and Space

Neoliberal governance both creates homelessness and is threatened by homelessness. One of the ways that homelessness is created is through gentrification. Neoliberal social policy places profits over people. Developers and financial institutions seek to gentrify neighborhoods to increase profits, not considering the people they are displacing. As cities seek to clean up blighted areas, property values rise, rents increase, and more people are pushed to the street. There is a conundrum: non-profit agencies serving people who are homeless are typically located in areas where they can reach the most people at the lowest cost. At the same time, those places are the most likely to be gentrified. As people experiencing homelessness get pushed farther away from gentrified areas, they are not only less able to become housed, but also farther away from services that may help them.[47] The voting public—and in the case of Myrtle Beach, the tourists—blame people who are homeless, not the structural conditions that caused them to be homeless in the first place.

The situation of Bernie and Georgia (a White couple in their sixties) highlight the problem with gentrification when it comes to housing low-income residents. Bernie and Georgia are both on fixed incomes; Bernie is retired and has cancer. Georgia was hit by a bus when she was a teenager and has survived on her disability checks since. Georgia and Bernie have been renting a non-subsidized home near a public kitchen for the past decade, and they go to the public kitchen for all their meals.

Gentrification and the post-pandemic housing boom have increased property values, and the owner of the house Bernie and Georgia were renting evicted them so the house could be sold. They could not afford rent in the expensive post-pandemic housing market and most of the low-cost motels are being demolished to 'clean up the city.' There were no motels they could afford available, even temporarily. Georgia and Bernie packed up their home and put all their belongings in storage, then walked over to the public kitchen in tears. They did not know where to go.

We arrived at the kitchen after the dinner meal to meet with Bob, the director of the kitchen, and he was incensed. "Remember that couple?" He pointed to Georgia and Bernie, the only people left at the tables.

"Yes. We've talked to them many times."

"You're not going to believe this," Bob said. He told us about Bernie and Georgia's eviction and said:

> I've been letting them sleep behind the building, but someone called code enforcement. The code enforcement people came by and told me I have to kick them off the property. I've been calling around all day trying to find them a place to stay. Everything has gotten so expensive. There's nothing out there.

We asked Bob where Bernie and Georgia were going to sleep. Bob stated, "In the woods. There is nowhere else for them to go right now."

We were back at the kitchen a few days later, and so were Bernie and Georgia. "Did they find a place to stay?" we asked.

Bob sighed:

> I have been calling people nonstop. I finally got a voucher for a deposit and three months' rent and found them a place, but they can't move in for another two months. These people are old and sick. They've been sleeping outside in the woods for two weeks and are not doing well. I don't know what else I can do for them.

Bob is not responsible for housing people, yet every day there is a new person who desperately needs help and has no recourse. These two humans are just "homeless people" to the person driving by. To the people they know however, this couple are victims of circumstance, doing the best they can do to survive.

Conclusion

The neoliberal policies of the Reagan, Bush, and Clinton years institution-alized homelessness and the non-profit industrial complex and created the very thing disdained by policymakers—dependency. The neoliberal social policies of the federal government over the last four decades have created an economy in which very few resources are available to lower-income people who need them. It is difficult to climb a ladder that has lost all of its rungs. The social safety nets of the past were the rungs on the ladder, which allowed many people to escape poverty. Affordable housing is scarce, and social welfare has been practically eliminated. As a result, most low-wage workers are at risk of becoming homeless. Low-income people, even those with full-time jobs, who would not have been homeless before the 1980s, have become the new face of homelessness.

For the masses, neoliberal social policies create a social construct of the poor as somehow "different," unworthy, or a drain on their community. Neoliberal policies operate under the premise, either explicitly or implicitly, that people who are poor are irresponsible and need to be "controlled." Lawmakers promote their policies by advertising them as allowing people to be less "dependent" on government, and neoliberal corporate policies, such as tax breaks, are advertised as freeing corporations from the strong arm of government. Additionally, policymakers will hold up rags-to-riches stories of individuals who "worked hard" and succeeded without relying on a government *handout*.

Critics argue that the benefits of neoliberal policies are enjoyed by the wealthy, but the rewards rarely trickle down to the working classes. They assert that neoliberal policies are rooted in social Darwinism and that sur-vival of the fittest approaches increase poverty by stigmatizing the poor while at the same time advantaging those who are already well off. It is interesting to note that neoliberal policies in the United States have not been applied in all areas. Even during neoliberal administrations, there has still been a significant level of government investment in the military, and financial bailouts for corporations are common. Thus, critics view neolib-eralism as a marketplace for ordinary citizens and welfare for corporations and people who are wealthy.

Interestingly, because homelessness has become a sedimented part of American society, it is not in the interest of the non-profit industrial com-plex to find structural solutions to housing everyone. For the social welfare industry to thrive, homelessness can never be eradicated. Homeless clients are necessary for the non-profit industrial complex to thrive, so it is not in the interest of the non-profits to eliminate homelessness. It is also not in the federal government's interest to fund affordable housing. Affordable housing is not profitable for businesses or developers.

The success of the neoliberal marketplace is exemplified by the competition for grants and resources necessary for non-profits to survive. Because of the profit-seeking nature of capitalism, the decision-makers seek to make choices that save the company money while at the same time benefiting themselves. The executives and administrators of for-profit and non-profit companies receive large salaries, while the caseworkers and lower-level workers share very little of the financial profits. This inequality is justified by the higher-ups believing those positions are more "worthy" because the people in them work hard.[48]

The neoliberal social policies passed over the last half century were not enacted in isolation. They went hand in hand with a changing economy, an economy focused on individualism and profits above all else, including the common good. At about the same time, the United States began to shift from a largely industrialized economy to a service-centered economy; homelessness became a "normal" part of the social landscape. Many of us (one of the authors included) can still remember the stereotypical homeless "bum" riding the freight trains in search of work or excitement. Still, this vision is no longer the reality faced by most of the current homeless population. Today, an unaffordable housing market, an economy that fails to offer a living wage to many workers, the incarceration epidemic, and a shortage of resources for the mentally ill are the main factors in the prevalence of homelessness in the United States.

Notes

1 Jackson A. (1976). *A place called home: A history of low-cost housing in Manhattan*. MIT Press.
2 Sunstein, C. (2004). Economic security: A human right reclaiming Franklin Delano Roosevelt's second bill of rights. *The American Prospect, 15*(10), A24–A26.
3 Reagan, R. (1981). Inaugural address: Putting America back to work. *Vital Speeches of the Day, 47*(9), 258–260.
4 Samson, C. (1990). Inequality, the new right and mental health care delivery in the United States in the Reagan era. *Critical Social Policy, 10*(29), 40–57.
5 Stoesz, D., & Karger, H. J. (1993). Deconstructing welfare: The Reagan legacy and the welfare state. *Social Work (New York), 38*(5), 619–628. https://doi.org/10.1093/sw/38.5.619.
6 Ibid.
7 Roberts, C. (2016, June 29). The great eliminator: How Reagan made homelessness permanent. *S.F. Weekly*. www.sfweekly.com/news/the-great-eliminator-how-ronald-reagan-made-homelessness-permanent/.
8 Tucker, W. (1990, February 6). The source of America's housing problem: Look in your own back yard (Policy Analysis No. 127). *Cato Institute Policy Analysis*. www.cato.org/sites/cato.org/files/pubs/pdf/pa127.pdf.
9 Kohler-Hausmann, J. (2015). Welfare crises, penal solutions, and the origins of the "Welfare Queen." *Journal of Urban History, 41*(5), 756–771. https://doi.org/10.1177/0096144215589942.

10 Stone, C. (2013, May 16). The facts about food stamps conservatives don't want you to hear. *U.S. News and World Report*. www.usnews.com/opinion/blogs/economic-intelligence/2013/05/16/facts-show-food-stamp-program-has-a-strong-record-of-efficienty.

11 Dreir, P. (2004, May 1). Reagan's legacy. Homelessness in America. *Shelterforce*. https://shelterforce.org/2004/05/01/reagans-legacy-homelessness-in-america/.

12 Stoesz, D., & Karger, H. J. (1993). Deconstructing welfare: The Reagan legacy and the welfare state. *Social Work (New York)*, 38(5), 619–628. https://doi.org/10.1093/sw/38.5.619.

13 Race and sex discrimination in the operation of the Job Training Partnership Act: Hearing before the Employment and Housing Subcommittee of the Committee on Government Operations, House of Representatives, One Hundred Second Congress, first session, July 17, 1991.: 4.G 74/7:D 63/11. (1992). U.S. G.P.O.: For sale by the U.S. G.P.O., Supt. of Docs., Congressional Sales Office, 1992.

14 McAndrews, L. (2018). *The presidents and the poor: America battles poverty, 1964–2017*. University Press of Kansas. www.jstor.org/stable/j.ctv5j020x.9.

15 Abramovitz, M. (2014). Economic crises, neoliberalism, and the U.S. welfare state: Trends, outcomes, and political struggle. In C. Nobel, H. Strauss, & B. Littlechild (Eds.), *Global social work: Crossing borders, blurring boundaries* (pp. 225–240). Sydney University Press.

16 Ibid.

17 Burt, M. R. (1992). *Over the edge: The growth of homelessness in the 1980s*. Russell Sage Foundation. www.jstor.org/stable/10.7758/9781610440998.5.

18 Weisman, J. (2004, June 9). Reagan policies gave green light to red ink. *The Washington Post*. https://www.proquest.com/newspapers/reagan-policies-gave-green-light-red-ink/docview/409643348/se-2.

19 Abramovitz, M. (2014). Economic crises, neoliberalism, and the U.S. welfare state: Trends, outcomes, and political struggle. In C. Nobel, H. Strauss, & B. Littlechild (Eds.), *Global social work: Crossing borders, blurring boundaries* (pp. 225–240). Sydney University Press.

20 National Coalition for the Homeless. (2006, June). *Fact sheet on The Stewart B. McKinney Homeless Assistance Act*. www.nationalhomeless.org/publications/facts/McKinney.pdf.

21 Ibid.

22 Gowan, T. (2010). *Hobos, hustlers and backsliders*. University of Minnesota Press.

23 See Chapter 1 for the federal definition of homelessness.

24 Roberts, S. (1988). Reagan on homelessness: Many choose to live in the streets. *New York Times*. Section A, p. 26.

25 McAndrews, L. (2018). *The presidents and the poor: America battles poverty, 1964–2017*. University Press of Kansas. www.jstor.org/stable/j.ctv5j020x.9.

26 Osborne, D., & Gaebler, T. (1992). *Reinventing government: How the entrepreneurial spirit is transforming the public sector*. Dutton Sign.

27 Willse, C. (2015). *The value of homelessness: Managing surplus life in the United States*. University of Minnesota Press. https://doi.org/10.5749/j.ctt17572nxllse.

28 Kingfisher, C. (2007). Discursive constructions of homelessness in a small city in the Canadian prairies: Notes on destructuration, individualization, and the production of (raced and gendered) unmarked categories. *American Ethnologist*, 34(1), 91–107. https://doi.org/10.1525/ae.2007.34.1.91.

29 Nightingale, D. S., & Pindus, N. M. (1997). *Privatization of public services*. The Urban Institute.

30 Safawi, A., & Reyes, C. (2021, December 2). States must continue recent momentum to further improve TANF benefit levels. *Targeted News Service. Center for*

Budget and Policy Priorities. www.cbpp.org/research/family-income-support/states-must-continue-recent-momentum-to-further-improve-tanf-benefit.

31 Shirivastava, A., & Thompson, G. A. (2022, February 18). Cash assistance should reach millions more families to lessen hardship. *Center on Budget and Policy Priorities.* www.cbpp.org/research/family-income-support/cash-assistance-should-reach-millions-more-families-to-lessen.

32 Feldman, G. (2019). Neoliberalism and poverty: An unbreakable relationship. In B. Greve (Ed.), *Routledge international handbook of poverty* (pp. 340–350). Routledge.

33 Ibid.

34 Gowan, T. (2010). *Hobos, hustlers and backsliders.* University of Minnesota Press.

35 Kuhn, R., & Culhane, D. P. (1998). Applying cluster analysis to test a typology of homelessness by pattern of shelter utilization: Results from the analysis of administrative data. *American Journal of Community Psychology, 26*(2), 207–232. https://doi.org/10.1023/A:1022176402357.

36 See Chapter 5 for a more thorough discussion of Housing First.

37 Poppe, B. (2010, June 16). Opening doors. *The Obama White House.* https://obamawhitehouse.archives.gov/blog/2010/06/15/obama-administration-unveil-national-strategic-plan-prevent-and-end-homelessness.

38 The National Academies of Science, Engineering, and Medicine. (2018). *Permanent supportive housing: Evaluating the evidence for improving health outcomes among people experiencing chronic homelessness.* National Academies Press.

39 Eide, S. (2020). *Housing first and homelessness: The rhetoric and the reality.* The Manhattan Institute.

40 O'Donnell, K. (2020, February 10). Trump offers no new funds for homeless, even as he pressures cities. *Politico.* www.politico.com/news/2020/02/10/trump-no-new-funds-homeless-113509.

41 O'Donnell, K. (2020, February 10). Trump offers no new funds for homeless, even as he pressures cities. *Politico.* www.politico.com/news/2020/02/10/trump-no-new-funds-homeless-113509.

42 National Low Income Housing Coalition. (2021, February 22). Robert Marbut removed as executive director of USICH. *National Low Income Housing Coalition.* https://nlihc.org/resource/robert-marbut-removed-executive-director-usich.

43 National Low Income Housing Coalition. (2020, February 10). NLIHA and NAEH release new materials responding to administration's false statements on homelessness. *National Low Income Housing Coalition.* https://nlihc.org/resource/nlihc-and-naeh-release-new-materials-responding-administrations-false-statements.

44 HUD Exchange. Annual Homeless Assessment Reports. AHAR Reports—HUD Exchange.

45 FACT SHEET: Housing Provisions in the American Rescue Plan Act of 2021 (hud.gov).

46 National Alliance to End Homelessness. (2021). *State of homelessness: 2021 edition.* https://endhomelessness.org/homelessness-in-america/homelessness-statistics/state-of-homelessness-2021/.

47 Anderson, M., & Tsikalas, S. (2021). Homelessness and the American dream: An inconvenient truth. *Research Outreach.* https://researchoutreach.org/articles/homelessness-american-dream-inconvenient-truth/.

48 Willse, C. (2015). *The value of homelessness: Managing surplus life in the United States.* University of Minnesota Press. https://doi.org/10.5749/j.ctt17572nxllse.

Chapter 3

The Evolution of Risk Factors for the New Homeless

"It's crazy. The same people keep getting arrested. In and out of jail. It is a waste of time and money to keep arresting people."

Martin (41-year-old Black male)

Introduction

In Chapter 2, we discussed how, by the 1970s, homelessness had shrunk dramatically. In the 1980s, however, the U.S. began to see a wave of people who became homeless due to a series of federal public policy decisions that shifted the focus of federal policy from the common good to the good of the individual. The neoliberal shift included disinvestments in social safety nets, affordable housing, and the rise of the non-profit industrial complex. Along with these changes was a reduction in public assistance for people with mental illness and an increase in the criminal justice industrial complex.[1] These changes significantly increased homelessness in the 1980s and created an economy in which homelessness today is no longer an anomaly.

Today, a significant portion of the housed population lives one medical or financial setback away from becoming homeless. The new homeless are poorer, younger, and more likely to have a mental illness, than the prior cohorts. Other changes in the homeless population include more individuals with substance abuse issues, more families, and more individuals who are unable to qualify for housing. Today, homelessness has become an institutionalized part of American reality.

A comprehensive view of the causes of homelessness must include all the aforementioned issues because the current level of homelessness does not have just one cause. Instead, it is a consequence of many intersecting public policy decisions that, taken together, have caused an economy in which not only is it easy to become homeless, but it has also become increasingly difficult to rehouse those who are unhoused. In this chapter, we discuss the history of psychiatric care in the United States and the impact of the closure

DOI:10.4324/9781003325581-4

of state-funded institutions on the levels of homelessness we see today. We then discuss the commodification of space in a neoliberal economy and the role the criminal justice system plays in the prevalence and sedimentation of homelessness. This chapter provides context for Chapters 7 and 9, in which we explore how mental health and the criminalization of homelessness affect people who are experiencing homelessness in Myrtle Beach.

Deinstitutionalization and the Closure of Psychiatric Hospitals

Some scholars and practitioners assert that the closure of state-funded psychiatric institutions caused the wave of homelessness, while others assert that the closures have nothing to do with today's homeless crisis. We maintain that neither of these views is entirely accurate. As we stated earlier, a perfect storm of many public policy decisions created the current homeless epidemic. The closure of state-funded institutions and the corresponding lack of adequate treatment for individuals with mental illness is just one piece of that puzzle, but it is an important piece. In the following section, we outline the history of psychiatric institutions and the impact that deinstitutionalization has on homelessness today.

Mental illness can be a cause of homelessness. Treatment of mental illness is costly and can require considerable medication management, behavioral therapy, and social support. Some individuals with mental health issues do not want to take their medications, and others cannot afford the medicine they need to treat their mental health. Even for people with insurance, the costs of medication and counseling can prohibit many individuals from getting the care they need. Regardless of why a person may not be treating their mental illness, the costs can be the same: a loss of friendships and familial relationships, job and income loss, and potentially a loss of housing.

Mental illness can also be a consequence of homelessness. Living on the street or in a shelter is exceptionally stressful for most people who have nowhere else to go. Rough sleepers may have issues with the weather, finding the services they need, locating places to eat and sleep, and the stress of not feeling safe and protected. Even if a person can find a shelter to stay in, they may feel anxiety related to the shelter's rules, safety, or living in an overcrowded environment. All these stressors can deteriorate the individual's mental health.

Whether it is a cause or consequence of homelessness, we know that today mental illness is overrepresented in the homeless community compared to the general population. A 2015 report by HUD found that about 45 percent of people who are experiencing homelessness have issues with their mental health, and 25 percent of those mental health problems are severe. These numbers far outweigh the four percent of housed individuals who report having a serious mental illness.[2] The prevalence of severe mental illness in the homeless population should be concerning to policymakers.

The pervasiveness of mental illness is a direct result of the lack of adequate facilities to replace psychiatric institutions after the deinstitutionalization of psychiatric patients from hospitals and asylums in the twentieth century.[3]

Nineteenth-Century Psychiatric Care

Before the nineteenth century, children with mental illness were cared for by their parents and other family members in their homes. If the child grew into an uncontrollable adolescent or adult, they were often sent to jails or madhouses.[4] "Patients" in these institutions were boarded without much care and were "controlled" with beatings, shackles, or other severe punishments. The public largely accepted the treatment of these patients because mental illness was typically viewed as a deficiency and a moral failing. Today, most people would consider the punishments endured by "patients" in madhouses and jails as torture.

By the mid-nineteenth century, a group of reformers, led by activist Dorothea Dix, began to rally for better treatment of people who were institutionalized. The reformers believed that patients would recover quicker if they were treated kindly instead of being locked away and beaten. Building on the European model of "moral treatment," Dix rallied for government funding for facilities that would serve psychiatric patients with more compassion. Soon, state-funded insane "asylums" began to be constructed across the country.[5] The goal of the new asylums was to treat mental illness as a recoverable problem that could be mitigated with care and compassion. Many of the newly constructed institutions sought to provide patients with life skills and give people work, such as farming, to keep them busy.[6] Policymakers, and much of the public, became convinced that moral treatment was more beneficial to the patients than merely hiding people away and doling out punishment for uncontrollable behavior.

By 1870, all states had at least one taxpayer-funded public psychiatric institution. These institutions were not perfect, however. Abuse and mistreatment of patients was common, and individuals were often unfairly institutionalized. Regardless, it was believed that the asylums were better than previous institutions at treating patients. Despite some initial success, it did not take long for asylums to become dumping grounds for people who wanted to rid themselves of their elderly, neurocognitively impaired, or difficult family members. The dumping of patients, combined with the reduction of available nurses during the Great Depression and World War II, led to a reduction in social and political support for these institutions.

Twentieth-Century Psychiatric Care

After World War II, a new movement began to make waves. Activists in the Mental Hygiene Movement argued that not only should asylum patients be treated better, but that mental illness should, and could, be prevented before it became debilitating to people's lives. Advocates argued that early treatment for mental illness could keep people from ever requiring institutionalization. Mental Hygiene advocates believed that child-rearing programs for parents and teacher education could help stem the tide of mental illness in children.[7]

The emergence of psychoanalysis and shock therapy contributed to the post-WWII view.[8] Psychiatrists and mental health advocates argued that psychoanalysis, along with newly invented and safer medications, could control the more severe effects of mental illness before institutionalization would become necessary. Pressure from the Mental Hygiene Movement, and the costs associated with publicly funded asylums, led to a decline in government funding and public support of mental institutions. In response, communities began building outpatient facilities to keep individuals out of institutions, and nursing homes were established for the elderly and patients with cognitive loss. Theoretically, outpatient facilities would provide care dedicated to the individual's specific mental health care needs while simultaneously reducing the number of patients who were institutionalized.

Despite efforts by reformers, by the mid-1960s, there were still over 60,000 psychiatric patients living in asylums.[9] Civil Rights advocates pushed for the closure of state-funded mental institutions. They asserted that the therapy and training envisioned by the proponents of moral treatment were not the reality when people were institutionalized, and the asylums that were supposed to be helping people were inhumane, understaffed, and violated individuals' civil rights. Like mental hygiene advocates, civil rights supporters argued that fewer people should be institutionalized, especially those who could be treated on an outpatient basis. They called for making antipsychotic medications more widely available so more people could lead "normal" lives.

Heeding the pressure from civil rights advocates, President John F. Kennedy passed the Community Mental Health Care Act of 1963.[10] The act reduced state funding for psychiatric institutions and appropriated funding for new community health centers to treat patients on an outpatient basis. It increased the standard of care for the public institutions that were still in operation and provided federal funding for more training of health care professionals. Additionally, grants became available to communities for establishing community health centers that could meet their needs while saving the government, and taxpayers, money.

To help people pay for their care, The Medicaid Act of 1965 and Medicare provided government-sponsored health insurance for people who had health conditions or impairments and/or were retired. To encourage people to use community mental health centers rather than institutions, Medicaid and Medicare programs included higher reimbursement rates for community-based care than for institutions, excluding all reimbursements for psychiatric institutions.

Following these reforms, a series of court cases accelerated the release of psychiatric patients from institutions. In the 1966 *Lake v. Cameron* case, the court decided that hospitals must care for mentally ill patients in the "least restrictive setting" possible, with hospitalization being used as a last resort.[11] The decision stated that psychiatric patients cannot be held in institutions if there is a less restrictive alternative, such as home care or outpatient therapy, available. The *Lake v. Cameron* decision is crucial because it led to the deinstitutionalization of most psychiatric patients. A latent consequence of this decision was that, due to the stricter eligibility requirements for inpatient treatment, some people who need to be institutionalized no longer qualify.

The 1975 *O'Connor v. Donaldson* case further limited who could be admitted to psychiatric institutions by restricting who could institutionalize a person against their will. Until 1975, authorities or family members could institutionalize individuals without their consent for various reasons including "promiscuity" or "hysteria." Additionally, affluent individuals often used institutionalization to rid themselves of "difficult" family members.

The *O'Connor v. Donaldson* decision found that "A finding of mental illness alone cannot justify a state locking a person up against his will and keeping him indefinitely in simple custodial confinement."[12] This decision found further that unless a person is considered an imminent threat to themselves or others, it is unconstitutional to institutionalize them without their consent. Thus, a patient hospitalized after a psychiatric breakdown can be released on their own recognizance if physicians feel that the person is not a danger, even if they are still mentally unstable. Although the guidelines outlined in the *O'Connor* decision benefit many individuals who might have been unnecessarily institutionalized otherwise, the decision did not consider psychiatric patients who, although not dangerous, might need to be placed in a medical setting for their needs to be met.[13]

By the end of the 1970s, the *Lake* and *O'Connor* cases, Medicare, Medicaid, and the public and political distaste for psychiatric institutions, led to the closing of most public asylums. At the same time, the more stringent requirements for admittance reduced the number of patients who were eligible for hospitalization. This meant that fewer hospital beds were needed for inpatient psychiatric care. Having fewer beds available increased the incentives for hospitals to deny admission to mentally ill patients. The result was that, by the 1980s, over 80 percent of psychiatric patients had been released from institutions.[14]

Deinstitutionalization and Homelessness

So, what does all this discussion of mental institutions have to do with the extent of homelessness today? The court decisions and government mandates focusing on the care of people with mental illness had unintended consequences, including an effect on the landscape of homelessness. Today, the most visible homeless, the ones who are the least likely to garner compassion from people passing by, are those who are mentally ill. Whether they were mentally ill before they became unhoused or if being homeless caused their mental illness, people have few options when it comes to taking care of their mental health. The available options are inadequate and unaffordable to most individuals, particularly if they are homeless.

Although most people should not be institutionalized for the rest of their lives, many individuals who might have been hospitalized in the past no longer have any treatment options. Because hospitals must release their charges into the least restrictive setting, people with severe mental illness often end up circling in and out of emergency rooms and hospitals without any provision for long-term care. In addition, the directive that someone with mental illness must pose an immediate threat to themselves or others to be admitted against their will means that often people who need to be hospitalized are not. So, although the goal of deinstitutionalization was to protect the rights of individuals, these policies mean that often people with mental illness can get no help at all.

Mental Illness and Housing

Another latent consequence of deinstitutionalization is the difficulty individuals who no longer qualify for institutionalization have with securing stable housing. It is difficult to qualify for housing if a person has a mental illness, particularly if the mental illness keeps them from working. Additionally, securing disability benefits has become increasingly difficult as new, more stringent criteria for inclusion have been passed at the state and federal levels.

The most significant decrease in funding for disability and housing subsidies came from the Social Security Disability Amendments of 1980, which reduced the ability of people to qualify for benefits and to be eligible for subsidized shelter in rooming houses or SROs.[15] In 1980, some public nursing homes focused exclusively on treating people with mental illness. President Reagan's 1981 Omnibus Budget Reconciliation Act (OBRA) ended federal funding for those community nursing homes. This shifted the burden of care for mentally ill patients to non-nursing homes, which were mainly privately run, expensive, and underfunded.[16]

The consequences of the 1981 OBRA are still apparent today. People who rely on Medicaid for their mental health care often find public hospitals unwilling or unable to treat them. If the patient can locate a facility willing to accept it, Medicaid disallows payment for inpatient care that lasts over 72 hours. This can leave individuals who need help unable to afford it.[17] Private hospitals are not an option for many people because the cost of hospitalization for mental illness can run as high as $30,000 per month.[18] Thus, while wealthy patients can get their mental health needs met, lower-income individuals are left out of a system in which they cannot afford to participate. So, where do people who cannot receive adequate services go? Individuals with mental health crises often end up in emergency rooms where they are treated and then quickly released, making them more vulnerable to becoming homeless or incarcerated.

The Criminal Justice System

The purging of psychiatric institutions did not immediately increase homelessness. Housing was plentiful in the 1960s and 1970s, so many newly released psychiatric patients did not become homeless right away. By the 1980s, however, cuts to HUD and other federal programs meant that housing, particularly public and low-cost housing, became more difficult to find. From the mid-1970s through the mid-1980s, close to 800,000 low-income housing units were lost due to urban renewal, gentrification, and inflation. Over a million single-room occupancy hotels (SROs) were shut down as well, leaving individuals who depended on Social Security/Disability income unable to afford any housing at all (see Chapter 4 for a more comprehensive discussion of the loss of low-income housing).

The destruction of publicly funded mental institutions and the reduction of low-cost housing had very few, if any, adverse effects for individuals who were wealthy enough to own a home and afford private health care. However, the new normal is often devastating for low-income and mentally ill individuals. The loss of housing and psychiatric resources created an additional risk factor for becoming homeless and staying homeless—the criminal justice system. Because individuals with untreated mental illness are disproportionately poor, the criminal justice system is often their first experience of receiving treatment for their mental health issues. At the same time, being involved in the criminal justice system can deteriorate people's physical and psychological health and increase their chances of becoming homeless.

Incarceration as a Cause or Consequence of Homelessness

The populations of both people who are homeless and people who are incarcerated have exploded since the 1980s.[19] Like mental illness, becoming caught up in the criminal justice system can be either a cause or consequence of homelessness. Due to mandatory minimum sentences, the commodification of space under neoliberal regimes, and the boom in the number of behaviors that are now considered criminal, merely being homeless can be a risk factor for incarceration. Although some arrests of people who are homeless are legitimate, many arrests are for petty crimes, crimes of survival, or a result of the implicit bias of the arresting officer. For example, if a police officer encounters a person who does not have a permanent residence, they are more likely to incarcerate them for loitering than they would someone who has a home. If that person has a mental illness, the officer is more likely to arrest them than to take them to a hospital for treatment. Once the individual is released, they are left with an additional risk factor of homelessness—a criminal record.

The National Alliance to Prevent Homelessness reports that almost 50,000 people across the country enter homeless shelters after leaving jails and prisons each year. This number does not include individuals who end up on the street and are not included in the count. The risk of becoming homeless is ten times higher for people who have been incarcerated than those who have not been incarcerated, partly because individuals who become incarcerated are more likely to be poor than those who are not incarcerated.[20] Once they are released, their criminal record makes it difficult to pass the background checks to become employed or qualify for subsidized housing.[21] The risk of becoming homeless increases if the person was homeless before they were incarcerated, is a racial minority, or has been imprisoned more than once.

Gender also plays a part in the likelihood of becoming homeless after incarceration. Formerly incarcerated females are more at risk of becoming homeless than males, but males are more likely to leave prison for the street, while females are more likely to end up in shelters. Black females have the highest risk of homelessness after incarceration.[22] Gaining any type of housing, subsidized or not, is difficult if a person has a criminal record. It is easy to stigmatize someone based on a criminal record, and the circumstances surrounding the incarceration are often ignored. Without a job or steady stream of income, gaining any type of housing on one's own can be close to impossible after incarceration.[23]

The Commodification of Public Space

As homelessness began to grow in the 1980s, cities began to look for ways to "clean up their cities." "Vagrancy" was seen as a threat to capitalism. Neoliberal urban cities seek to attract capital investments and consumers, and anything that deters capitalists from investing in cities is viewed as deviant or undesirable.[24] For many city leaders, homelessness is not considered a housing problem but an intentional deviant act that could dissuade businesses from investing in an area. To sort out this problem, city leaders implement anti-homeless laws that put the interests of the business owners above the interests of people who are homeless. For example, if a business does not want someone who is homeless to stand or sit near their property, anti-homeless laws allow for the arrest of the "criminal."

Anti-Homeless Laws

Most U.S. municipalities have laws that criminalize the behaviors associated with being human and homeless. Although it is not technically illegal to be without a home, it has become illegal in practice because there are so many laws criminalizing the activities necessary for human survival if they are performed in public. Laws against crimes of survival, such as sleeping and camping, loitering, sitting, standing, begging, food sharing, living in cars, public urination, and scavenging, are all common. Rather than focusing on affordable housing, the availability of public restrooms, and public spaces to

Figure 3.1 Anti Homeless sign

accommodate these unavoidable human behaviors, municipalities often use anti-homeless laws to regulate these behaviors.

Anti-homeless laws intend to create obstacles for people who are sleeping rough so they will not stay. There is an assumption that people have a "choice" when it comes to where they experience homelessness and that if it becomes difficult to be homeless in one place, people will move on to a friendlier location. Policymakers who establish anti-homeless laws often believe that they can make the individual so uncomfortable that they will "choose" to become housed.

The National Homelessness Law Center has been tracking anti-homeless laws for almost two decades. In 2021, they reported that all but two states (Missouri and Wyoming) have anti-homelessness laws in place.[25] Anti-homeless laws ignore the structural causes of homelessness and the fact that being a human requires people to sit, stand, urinate, and sleep. The laws are designed with the assumption that homelessness is caused by the poor life choices of the individual. In part due to the prevalence of the American Dream ideology, the public often views people who are experiencing homelessness as underserving of aid. They typically accept anti-homeless laws and often advocate for more, even though anti-homeless laws do nothing to address the root causes of homelessness and may even extend the length of time people are without a home.

A story from Fort Lauderdale, FL, highlights this type of thinking. Fort Lauderdale has a law against feeding people who are experiencing homelessness. When a 90-year-old man was arrested for handing out plates of food in a public park, the mayor, Jack Seiler, justified the arrest by stating, "I'm not satisfied with having a cycle of homelessness in the City of Fort Lauderdale."[26] The mayor assumes that punishing the person who is feeding people will discourage others from doing the same, while ignoring the reason the man was feeding them in the first place.

The Criminal Justice System Contributes to Homelessness

The criminal justice system can be a risk factor for becoming homeless even when no other risk factors are present. For individuals who are insecurely housed, the fines correlated with incarceration can contribute to the loss of housing as the individual must weigh the costs of paying the court or paying their rent. It is a catch-22. If they do not pay their rent, they could be evicted, but if they pay their rent and not the court, they may be incarcerated and lose their ability to pay their rent. It is difficult to earn money in jail to pay rent for housing you are not living in.

Getting caught up in the criminal justice system is hazardous for those who are already homeless. Being ticketing or arrested for minor infractions, such as loitering, can result in fines and prison stays. Fines and fees associated with the criminal justice system can increase the length of time a person is homeless because it is difficult to save money when one is trying to pay court costs. It can also decrease the individual's ability to pay for basic needs such as food and medication.

Fear of leaving their belongings, not being able to find transportation to their court dates, and/or not being able to leave work can keep individuals from meeting their obligations to the court. Individuals who are sleeping rough may not have a mailing address to receive notice of court dates, and if they do not show up to court, it may result in a warrant for their arrest. Once an individual has a criminal record, it becomes difficult to pass the background checks that are often necessary to become employed or to secure permanent housing. Additionally, an unpaid fine can have a negative impact on a person's credit score, which creates another obstacle to qualifying for housing, especially public housing. In addition to poor credit, fines and fees can lead to lost driver's licenses, arrest warrants, and incarceration. These repercussions can cause extreme financial hardship for those already struggling to pay for food, medicine, rent, or transportation.

It took us very little time working with and interviewing people who are experiencing homelessness for us to understand that if a person does not have a criminal record before they become homeless, it will not take long before a criminal record is one more obstacle to housing.

Broken Windows Policing

Criminalizing the unavoidable human behaviors of people who are experiencing homelessness follows the broken windows model of policing. The idea behind broken windows policing is that if law enforcement cracks down on minor crimes, more serious crimes will not occur. In contrast, it is believed that more serious crimes will happen if penalties are not imposed for minor infractions. Think of it this way: if you walk by a building that looks nice and well-kept, you might not even think about throwing a rock and breaking a window. If, however, that building looks abandoned and not cared for, you may not be as hesitant to throw the rock and break the window.

Police officers using broken windows policing will look for people who are homeless and arrest them for minor infractions, such as sitting and standing. Theoretically, if people know they can and will be arrested for loitering and other petty 'crimes,' other people will not exhibit those behaviors. They may even avoid the city altogether. In theory, if a person knows they can get away with petty crimes, or crimes of survival, they will be more likely to continue these activities.[27]

The problem with using broken windows policing for homelessness is that the "crimes" committed are often unavoidable. If a person has nowhere

Figure 3.2 Photo in a local park used to prevent people from sleeping there

to go, sleeping, standing, and sitting in public are unavoidable human activities. Another problem with policing homelessness is that policing does not solve the root causes of homelessness. People become homeless due to various factors, most of which do not involve a person actively choosing to become homeless.

Policing Encampments

In the absence of permanent housing, people who are homeless often try to protect and shelter themselves in tents, either alone or as part of a community of tents. Encampments with numerous tents are sometimes organized similarly to neighborhoods with houses. People know their neighbors and often look out for each other. Across the country, many of the more established encampments even have mayors or other community leaders. Some encampments have devised systems for the removal of trash and bodily waste.

Homeless encampments, even those that are well-maintained, are illegal in most areas of the country. In Tennessee, setting up a tent in public is a felony offense which carries up to six years in prison.[28] Although people who sleep outside typically try to stay away from the public eye, homeless encampments are regularly raided and destroyed by police.

Rather than encouraging encampment residents to "choose" to become housed, sweeping encampments can reduce the residents' ability to care for themselves financially, mentally, and physically. When no other housing options are available, the destruction of homeless encampments can harm the encampment residents and the public safety and health of all community members. For instance, when police raid encampments, they disperse the residents into the community, reducing their social networks and sense of security without a backup plan for services to meet their needs. When police take personal belongings, such as pillows and blankets, during the raids, it can cause an increase in individuals' pain and illness from sleeping on the street in the cold. If clean syringes are taken from those who use them for street drugs or for medications such as insulin, they will be more likely to use dirty needles, increasing their chances of incurring an infection or other diseases. The camp residents may lose their IDs, birth certificates, medication, or other important paperwork. These losses create roadblocks on the path to housing and may increase the time the person experiences homelessness.

The concern over the physical and mental health of individuals who are the victims of these police raids has led the American Medical Association to condemn policies that promote sweeps of homeless encampments. This condemnation, however, has not led to an actual decrease in sweeps by police. As housing grows progressively more unaffordable and the wages of unskilled and semi-skilled professions have stagnated, homeless encampments are becoming more prevalent across the country. With the proliferation of camps has come an expansion of policing. Encampments exist because the people in the camps have nowhere else to go. Still, the sweeping of these camps continues, usually without offering the residents of the camps an alternate place to stay or providing other options.

The policing of encampments is not only mentally and physically exhausting to those being targeted, but it is also costly to taxpayers. Rather than taxpayer dollars being spent to build public housing, public bathrooms, or to improve a city's infrastructure, the taxes are spent maintaining jails and prisons and paying the salaries of police officers, judges, clerks, and other personnel necessary to process the crimes. For example, a 2015 study conducted in Santa Clara County, California, found that from 2007–2012, over five hundred million dollars were spent on direct services to homeless individuals. Over a third of this was spent on services related to the costs related to anti-homeless policies such as fees, probation officers, jail wardens, judges, and in-custody mental health care.[29] Another study of four cities found that the yearly costs associated with the clearing of encampments ranged from over three million dollars in Houston, TX, to over eight million dollars in San Jose, CA.[30]

In 2009, ten homeless individuals sued the City of Boise, Idaho, after being given citations for behaviors such as sitting and standing. The case, *Martin v. City of Boise,* was finally decided a decade later. In 2019, the Ninth Circuit Court of Appeals concluded that the Eighth Amendment to the Constitution prohibits laws that criminalize sleeping, sitting, or lying down in public when there is no other alternative available.[31] This decision is law in nine western states and sets a precedent for future court decisions. Two states within the Ninth Circuit's jurisdiction (Alaska and Arizona) still have camping bans.

The Eighth Amendment is meant to protect citizens against excessive punishment. It is reasonable that a person should not be arrested for sitting down on a public bench if they have nowhere else to go. Although some homeless advocates view this decision as a win, the ruling is very narrow, and it does not apply nationally; it is only in effect in the Ninth Circuit. In addition, even in the Ninth Circuit, if shelter beds are available, arresting people who are experiencing homelessness is still legal. The most significant impact of this decision is that it limits the ability of some cities to arrest people who are just passing through, or removing them from the city limits.[32]

Cities often justify clearance policies as "tough love." City leaders assert that once the camps are cleared, the encampment residents will be more likely to enter city-operated shelters. Academic studies, however, show the opposite. Sweeps of encampments do little to increase shelter usage or resolve the problem of people staying in the encampments. In communities with many low-visibility places, such as woods, people are likely to pack up and move on to another location or re-establish the encampment at the former site once the city has cleared the area.

Encampment sweeps often erode trust in authority figures and create an adversarial relationship between people who are unhoused and law enforcement or outreach workers. For example, 21 percent of people surveyed at an encampment in Honolulu, HI, said they were less able and less willing to enter shelters after sweeps. Sixty-eight percent said that the sweeps did not affect whether they went to shelters. Many of those who were surveyed asserted that the conditions in shelters were not any better than staying outside.

Other lower-level courts have found that sweeps on homeless encampments violate the Fourth Amendment's right to protection of property, the due process rights protected by the Fourteenth Amendment, and the First Amendment's right to free speech. These decisions, however, have not had an overall effect on most local jurisdictions' policies.

Conclusion: Mental Health Care and Policing in a Neoliberal Economy

When mental health issues are treated as an individual problem, and people are labeled in relationship to their problem without considering the socioeconomic, cultural, and structural conditions associated with it, it pathologizes the individual. If a person cannot work and cannot be productive, they are perceived as deviant or othered.[33] If individuals are prescribed medication and do not take it, their medical condition is viewed as their fault.[34] The person becomes labeled as their illness (i.e., mentally ill or drug addict). If these labels lead to a loss of housing, society views the individual's situation as a product of their own choices.

As with treating mental health issues, the way individuals in any society are policed reflects that society's values. In a neoliberal economy where the goal is for people to be productive, anyone who interferes with an effective market can be labeled and sanctioned as deviant. The purpose of most anti-homeless policies is to keep people who are experiencing homelessness out of sight.[35]

When police enforce anti-homeless laws, they keep their jobs and supply jobs to workers in the jails and courts. The police enforce laws that benefit business owners and attract more capital to cities. If a person chooses the "wrong" place to lay their head at night, they can be viewed as a criminal even if there is no "right" place to lay their head.[36] The person experiencing homelessness is not seeking to contest authority, but just being in the city is often considered deviant. Unknowingly, the person experiencing homelessness also provides numerous jobs to city and state employees in the criminal justice system, because this is how a neoliberal capitalist economy works.

In this chapter, we described how mental health care and policing affect the prevalence of homelessness and how difficult it can be to exit homelessness under the current social structure. It wasn't the deinstitutionalization of psychiatric patients that caused the significant swell of homelessness in the 1980s: it was the fact that there was no accessible or affordable alternative. There still isn't.

Notes

1 Jackson, A. (1976). *A place called home: A history of low-cost housing in Manhattan.* MIT Press.
2 Tarr, P. (2018, November 19). Homelessness and mental illness: A challenge to our society. *Brain & Behavior Research Foundation.* www.bbrfoundation.org/blog/homelessness-and-mental-illness-challenge-our-society/.

3 Yohanna, D. (2013). Deinstitutionalization of people with mental illnesses: Causes and consequences. *Journal of Ethics*, *15*(10), 886–891. https://doi.org/10.1001/virtualmentor.2013.15.10.mhst1-1310.

4 This was the term used in the nineteenth century.

5 Dantonio, P. (n.d.). History of psychiatric hospitals. *Penn Nursing*. www.nursing. upenn.edu/nhhc/nurses-institutions-caring/history-of-psychiatric-hospitals/.

6 Yohanna, D. (2013). Deinstitutionalization of people with mental illnesses: Causes and consequences. *Journal of Ethics*, *15*(10), 886–891. https://doi.org/10.1001/virtualmentor.2013.15.10.mhst1-1310.

7 Toms, J. (2010). Mind the gap: MIND, the mental hygiene movement and the trapdoor in measurements of intellect. *Journal of Intellectual Disabilities*, *54*(Suppl 1), 16–27. https://doi.org/10.1111/j.1365-2788.2009.01234.x.

8 Dantonio, P. (n.d.). History of psychiatric hospitals. *Penn Nursing*. www.nursing. upenn.edu/nhhc/nurses-institutions-caring/history-of-psychiatric-hospitals/.

9 Toms, J. (2010). Mind the gap: MIND, the mental hygiene movement and the trapdoor in measurements of intellect. *Journal of Intellectual Disabilities*, *54*(Suppl 1), 16–27. https://doi.org/10.1111/j.1365-2788.2009.01234.x.

10 National Council for Mental Well-Being. (2021). *Hope for the future CCBHHs expanding mental health and addiction treatment*. www.nationalcouncildocs.net/wp-content/uploads/2020/03/2020-CCBHC-Impact-Report.pdf.

11 Lake v. Cameron. (1966). 124 U.S. App. D.C. 264, 364 F.2d 657.

12 O'Connor v. Donaldson. (1975). 422 U.S. 563.

13 Flynn, K. (1985). The toll of deinstitutionalization. In P. W. Brickner, L. K. Sharer, B. Cunanan, A. Elvy, & M. Savarese (Eds.), *The health care of homeless people* (pp. 189–190). Springer Publishing Company.

14 Ibid.

15 Collin, R. W., & Barry, D. J. (1987). Homelessness: A post-industrial society faces a legislative dilemma. *Akron Law Review*, *20*(3), 409–432.

16 Yohanna, D. (2013). Deinstitutionalization of people with mental illnesses: Causes and consequences. *Journal of Ethics*, *15*(10), 886–891. https://doi.org/10.1001/virtualmentor.2013.15.10.mhst1-1310.

17 Ibid.

18 Stensland, M., Watson, P. R., & Grazier, K. L. (2012). An examination of costs, charges, and payments for inpatient psychiatric treatment in community hospitals. *Psychiatric Services (Washington, D.C.)*, *63*(7), 666–671. https://doi.org/10.1176/appi.ps.201100402.

19 Metraux, S., & Culhane, D. P. (2004). Homeless shelter use and reincarceration following prison release. *Criminology & Public Policy*, *3*(2), 139–160. https://doi.org/10.1111/j.1745-9133.2004.tb00031.x.

20 Couloute, L. (2018, August). Nowhere to go: Homelessness among formerly incarcerated people. *Prison Policy Initiative*. www.prisonpolicy.org/reports/housing.html.

21 Gowan, T. (2002). The Nexus: Homelessness and incarceration in two American cities. *Ethnography*, *3*(4), 500–534. https://doi.org/10.1177/1466138102003004007.

22 Couloute, L. (2018, August). Nowhere to go: Homelessness among formerly incarcerated people. *Prison Policy Initiative*. www.prisonpolicy.org/reports/housing.html.

23 Marxists would argue that the effects of incarceration are intentional. The criminal justice system is a money maker in a neoliberal capitalistic economy. People who experience homelessness are commodified in numerous ways to make money for a variety of industries. They serve as a source of the surplus labor pool, willing to work for low wages which benefit companies. More importantly for this chapter, the criminalization of homelessness contributes to keeping the police, social workers, the legal system, courts, and psychiatrists in business. Wilson, T. D. (2019). A note

on capitalist commodification of the homeless. *Review of Radical Political Economics, 51*(2), 298–309. https://doi.org/10.1177/0486613417741308.

24 Dasse, M. (2019). The neoliberalization of public spaces and the infringement of civil liberties. *Angles: New Perspectives on the Anglophone World, 8.* https://doi.org/10.4000/angles.595.

25 National Homelessness Law Center. (2021, November). *Housing not handcuffs state law supplement.* https://homelesslaw.org/wp-content/uploads/2021/11/2021-HNH-State-Crim-Supplement.pdf.

26 Willoughby, K. L. (2014, November 5). Fort Lauderdale arrests 90-year-old for feeding homeless. *Christian Examiner.* www.christianexaminer.com/news/fort-lauderdale-arrests-90-year-old-for-feeding-homeless.html.

27 Kelling, G. L., & Wilson, J. Q. (1982, March). Broken windows. *The Atlantic, 249,* 29–38.

28 Watt, N. (2022, August 9). In Nashville, it's against the law to live in a tent on public land: Is that the best way to deal with homelessness? *CNN.* https://www.cnn.com/2022/08/09/us/homelessness-in-nashville.

29 Flaming, D. J., Toros, H., & Burns, P. J. (2015). *Home not found: The cost of homelessness in Silicon Valley.* Economic Roundtable. https://economicrt.org/publication/home-not-found/.

30 Dunton, L., Khadduri, J., Burnett, K., Fiore, N., & Yetvin, W. (2020). *Exploring homelessness among people living in encampments and associated cost.* U.S. Department of Housing and Urban Development. www.huduser.gov/portal/sites/default/files/pdf/Exploring-Homelessness-Among-People.pdf.

31 Eighth Amendment—Criminalization of homelessness—Ninth Circuit refuses to reconsider invalidation of ordinance completely banning sleeping and camping in public-Martin v. City of Boise (2019). *Harvard Law Review, 133*(2), 699–706.

32 Ibid.

33 Esposito, L., & Perez, F. M. (2014). Neoliberalism and the commodification of mental health. *Humanity and Society, 38*(4), 414–442. https://doi.org/10.1177/0160597614544958.

34 DeFehrm, J. N. (2016). Inventing mental health first aid: The problem of psychocentrism. *Studies in Social Justice, 10*(1), 18–35. https://doi.org/10.26522/ssj.v10i1.1326.

35 Beckett, K., & Herbert, S. (2009). *Banished: The new social control in urban America.* Oxford University Press. https://doi.org/10.1093/acprof:oso/9780195395174.001.0001.

36 Wright, T. (1997). *Out of place: Homeless mobilizations, subcities, and contested landscapes.* State University of New York Press.

Chapter 4

Theoretical Explanations of Homelessness

"What they don't understand is that they need people like me to do the dirty work. The rich won't do it, but how do they expect us to live on nine dollars an hour? People would work more if you treated them better"
(Kate, a 30-year-old White female)

Introduction

In the previous chapters, we discussed the social conditions and policies that created the "new" homelessness found in the United States today. This chapter outlines how sociologists, and academics in other disciplines, use theory to explain various aspects of homelessness. There is so little research focusing specifically on this issue that Nicholas Pleace, who studies homelessness in the United Kingdom, calls the current theories "uncomfortably close to being an inconsistent mess."[1] Due to this undertheorizing, several of the theories outlined here are modified to apply to homelessness.

Social scientists use theory to explain human behavior. Like scientific theories that examine cause and effect, social scientists explore the connection between two or more social facts or conditions. There are three predominant theoretical frameworks for exploring issues of poverty and homelessness.

Micro-Level theories focus on the characteristics of individuals and, until recently, dominated the social science literature on poverty and homelessness.[2] These theories focus on identity management, drug use, and the effects of mental illness on one's ability to become and stay housed.[3] These theories also dominate social work training, published articles, and industry practices. Social work research using micro-level theories focuses on relationships between service providers and clients, interactions between people who are housed and those who are unhoused, issues of health, drugs, and safety, or the personal pathologies of homeless individuals. Most sociologists, however, understand that most micro-level theories are not conducive to finding sustainable solutions to homelessness.

DOI:10.4324/9781003325581-5

Structural theories are macro-level theories that examine the institutions (the economy, health care, housing, etc.) that enhance or limit opportunities for people in a society. In any given society, a person's actions and decisions are influenced by the structural conditions in which they live.[4] When studying homelessness, structuralists focus on how institutions affect the ability of people to become and stay housed.

A third framework explores the intersection of the individual and society. Intersection theories combine micro and macro effects. These theories examine the relationship between the structural environment and personal choices. Intersection theories examine how social structure and institutions influence one's ability to make choices, as well as the choices one makes. These theories outline how different people may become at risk as the structural environment shifts.

In this text, we take an intersectional approach to examining homelessness. We find that regardless of the time and effort a person puts into getting ahead or what personal problems they may have, the structure of the U.S. economy creates a social environment in which individuals who are born into poverty are at a higher risk of becoming homeless than someone who is not born into poverty. Additionally, the current post-industrial, neoliberal economy positions low-income people to have more involvement with the criminal justice system and higher rates of mental illness than higher-income people, neither of which they have the financial ability to handle.

Using Grounded Theory to Understand Issues of Homelessness

We did not set out to explore homelessness from a specific theoretical perspective. Because we were conducting needs assessment surveys, we might have been more likely to veer toward an individualistic (micro-level) analysis than a structural or interactionist perspective. However, at first, we did not know what we would find, so we refrained from organizing our survey via the lens of any specific theory. We knew that we wanted to learn more about the causes of homelessness and the needs of people who are homeless by asking people about their needs, so before we began, we looked for other studies that asked individuals who were homeless about their needs. We found almost none.[5] When we moved on to exploring the theories, we were again met with a dead end. We found few theories of homelessness and even fewer that did not place the blame for being homeless on the person experiencing it. Due to this dearth of research, we did not begin this study by trying to find support or reject a specific theory or hypothesis. Instead, we decided to use grounded theory to understand the causes and consequences of homelessness from the perspective of the individual.

Grounded theory is an inductive process in which hypotheses and theories come from the analysis of the research. In a study using grounded theory, the data collected are used to generate knowledge rather than verify specific hypotheses. Grounded theory is helpful for understanding complex issues in which few theoretical explanations have been developed. Whereas most scientific studies seek to test a hypothesis or answer specific research questions, grounded theory is more likely to incorporate a contextualized and explanatory analysis of social circumstances.

Grounded theory assumes that it is the responsibility of the person (or persons) conducting the research to explain, in real time, the behaviors of the people in which they are interested. The assumption is that human behavior is unique in that actions occur at a specific time and place; thus, the theory and data collected should evolve as the study continues.[6] For example, as we showed in Chapter 1, the meaning of homelessness has changed over time, as have the types of people who are likely to become homeless. In addition, homelessness in one municipality may mean something much different than it does somewhere else. If a person is homeless in a city with plenty of services and social safety nets, they may have a much different experience than in a city with few supports and safety nets. Not only will the experience be different, but the way the community perceives the problem may also be different.

After conducting our first round of interviews, we began to look for themes. The themes we found will be discussed more thoroughly in Section Two of this text. Still, the most critical finding was that the micro-level theories, which often blame the victim and are typically used to discuss homelessness, are inadequate to explain the causes and consequences of people who are experiencing homelessness in Myrtle Beach, South Carolina, and the surrounding county.

It did not take long until we realized that social structure is much more influential on whether a person in Myrtle Beach becomes homeless than how hard they are willing to work. We found people who wanted to work but could not or individuals who were working but were not paid enough to afford even the smallest apartment. We saw people who had mental health problems, criminal records, or who lacked reliable transportation. Most of the individuals we interviewed would do anything to find a path to housing, but they were met with bureaucratic obstacles at every turn. They were constantly told no, put on a list that could take years, or shuffled from place to place. Because most of the themes we found lead to structural explanations for homelessness, or how individual responses are affected by structural conditions, this chapter will focus on structural and intersectional theories. We find these theories are most applicable to what we have heard and experienced over the past six years. These theories are not meant to be comprehensive, as this is not a textbook on theory. The approaches we describe are the ones we found most helpful in explaining homelessness in a neoliberal economy as they relate to individuals' ability to achieve the American Dream.

Structural Theories

Marxist Theory

Karl Marx argued that capitalism creates social conditions in which poverty thrives. Today's Marxists view globalization, deindustrialization, the lack of affordable housing, and a decrease in labor union strength, as creating a system that benefits the elite at the expense of the poor. This view infers that in a capitalist society poor individuals are exploited by corporations who seek to get as much work out of their employees as possible at the lowest cost.[7]

Marxists assert that capitalism is only sustainable if some people are excluded from the ability to benefit. For example, a Marxist would argue that companies like Walmart pay their workers as little as possible so that the company can maximize its profit. The workers are employed there not because the work is fulfilling, but because they feel they must keep working if they ever want to succeed. They are paid just enough to believe that if they work hard enough, eventually, they can save enough money to live the American Dream, complete with a house and a picket fence.[8]

At the center of Marxist theory is the idea of a surplus labor force and the exploitation of labor. The employees of any organization are often willing to work for unreasonably low wages because they understand that they are replaceable. They know there is a surplus of labor and that if they quit, there will always be someone desperate enough to take their place, regardless of how they are treated. Wages will only increase when employers are forced to start competing for workers.

Marx, and his colleague Friederich Engels, referred to two other groups in their analysis of capitalism. The lumpenproletariat, or dangerous class, is a category that includes people such as escaped slaves, vagabonds, or "jail-birds."[9] Marx and Engels argued that in capitalist systems, the lumpenproletariat class is less valuable than the working classes (proletariat) because members of the lumpenproletariat are not productive; a person's value is derived from their ability to produce goods.[10] The working classes keep working because they fear becoming part of the lumpenproletariat. Today, people who are incarcerated or homeless would be the lumpenproletariat and are the surplus labor force of which the working classes are afraid.

Marxists argue that capitalism relies on the sense of false consciousness many working-class individuals have. An individual with a sense of false consciousness is more likely to identify with people of higher social standing because they believe that they are more like their employers than their peers. They believe they will eventually be able to work themselves to their employer's position. For example, a person who struggles to support their family with the wages they earn might agree with tax cuts for people who are wealthy because they expect to be rich themselves one day, despite the improbability that wealth is in their future.

One consequence of false consciousness is that it causes low-income people to be less likely to stand up for themselves and demand higher wages because, in their minds, their turn for success will come with hard work, tenacity, and perseverance. They are more likely to criticize others like themselves than to question those above them in social standing.

Marxists assert that false consciousness creates workers who have accepted their social and economic conditions. For any social change to occur, workers must become dissatisfied and replace their sense of false consciousness with class consciousness. Class consciousness means that the worker identifies with the people in the same socioeconomic position as they are. The class-conscious individual understands the exploitative nature of capitalism and realizes that the only way to change the system is to consolidate with others like themselves and gain power in turn.[11]

Marxists theorize that capitalism creates a system in which a person's worth is directly tied to their ability to be a source of labor. Homeless shelters often take advantage of this idea of the link between work and worthiness. It is common for homeless shelters to require residents to complete chores around the shelter in exchange for their beds. In Myrtle Beach, we see Springhouse residents working in the kitchen and laundry room, acting as drivers, and working at the front desk. Springhouse will often offer courses such as workforce development, job training, or job readiness to increase the residents' productive value. If residents attend classes and begin working, they are considered "worthy" of the help they are given.[12] A Marxist would assert that work requirements are just one of the ways for the capitalist class to regulate the behavior of the poor without doing much to help the individual.[13]

People who are homeless and use service providers become a valuable mechanism for capitalism by providing jobs. If homelessness did not exist, there would be fewer jobs for police, judges, and social workers. Homelessness also contributes to the employment of psychiatrists, emergency room doctors, ambulance drivers, EMTs, and all the other employees of hospitals. Additionally, thousands of non-profit companies and their private, state, and federal funders make a living by creating and funding programs for people who are experiencing homelessness.

The stigmatization of people who are experiencing homelessness also benefits the neoliberal economy. If a person does not have a home, it is assumed that they "must" have a problem that needs to be solved. It does not matter if many people who are housed and have a mental illness or addiction are not labeled in the same way. Blaming individuals who are homeless for their problems is another way to make the rest of the population feel better about their lives and reinforces the American Dream. "Those people" just must not have worked hard enough.[14]

As we showed in Chapter 3, the criminalization of homelessness is also a byproduct of capitalism. People without permanent housing are viewed as "offensive" to housed individuals living, working, and consuming goods and services, particularly in cities. Marxists assert that in a capitalist society, the heads of corporations and other wealthy individuals have the power. When people who are homeless panhandle, their presence is often viewed as a threat to businesses. The police may clear out and arrest individuals living in homeless encampments if businesses find them offensive. It is not for the safety of the individuals living in them. Instead, it is so that nearby retailers' profits and landowners' capital will not be threatened. The individual, regardless of whether police officers formally arrest them, is pushed into shelters or away from businesses so that their presence does not threaten the capabilities of capitalists to increase their wealth.[15]

Guy Standing

Guy Standing's theory of the precariat focuses on the effects of neoliberal political thought by exploring the global processes that set the stage for poverty and economic insecurity.[16] This theory is helpful to include in our analysis of homelessness because of the neoliberal cuts to social safety nets from the 1980s through today, which was one factor in the dramatic increase in homelessness.

According to Standing, the precariat is similar to Marx's proletariat, although Standing focuses specifically on neoliberal economies. The precariat consists of millions worldwide who have become financially unstable due to neoliberal economic practices. In this view, the global marketplace transfers any risk the owners of production may incur onto their workers.[17] Standing argues that globalization has changed the labor market. The new knowledge-based economy in the United States replaced the previous production-based market and shifted access to knowledge upward. Those who succeed in the new economy are the ones who have the information, while those with less knowledge are left in low-wage service sector industries.

This theory posits that the neoliberal marketplace in which goods and services, including social welfare, have been privatized has resulted in a growth of unemployment, insecurity, and poverty in the world's most developed nations, including the United States.[18] Because corporations are profit-seekers, businesses often move their production to countries where labor is less expensive and goods are less costly to produce. The movement of capital creates a system in which poverty and homelessness in the wealthier countries flourish along with the lower-income nations. Like the Marxist view of a surplus labor force, Standing argues that capitalists rely on the insecurity of the employees in the more well-off countries for their corporations to thrive. The insecurity of workers means they are more likely to be willing to work for lower wages, advantaging the corporations. As obstacles to success increase, the precariat grows.[19] The growth of the precariat, along with the increase in the number of extremely wealthy individuals, leaves little room for the middle class.[20]

Concerning homelessness, Standing asserts that the changing, unstable, globalized economy has resulted in an explosion of "poor work." Poor work is work in post-industrial countries where the employee at the bottom can never work hard enough or long enough to be financially sound. Although the standard of living has increased in the post-industrial era, the gap between the wealthy and the poor has grown, and people with low incomes are not better off.[21] The precariat suffers from job insecurity and housing insecurity, which has a latent consequence of causing problems with their mental health.[22]

Despite the ever-present belief in the American Dream, Standing asserts that the American Dream is far out of reach for much of the population in the United States. Individuals with low incomes, and their families, are at constant risk of becoming homeless. The insecurity faced by the precariat will continue and grow more devastating over time. Standing argues that rather than an American Dream available for all, the post-industrial economy is more like a river where most people are relieved if they stay afloat.

Standing posits that the solution to the levels of economic insecurity brought on by the new global economy is for governments to ensure that financial security is treated as a fundamental right for all. He argues that the best solution for financial security is for governments to provide a universal basic income to all people. A basic income, available for all, will allow all citizens to strive to seek opportunities over and above that provided by the government, allowing them to be more productive. Standing predicts that social unrest and violence will follow if the level of stratification between the rich and poor we see today continues without governmental involvement.

Michel Foucault

Michel Foucault's theory of inequality takes a different approach than Marx and Standing. Foucault argues that in any society, there are multiple sources of power and that all societies are products of discourse between existing power structures and individuals. The social structure and political system work together to create the dominant ideology that guides public behavior and attitudes toward work; in the United States, that dominant ideology is that of the American Dream. Because individuals believe in the American Dream, they think the U.S. is a meritocratic system. They do not fight for changes to the system because they are convinced it is just. This belief helps to maintain the existing power structure of society.

Foucault argued that the goal of power is to maintain social control by using social institutions such as religion, politics, and education to promote the dominant ideology. These institutions normalize the practices that justify the status quo.[23] This normalization creates collective agreement on the dominant ideology and helps to maintain social cohesion. For example, why do most people agree that sixteen is the correct age for children to begin driving cars or that at age eighteen, they can vote and go into the military but not drink alcohol? The collective agrees upon these norms because they have been internalized through participation in social institutions. Thus, the age one may participate in life milestones such as voting, driving, and joining the military is seldom questioned.

In Chapter 1, we discussed the notion of homelessness as a social construct and showed that homelessness is not an inevitable outcome of every society. Rather than fighting for a better provision of services, communities in the late twentieth century began accepting homelessness as a social fact. The overwhelming belief in the American Dream ideology created a society in which it became easy to place the blame for homelessness on the individual. The idea that hard work is the key to success contributes to the stigmatization of people who lose their housing and the view that they are deviant and need discipline. Whether that discipline is enacted as a social sanction, such as having people distrust them, or a formal sanction through policing is up to the community. The condition of homelessness, however, is understood collectively as a negative condition.

According to Foucault, the stigma of homelessness serves to maintain social control. The American Dream ideology is meant to keep people working and working hard. In theory, the stigma surrounding homelessness should be enough to keep people working even when they are not rewarded for doing so. The rewards for following the rules start early in life. Rewards will appear once a child enters school if not begun at home. In school, children are given stars or badges for good behavior and sanctions when their behavior declines. This reward system encourages conformity when individuals are young, and the reward system continues through adulthood. Even when the rewards are no longer present, they continue to conform to societal expectations because they have become resistant to sanctions.[24]

Foucault argued that the state uses biopolitics (the state creating social norms and enforcing these norms through stigma) to separate people into classes where some people are accepted by society and others are not. To be a member of the "accepted" class, one must meet the social norms defined by the state.[25] Foucault uses the term panopticon to establish norms to get people to adhere to those norms without punishment. For example, the NSA regularly monitors social media, phone calls, and emails. Most people accept this as a fact of living in the twenty-first century and tend to self-guard against abnormal behavior.[26] These norms, however, are not accepted overnight. If citizens in the early 1900s had been told that the government could monitor their conversations and daily activities, it would have frightened them. Today this is accepted as a fact of life.

As we showed in Chapter 2, in a neoliberal economy, the government turns over most of the responsibility for providing social services to a series of non-profit and private organizations. Foucault argues that these organizations do not try to end poverty and homelessness because they would go out of business if they did. Instead, these organizations become a part of the economy.[27] Neoliberalism, as practiced in the U.S., places the market risk in the hands of individuals—not the government.[28] Policymakers will not seek to reduce homelessness by creating low-income housing if it is not profitable because that would interfere with the free market. Additionally, spending money on non-productive people (such as people who are homeless) wastes money in a neoliberal marketplace. Thus "homelessness" becomes a business opportunity in which the goal is not to end homelessness but to profit from it. Ending homelessness would not be rational as it would cause businesses to close and people to lose their jobs.

The Interaction Between Structure and Agency

Pierre Bourdieu

Pierre Bourdieu wrote about many theoretical concepts but here, we focus on a subset of ideas related to his theory of class.[29] Bourdieu had an integrated perspective of class. He argued that capitalistism and neoliberalism reproduce social classes. He asserted that to understand social class, one must take social structure and individual agency into account. Bourdieu did not suggest that it is only capitalism and social structures that restrict social mobility, but that the choices the individual makes, or are able to make, are constrained or enhanced by the structural environment.

Like Foucault, Bourdieu was interested in the concept of power and how people in higher social classes maintain their power. He was also interested in how power, or the lack of power, affects individual experiences. Also like Foucault, Bourdieu was critical of neoliberalism. He examined neoliberal reforms in France and found that at the heart of neoliberal regimes are the interests of those who are in power. The government privatizes services so that the government will save money and businesses will profit while the people using the social services are no better off.

Regarding social reproduction, Bourdieu used the term habitus to refer to the culture in which each person is raised. The individual's culture and corresponding habitus is a collection of habits, mannerisms, tastes, and preferences that result from socialization and the beliefs and behaviors of the people around us. For example, a child who grows up in an apartment their parents pay rent on is likely to expect to live in an apartment and pay rent when they grow up. In contrast, the child who lives in a mansion will likely expect to have a mansion of their own one day. Bourdieu argued that habitus is influential in social reproduction and can inhibit social mobility for people in lower classes.

Another part of a person's habitus and social reproduction is social and cultural capital. Cultural capital includes information, knowledge, and speech patterns acceptable to higher social classes. For example, a child who vacations in Italy gains more cultural capital than a child whose parents take them camping on a local lake for vacation. Even one's taste in food can symbolize a person's social class.[30] Children from lower classes are more likely to enjoy fatty, cheap food because that is the food their parents can afford to feed them. Understanding the table manners, behaviors, and attitudes of the upper classes helps individuals show that they belong.

Social capital is important for the maintenance of social reproduction as well. Social capital includes weak ties and relationships between people. Although most people have some social capital, the social capital of lower-class individuals is often less valuable in terms of social mobility than that of wealthy individuals. This ensures that the information and resources are kept within the high-status group.[31] For example, whereas the interconnectedness between people in the upper classes may help parents get their children into good schools, provide references for the best clubs, and information for high-status jobs, lower-class social capital may be used to help with small loans, sharing food, or helping with childcare.

The social capital of people in the lower classes can also be negative. For example, if a low-income person does not have enough money for their rent, a friend may suggest going to a title loan company for an advance on their paycheck. Title loan companies charge high interest rates and can hurt one's ability to pay their other bills.

Bourdieu argued that people believe that they win or lose based on merit without understanding how social capital, cultural capital, and habitus keep them in their place. The social structure of any system is important in the maintenance of inequality and social classes because the ability of individuals to make rational choices and to be able to act on those choices depends on the structural environment.[32]

Nicholas Pleace

In the 1990s, a "new orthodoxy" began to shape research on homelessness. Like Bourdieu, Nicholas Pleace, a primary proponent of the "new orthodoxy," argues that homelessness is not caused entirely by structural factors or individual attributes.[33] Instead, structural conditions such as the cost of housing, the availability of jobs, health care, the criminal justice system, and the policies relating to homelessness, among others, create a social environment in which some groups of people are more at risk of becoming homeless than others. Pleace argues that homelessness is caused by a combination of individual and structural factors that, when taken together, create the circumstances conducive to the person becoming homeless.

For example, the lack of adequate facilities for people with mental illness creates a situation where mental illness is a risk factor for homelessness. Mental illness alone does not cause homelessness. However, if there are not adequate and affordable facilities for a person with mental illness to get the care they need, they are more likely to become homeless than someone with access to care. Shifts in social structures can also increase the risk factors of being homeless. In the past two decades, most criminal records have been digitized. Therefore, if someone commits a crime, their criminal record can follow them wherever they go. While in the past one might have been able to move to another state for work or school without anyone knowing about their criminal record, this is not possible today. Having a criminal record means getting financial aid for school or passing a criminal background check for housing or employment is more difficult. Thus, a criminal record in the twenty-first century causes more people to be at risk of homelessness. In contrast, if the record did not follow the person, they may be able to start over without the stigma because they would be more likely to be approved for employment or housing.

People's social support plays a part as well. Someone with a social safety net of family and friends to support them has a lower risk of being home-less than someone without these safety nets. When one with strong safety nets has a financial crisis, there is a support system to fall back on. A person without those safety nets may find themselves out in the cold.

Pleace argues that the structural environment does not cause homeless-ness but creates increased risks. Those risks, however, should be understood as not the same for everyone. A low-income person who gets a DUI has a greater chance of becoming homeless than someone who is wealthy and commits the same crime. In addition, Pleace argues, policies that prevent homelessness in the first place would be more successful than offering assis-tance after the person loses their housing.

Structuration

Anthony Giddens' theory of structuration asserts that social structures repro-duce social systems. At the heart of social structures, policies and resources limit what people can achieve. For example, if the minimum wage for work-ers is below what people need to afford housing, minimum-wage policies can contribute to homelessness. Social structure also provides the funda-mental outline for interactions between individuals.[34] If inequality between groups is present as part of the social structure, it affects power relationships and the way people interact with each other.

According to Giddens, society's social structure affects its citizenry's con-duct. For example, theoretically, if jobs are plentiful, education is good, housing is affordable, and political systems are stable, nations will have lower levels of homelessness because the social structure would be set up for peo-ple to succeed rather than to fail. Giddens asserts that a person's agency (their will and effort) and ability to act on their wants and needs are affected by society's social structures (housing costs, availability of education and jobs, etc.). The agent (the person) acts in a particular manner depending on the social structure they face, and social structures can either enhance or inhibit opportunities for individuals. Thus, a person may be less likely to drop out of school if they live in a high-income neighborhood, attend a good school with adequate educational resources, and feel social pressure from their peers to do well.

Giddens' theory of structuration suggests a reciprocal relationship between social structure and individual agency. Both structure and agency are equally important, and a person's habitus (social environment, values, norms, and beliefs) is a link between the two. Whereas the previously described theories place all the blame for inequality on structural factors, Giddens posits that individual actions and decisions are also important. Structuration is not a theory that blames the person for their choices, however, as it acknowledges that individual agency is strongly affected by the social structure and the habitus of the community in which the person resides.

When applying structuration to homelessness, one needs to consider: 1. The agency of the homeless individual (Do they want to, or are they able to, work and support themselves?); 2. The social structure (Are there jobs, affordable housing, job training, and education available? Are there logical rules and requirements); 3. A person's habitus (What are the norms and values of the community? Are there people supporting the person? Are there people who believe in the ability of the person? Are they in a social environment with support, or does stigma surround them?).

Giddens argues that individuals are rational actors who engage in everyday behaviors influenced by their environment. The actor's agency is affected by the social structures in place, and both structure and agency contribute to their success or failure. The person's habitus or social environment can encourage or discourage the person, thus acting as the mediator between structure and agency and affecting what the individual is capable of and interested in doing.

Giddens' theory rests on the "duality" of structure, whereby human agents make conscious choices based on the options given to them by existing power structures. Thus, some people may be more likely than others to become homeless, given their structural environment. Giddens would argue that we can neither blame the person nor the structure entirely for the fact that they became homeless. Instead, it is a combination of circumstances in which the person makes choices using the knowledge they have at the time.[35]

Giddens argues that power relations are dialectical in that power is a two-way street. People who are homeless do not have much power, but they are never entirely without any power and can resist the constraints that social structures may place on them. Because most people behave in predictable ways, they do not resist limits. By resisting, however, and acting in less predictable ways, they may begin to gain some of their power back. For example, if a teenager is in a school in which very few people graduate, they could try to graduate and go to college, thus being better off than if they just followed the crowd and dropped out.

Conclusion

The theories we have covered in this chapter are in no way a comprehensive analysis of the social science theories of poverty and homelessness, nor are our explanations meant to analyze each theory comprehensively. We would need an entire book to discuss each theory and give them adequate space. This chapter is intended to be an overview of different ways that social scientists study social problems such as homelessness to provide the reader with more of an understanding of why comprehensive solutions to homelessness have not been found.

Because we used grounded theory in our study, we conducted our research and then analyzed theories that corresponded best with our findings. Our perspective on homelessness is that although people are individual actors, their choices and decisions are influenced by social structure. People living in an economy with strong social safety nets can make different decisions than those with fewer social safety nets.

We believe that poverty and homelessness result from a society that does not take collective responsibility for the economic good of its citizens. The structure of the U.S. economy not only does little to solve homelessness but is also set up in a way that homelessness thrives. Stereotypes of the poor, and the stigma associated with poverty and homelessness, play a part in the reproduction of social classes and the preponderance of homelessness. Without pressure from their constituencies, policymakers feel no pressure to fix policies contributing to homelessness.

Notes

1 Pleace, N. (2016). Researching homelessness in Europe: Theoretical perspectives. *European Journal of Homelessness, 10*(3), 19–44.
2 Neale, J. (2007). Homelessness and theory reconsidered. *Housing Studies, 12*(1), 47–61. https://doi.org/10.1080/02673039708720882.
3 Barrett, A. L., Lewis, D. W., & Jones, S. J. (1992). Are the homeless to blame? A test of two theories. *The Sociological Quarterly, 33*(4), 535–552. https://doi.org/10.1111/j.1533-8525.1992.tb00142.x.
4 Clapham, D. (2003). Pathways approaches to homelessness research. *Journal of Community and Applied Social Psychology, 13*(2), 119–127. https://doi.org/10.1002/casp.717.
5 More specifically, we found one study that asked people experiencing homelessness about their needs (conducted from 1989–1995). Rand Corporation. *Homelessness Questionnaire.* www.rand.org/health-care/surveys_tools/homelessness.html.
6 Charmaz, K. (2003). Grounded theory. In M. S. Lewis-Beck, A. Bryman, & T. F. Liao (Eds.), *The SAGE encyclopedia of social science research methods.* SAGE.
7 Today, the bourgeoise includes wealthy individuals as well as the wealthy owners of corporations and CEOs.

8 See more about the American Dream in Chapter 6.

9 Bussard, R. L. (1987). The 'dangerous class' of Marx and Engels: The rise of the idea of the lumpenproletariat. *History of European Ideas*, *8*(6), 675–692. https://doi.org/10.1016/0191–6599(87)90164–1.

10 Marx, K. (1967). *Capital (1)*. International Publishers (original work published in 1987).

11 Lyon-Callo, V. (2008). *Inequality, poverty, and neoliberal governance: Activist ethnography in the homeless sheltering industry*. University of Toronto Press.

12 See Chapter 6 on employment for how the homeless shelters prioritize work in Myrtle Beach.

13 Hennigan, B. (2018). From Madonna to Marx: Towards a retheorization of homelessness. *Antipode: A Radical Journal of Geography*, *51*(1), 148–168. https://doi.org/10.1111/anti.12410.

14 Wilson, T. D. (2019). A note on capitalist commodification of the homeless. *Review of Radical Political Economics*, *51*(2), 298–309. https://doi.org/10.1177/0486613417741308.

15 Hennigan, B. (2018). From Madonna to Marx: Towards a retheorization of homelessness. *Antipode: A Radical Journal of Geography*, *51*(1), 148–168. https://doi.org/10.1111/anti.12410.

16 Standing, G. (2014). The precariat. *Context*, *13*(4), 10–12. https://doi.org/10.1177/1536504214558209.

17 Madanipour, A., Cars, G., & Allen, J. (1998). *Social exclusion of European cities: Processes, experiences and responses*. Jessica Kingsley Publishers and Regional Studies Associations.

18 Standing, G. (2010). *Work after globalization: Building occupational citizenship*. Edgar Elgar Publishing Limited.

19 Standing, G. (2014). The precariat. *Context*, *13*(4), 10–12. https://doi.org/10.1177/1536504214558209.

20 Ibid.

21 Dorling, D. (2014). *All that is solid: How the great housing disaster defines our times, and what we can do about it*. Penguin.

22 Standing, G. (2014). The precariat. *Context*, *13*(4), 10–12. https://doi.org/10.1177/1536504214558209.

23 Foucault, M. (1980). *Power/knowledge*. Vintage.

24 Foucault, M. (1977). *Discipline and punish: The birth of the prison*. Pantheon Books.

25 Foucault, M. (1978). *The history of sexuality*. Pantheon Books.

26 Foucault, M. (1980). *Power/knowledge*. Vintage.

27 Willse, C. (2010). Neo-liberal biopolitics and the invention of chronic homelessness. *Economy and Society*, *39*(2), 155–184. https://doi.org/10.1080/03085141003620139.

28 Foucault, M. (2008). The birth of biopolitics: Lectures at the College de France, 1978–1979 (M. Senellart & A. I. Davidson, Eds.). Palgrave Macmillian.

29 For a more complete analysis of Bourdieu's theory of class see Maryah Stella Fram's article in the Social Service Review. Fram, S. R. (2004). Research for progressive change. *Bourdieu and Social Work*, *78*(4), 553–576. or Bourdieu, P. (1986). The forms of capital. In J. G. Richardson (Ed.), *Handbook of theory and research for the sociology of education* (pp. 241–258). Greenwood Press.

30 Bourdieu, P. (1984). *Distinction: A social critique of the judgment of taste* (R. Nice, Trans.). Harvard University Press. (Original work published 1979)

31 Bourdieu, P. (1986). The forms of capital. In J. G. Richardson (Ed.), *Handbook of theory and research for the sociology of education* (pp. 241–258). Greenwood Press.

32 For a more thorough description of Bourdieu's theories including a discussion of doxa, symbolic capital and field, please see: Bourdieu, P. (1991). *Language and symbolic power* (J. Thompson, Ed., G. Raymond & M. Adamson, Trans.). Polity Press.

illustrated, reprint edition at Google Books. Harvard University Press. Bourdieu, P. (2021). *Forms of capital: General sociology, volume 3 lectures at the Collège de France 1983–1984*. Polity Press.

33 Please, N. (2000). The new consensus, the old consensus and the provision of services for people sleeping rough. *Housing Studies, 15*(4), 581–594. https://doi.org/10.1080/02673030050081113.

34 Giddens, A. (1984). *The constitution of society: Outline of the theory of structuration*. University of California Press.

35 Ibid.

Research on Homelessness in Myrtle Beach, SC

Chapter 5

Counting and Providing Services for People Experiencing Homelessness

"Without a place to live, life is unmanageable."
—Joel (60-year-old White male)

Introduction

In this chapter, we set the stage for the rest of this book and provide information that is the backdrop for our research in Myrtle Beach. We begin by examining how the extent of homelessness is calculated in the United States. Then we provide a more nuanced analysis of the prevalence of homelessness in Horry County, where Myrtle Beach is located. We conclude this chapter by exploring the primary non-profit agencies responsible for serving the needs of the homeless community in Myrtle Beach.[1]

Counting People Who Are Experiencing Homelessness

It is difficult to get an absolute number of people who experience homelessness in Myrtle Beach, or in any other U.S. city, despite the U.S. government's efforts to do so. As discussed in Chapter 3, HUD (The U.S. Department of Housing and Urban Development) has been using the Point in Time Count since 1983 to understand the extent of homelessness in the United States. The government uses these counts to target resources where they are most needed. Theoretically, this should be the way resources are allocated. We say "theoretically" because the PIT count is notoriously flawed. As discussed in Chapter 1, HUD's narrow definition of homelessness excludes many people from being counted. Additionally, despite the good intentions and effort of professionals and community members, the reliance on volunteers to do the work contributes to the vast undercount of the number of people unhoused at any time.[2]

DOI:10.4324/9781003325581-7

Another issue associated with the PIT count is the criminalization of homelessness. Hundreds, if not thousands, of individuals who are incarcerated on any given night will be homeless upon release. They are not included in the PIT count if they are incarcerated during the count. The significance of jails in undercounting homelessness is evident when examining the results of the 2017 PIT count in Houston, Texas. That year, Houston's CoC (Continuum of Care) decided to expand the PIT count to include those individuals who were in the county jail but would not have a place to stay when they left. After the Houston CoC included those incarcerated individuals who would be without housing upon their release, their count increased by 57 percent.[3]

Fear of the police can also lead people who are sleeping rough to hide from anyone who wants to ask them questions. For example, because Myrtle Beach has a tourist-centered economy, the city is incentivized to keep homelessness out of public view. The local police often encourage people experiencing homelessness to remove themselves from public view, sometimes ticketing or arresting them for minor infractions such as loitering.[4] This method of policing has pushed many people who are sleeping rough in Myrtle Beach farther and farther into the woods so that they will not be found, ticketed, or arrested. This exodus into the woods makes it difficult for PIT count volunteers to locate and count them.

Comparing HMIS Data to the PIT Count

Most people involved in the PIT count, including the volunteers and people working to organize the count, understand how difficult getting a reliable count can be. It can be frustrating because the PIT count takes a lot of planning, human resources, time, and effort. South Carolina has sought to document the true extent of homelessness for the last several years using other means. Starting in 2018, South Carolina began to use information gathered from their Homeless Management Information System (HMIS), in addition to reporting the numbers from the PIT count.

The HMIS system is a website for service providers to keep track of the agencies that people who are homeless, or at risk of homelessness, use. Each person who enters the system is given a unique identifier, and all the service providers who have access to HMIS can record the services they provide to the individual. For example, if a person visits one agency to receive help with housing and another to access clothes or food, all the other agencies using HMIS can see where the person has been and what resources they have accessed. The service providers can also see the outcomes of these services. For instance, if a person was housed and subsequently lost their housing, it would be documented in the HMIS system. Although the HMIS data only tracks people who are seeking help for issues related to homelessness and not those who may be experiencing homelessness but are not seeking help from service organizations, using HMIS is a more accurate reflection of the actual number of people experiencing homelessness in the state. In 2020, the *South Carolina State of Homelessness Report* shows that the PIT count found 4,268 people who were homeless on a single night in January; however, throughout the year, there were over twice as many (10,986) unique individuals logged into the HMIS system in South Carolina.[5]

Table 5.1 compares the numbers counted in 2020 via the PIT count and HMIS. About 65 percent of the individuals who were entered into HMIS for the first time were sleeping rough. This percentage is higher than the PIT count volunteers found. This discrepancy is likely because individuals who sleep rough are less likely to be found and counted during the PIT count.

In both the PIT count and the HMIS count, males are overrepresented and females are underrepresented. People who are Black are overrepresented in both calculations, but the percentage of people who are Black is higher in the HMIS system (58 percent) compared to the PIT count (50 percent).

Table 5.1 Comparison of HMIS and Point in Time Count Data in South Carolina

	HMIS	Point in Time Count
Total	10,986	4,268
Housing Status		
Sheltered	NA	2,564 (60.1%)
Unsheltered	7140 (65%)	1,703 (39.9%)
Single	7,748 (86.2%)	3,419 (80.1%)
Family or household	1263 (11.5%)	840 (19.7%)
Unaccompanied Youth	209 (2.3%)	54* (1.2%)
Gender		
Male	6,843 (62.3%)	2,695 (63.1%)
Female	4041 (36.8%)	1,564 (36.6%)
Transgender/Gender nonconforming	14 (<01%)	5 (<.01%)
Race		
Black	6314 (57.5%)	2147 (50.3%)
White	3940 (35.9%)	1882 (44%)
Native Am/Pac Islander	71 (.9%)	61 (1.4%)
Asian	24 (.02%)	12 (.02%)
Other	121 (1.1%)	166 (3.9%)
Other Characteristics		
Chronically Homeless	1735 (19%)	856 (20.1%)
Disabled	4,776 (52.6%)	NA
Veterans	2335 (25.7%)	428 (1.0%)
Receiving income (From any source)	5,076 (55.9%)	NA
Domestic Violence victim	1,329 (12.1%)	366 (8.5%)

In both cases, the percentage of people who are Black and experiencing homelessness is much higher than the state average (the state average is 27 percent). There is also a disparity in the status of veterans. Nine percent of all South Carolina citizens are veterans, and eleven percent of the cases documented in the PIT count are veterans. In contrast, 26 percent of the cases entered into the HMIS system are veterans. The higher percentage of cases in the HMIS data is likely due to the abundance of federally funded programs available for homeless veterans. If veterans become homeless, they are more likely to seek out services because there are programs available specifically for them.[6]

We were initially surprised when we found that over half of the people whom we speak to in the homeless community have severe disabilities that would, or should, prevent them from working. Over half (52.6 percent) of the people seeking help with issues associated with homelessness and are logged into the HMIS system in South Carolina report having one or more disabling conditions. Knowing this, it seems reasonable that a concentrated effort should be made to connect people who have disabilities (many of whom cannot work) to housing that they can afford.

A final point to note is the percentage of people coming through the social services organizations in Horry County who have an income. The stereotype of the homeless bum sitting around waiting for a handout helps perpetuate the stigma associated with homelessness. In most cases, however, this is inaccurate. The data collected in HMIS shows that over half of the people using services in the TCHC (Total Care for the Homeless Coalition) counties have an income, and many of these have income from work. The income, however, is not enough to afford housing.

The *2020 South Carolina State of Homelessness Report* finds that a minimum-wage worker in Horry County would need to work at least 86 hours per week to afford an apartment. Individuals who work only forty hours per week need to make at least $15.20 an hour to afford an apartment. There are almost no employment opportunities for a less educated worker to make enough money to afford an apartment in Horry County. If a person does make enough money to afford an apartment, the jobs in the county are often seasonal, with work only available for six months out of the year. Individuals living on their Social Security or disability check are priced out of the rental market, as are people making less than $15.20 an hour or working in seasonal occupations. Bruce, a 69-year-old White male who became homeless for the first time at 68 years old, expresses this sentiment: "I worked my whole life. Now I am retired. I get a Social Security check, but it is only enough to afford food or housing. If I wanted to eat, I did not have enough to pay my rent, so I had to come here (the homeless shelter)."

In sum, although the PIT count vastly underestimates the number of homeless, it can help us to understand trends or patterns of homelessness, particularly when examining national trends in homelessness over time.

Although the HMIS system can only allow us to understand the traits of people actively seeking services to help them become housed, it is likely more accurate in helping us understand the actual extent and numbers of homeless in South Carolina. HMIS can also give us a more nuanced and complete understanding of specific individuals over time. It may be time to implement a system like HMIS at the national level. HMIS can give us information that the PIT count does not, provide a more accurate assessment of needed services, and help dispel stereotypes. For example, knowing that over half of the homeless have an income, and that income is insufficient to afford housing, should help show the public the need for more affordable housing.

In 2020, the PIT count found 807 people who were sleeping rough or in shelters in Horry County, most of those residing in Myrtle Beach. As we demonstrated previously, this number is far lower than the actual number of people who are homeless in the area at any point in time. Even if this number is accurate, there are not enough resources to meet the needs of 807 people. In the next section, we describe the largest organizations that serve people who are experiencing homelessness in Myrtle Beach. These are all organizations we have worked with, or gained an understanding of, through the interviews we conducted.

Non-Profit Organizations Serving People Experiencing Homelessness in Myrtle Beach

Because Myrtle Beach has a tourist-centered economy, the issue of homelessness is complex. Developers and the political elite in Myrtle Beach have long argued that homeless individuals can hurt the tourist economy and stem development. On the other side, the seasonal job market and low wages, combined with high (relative to the wages) housing prices, lead people on the margins to be at risk of losing their permanent housing. The street is sometimes their only option, with few shelters available and over a three-year wait for affordable housing. Support for people experiencing homelessness is laissez-faire; services are fragmented, and there is little collaboration between agencies. Agencies can also be competitive and contentious at times.

Shelters

The majority of the businesses serving people who are homeless are non-profit organizations. In Myrtle Beach, only one organization is responsible for the men's, women's, and family shelters. Here we will call it Springhouse. Springhouse was formed in 2013 and was intended to be an umbrella organization that controlled all the services for people experiencing homelessness in Myrtle Beach. All the other non-profits that served the needs of the homeless community at the time were asked to allow Springhouse to become their umbrella. Although it was not mandatory for organizations to allow Springhouse to be their umbrella, there were consequences for organizations that did not agree. If organizations did not comply with the request to be placed under the Springhouse umbrella, they would be at risk of losing their funding stream from the City of Myrtle Beach. Despite the revenue loss, most other non-profits declined to be folded into the Spring-house umbrella. Today, most of the money the city allocates for homeless programs goes to Springhouse.[7]

It appears that the most influential factor in the non-profit organizations' decisions to risk losing much of their revenue stream, aside from the potential loss of autonomy, was the philosophy that guides Springhouse. From the start, Springhouse has been run using a toxic charity model of providing resources (see Chapter 7 for further discussion of toxic charity). At the core of the toxic charity model is the belief that if a person who is homeless is given a handout, they will become dependent on charity and will never become self-sufficient. Springhouse required, and wanted other organizations to require, people who stayed at their shelter to pay rent and work for their beds. A 2014 news article about Springhouse quoted a city council member as saying, "The focus of the organization is to change how the homeless are taken care of in the city, mainly having them earn their keep if they want service."[8]

Shortly after Springhouse took over, they turned the emergency shelter already in place into a high barrier-to-entry men's work/stay shelter. Initially, to stay at the men's shelter, a person had to agree to become a part of a labor pool that Springhouse had started, and to pay rent to live there. It is unclear how much rent Springhouse initially required. They took in $70,000 from residents in the first year, and the city provided them with almost $178,000.

Springhouse no longer runs the labor pool, but work and "getting a job" remains a strong focus. It is unclear how much Springhouse charges people to stay there today. When we asked the employees of Springhouse how much they charged, it was difficult to get a clear answer. One Springhouse resident, Bruno, a 53-year-old White male who lives at the shelter and works full-time at a furniture store, told us, "Most of my money goes to rent and savings. They charge us to live here." Other residents described the difficulties they faced trying to save money while paying Springhouse 'rent' for their bed.

Springhouse initially sought to give individuals ID cards that would identify them as "clients" of Springhouse. They were to use the ID cards when they received services in other places so that Springhouse could be sure they did not "double dip." This program did not last long because the other non-profits did not believe that charging people or that investigating individuals for using services relating to issues of homelessness was ethical.

Before Springhouse took over, there was no separate women's shelter, but there was a domestic violence/emergency shelter for women and children. The domestic violence shelter decided they could not afford to lose city money, so they agreed to let Springhouse take their emergency shelter over. In 2015, Springhouse closed the emergency shelter and created a women's shelter with similar programs to what they had implemented in the men's shelter. Since they considered domestic violence victims too risky, women who needed an emergency stay had to travel to the next county for help.[9]

The family shelter decided not to be included under the Springhouse umbrella because they disagreed with charging people money to stay there. The city cut off its funding, and within two years, the family shelter ran out of money. Without any funding support, the organization could not keep its doors open. Springhouse reopened a family shelter in 2017.

Today, Springhouse continues to run the men's, women's, and family shelters. They currently have beds for nearly 200 men, women, and children; far fewer beds than needed. All three shelters align better with a high-barrier transitional housing model than a traditional shelter. Men, women, and families who stay in the shelters live there until they are either asked to leave due to a rule violation, are given a bus ticket to go "home," or find housing they can afford. Springhouse advocates for residents to "earn" their way to housing. People who are employed have more space in the shelter and are expected to eventually move into transitional housing before they can become permanently housed through the CoC. The barriers to entry are, as one city employee told us, "higher than any shelter we've ever seen." There are curfews, and the shelter regularly brings in the police with dogs to ensure there are no drugs in the building. The men's shelter has recently added an emergency stay component where men without a place to sleep can come in at 8:00 pm, but they must be back outside by 6:00 am.

Housing Support

Only one organization in the area applies for and receives federal funding for housing individuals and providing rental assistance. The Housing Group receives federal subsidies for many programs, including Permanent Supportive Housing (PSH), Supportive Services for Veterans and Families (SSVF), Veterans Affairs Supportive Housing (VASH), and Coordinated Entry, among others. The lack of affordable housing in the county and the restrictive guidelines of the HUD programs, and for other grants the Housing Group receives, make their job difficult. Although they assist every person they can, if a person does not qualify for any federal programs, there is not much the Housing Group can do.

The Housing Group's case managers use a Housing First approach. The main purpose of Housing First is to get people housed and then work to address the underlying issues they may have. These issues could include help for mental or physical illnesses or disabilities, access to paperwork such as birth certificates or Social Security cards, or treatment for drug or alcohol addiction or PTSD (Post-Traumatic Stress Disorder). The Housing Group then helps participants who work with their case managers achieve their overall goal of finding permanent housing of their own. See the Conclusion for a more thorough discussion of Housing First.

Food

Myrtle Beach has a public kitchen for anyone who wants a hot breakfast or lunch Monday through Friday. The Neighborhood Kitchen's clientele are primarily people who are experiencing homelessness, but anyone is welcome to stop in to enjoy a freshly cooked meal. In 2021, they served over 79,000 breakfast and lunch meals and over 76,000 after-school snacks, teen dinners, and summer camp meals for children through their Children's Hunger Initiative program.

When Springhouse requested to take over the Neighborhood Kitchen, the Kitchen chose not to participate and lost its annual $30,000 per year funding from the city. Not only did they not want a fledgling operation such as Springhouse to tell them what to do, but to get city funding, they would have also been required to charge people for meals. When the city denied the funding request from the Neighborhood Kitchen, a local paper quoted the City Manager as saying, "We need to get away from giving things to people." Another City Councilman stated, "If they can walk around with bottles of wine, cigarettes, and a cell phone, they can pay for a meal."

The Neighborhood Kitchen responded by accepting that they would not get any city funding. Today, the Neighborhood Kitchen only has two employees and relies on volunteers and donations.

A second public kitchen in the nearby city of Conway serves lunch and dinner to low-income individuals who live outside the city limits. Additionally, Springhouse's men's shelter serves dinner in their parking lot seven evenings a week. On Saturdays, several churches pick up people from a public park and take them to their churches for lunch.

Medical Care

Receiving medical care is expensive and necessary whether one is housed or not. Luckily for the residents of Myrtle Beach and the surrounding area, there is Big Lake Medical Center (BLMC). BLMC provides services and referrals for physical and mental health and runs a mobile dental unit. Their health care and dental services are offered on a sliding pay scale, and they pride themselves on not refusing service to anyone who cannot pay. They also have a group that travels around giving vaccinations and testing people for HIV. BLMC did not choose to participate under the Springhouse umbrella, but they have stayed in business without city funding due to their paying clients and the grants they receive.

Big Lake also makes appointments for people to see mental health care providers. In 2019, BLMC served almost 3,000 homeless patients. Males made up 54 percent of the people BLMC served.[10] The most common conditions BLMC saw in 2019 were depression and mood disorders. They also saw a substantial percentage of people with high blood pressure, anxiety, PTSD, diabetes, and HIV/AIDS. Despite the prevalent stereotypes about the link between homelessness and addiction, only about seven percent of the people BLMC treated reported alcohol- or drug-related disorders.

Clothing

There is also a community closet where low-income people (including those who are homeless) can go for clothes once a week. Interestingly, when we began this study, we were under the impression that it would be problematic for people who are experiencing homelessness to find clean clothes. In our first round of interviews, we asked whether finding clothing was a problem for people living on the streets. One day when we were standing outside the Neighborhood Kitchen, we asked Conrad, a 64-year old Black male, who is sleeping rough, if he ever had trouble finding clothes. "No, Ma'am," he responded, looking down at what he was wearing. "I have plenty. When these get dirty, I just give them away and go get more." He picked up a backpack to show us. "I have another set of clothes in here in case I need them." We find that most of the individuals we speak to, sheltered and unsheltered, have no problem finding and wearing clean clothes. The only two people who have identified clothing as something they needed were very tall men. "There are plenty of clothes out there," Hendrick (29-year-old Black male) stated, "Just not in my size. I have big feet and big shoulders."

Conclusion

Although it is difficult to count the absolute number of people who are homeless in Horry County at a single point in time, the HMIS system allows us to see how many individuals are seeking services. We know more people experience homelessness than the data indicates, particularly the PIT count data. Despite this underestimation, we can use these numbers to show the necessity for services to meet the needs of people experiencing homelessness.

Some of the organizations in Horry County and Myrtle Beach that were created to meet the needs of individuals experiencing homelessness are adequate to meet the demand. For example, of the 250 people experiencing homelessness we interviewed, over 90 percent can obtain food when hungry, and 78 percent can obtain clothing. This data suggests that the public kitchens and community closets are meeting the most basic needs of the homeless community.

Other organizations, such as BLMC, do a terrific job at what they do. Overall, the homeless individuals we spoke felt that they had access to medical care. Eighty percent felt they were able to get emergency medical treatment when they need it[11] and 58 percent of respondents reported they had options for dealing with feelings of sadness or depression.[12] Thirty-four percent of our sample had used BLMC. Of the people who used their services, 90 percent felt they received good care.

The third group of non-profits is insufficient to meet the growing need for their services, whether due to a lack of effort or, as in the case of the Housing Group, insufficient resources available. The Housing Group houses hundreds of people yearly, but there is not enough affordable housing for everyone who needs it. Others, such as shelters and the ability of the CoC to connect people to housing, are insufficient.

The resources described here are by no means a comprehensive list. They are, however, the largest organizations and the ones we hear people who are experiencing homelessness discuss most often. We include a discussion of these large non-profits as they provide context for the following chapters that describe our research and the ease or difficulty of people experiencing homelessness have when trying to become housed. These organizations also symbolize the contradictory ideologies service organizations have regarding allocating services.

Notes

1 All of the names we assign to agencies are pseudonyms.
2 National Law Center on Homelessness and Poverty. (2017). *Don't count on it; how the HUD point-in-time count underestimates the homeless crisis in America.* https://homelesslaw.org/wp-content/uploads/2018/10/HUD-PIT-report2017.pdf.
3 U.S. Department of Housing and Urban Development. (2017, December). *The 2017 annual homeless assessment report (AHAR) to congress.* www.huduser.gov/portal/sites/default/files/pdf/2017-AHAR-Part-1.pdf.
4 See Chapter 8 for a detailed outline of anti-homeless laws and policies in Myrtle Beach.
5 South Carolina Interagency Council on Homelessness. (2020). *2020 South Carolina state of homelessness report.* www.schomeless.org/media/1172/final-edits-actual-final-scich-state-of-homelessness_final.pdf.
6 Ibid.
7 O'Dare, T. (2014, August 1). Myrtle Beach officials: Homeless aid program headed in right direction. *My Horry News.* www.myhorrynews.com/news/local/horry_county/myrtle-beach-officials-homeless-aid-program-headed-in-right-direction/article_ab0f28a8–19ca-11e4-a638–001a4bcf6878.html.
8 Ibid.

9 O'Dare, T. (2015, July 9). Myrtle Beach emergency shelter for abused women shuts down, changes direction. *My Horry News*. www.myhorrynews.com/news/local/myrtle-beach-emergency-shelter-for-abused-women-shuts-down-changes-direction/article_56f82960–2638–11e5–9421–0f233019af7b.html.
10 From website data. Contact authors for source data.
11 Most of these individuals are referring to access to emergency rooms, which are not adequate for treating chronic physical or mental health problems.
12 Many of these individuals were referring to informal, social support; not professional mental health counselors.

Chapter 6

Work, Effort, and the American Dream

"Since the founding of our county, 'home' has been the center of the American Dream."

Barack Obama[1]

Introduction

In his 1931 book *Epic of America*, James Truslow Adams coined the term
"American Dream" to highlight the idea of America as a place where
dreams can come true, where anyone can succeed if they try hard enough.[2]
This idea has become one of the dominant ideologies of the U.S. It posits
that every person, even those who are born poor or immigrate to the U.S.
with nothing but their clothes, can be successful with enough hard work
and determination. In the eighteenth and nineteenth centuries, the idea
of America as a place of opportunity caused waves of immigration. People
from all over Asia and Europe immigrated to the U.S. for a new life working
in gold mines, railroads, and factories.

At the time of Adams' writing, the new life immigrants were looking for
in America included becoming part of a newly burgeoning middle class. By
the 1950s, the American Dream had evolved to include a family, a job, and
a house in the suburbs. This ideology is still so entrenched in the American
consciousness that even people with little to show for their hard work often
believe that if they persevere, the American Dream will eventually become
theirs.

Although the American Dream sounds idyllic, it has not materialized for
many people in the U.S. Most people do not move out of the class they
were born into, and for those born into low-income families, merely working hard will typically not bring the rewards the American Dream promises.
Although homeownership is the key to middle-class status and obtaining
the American Dream, the cost of homeownership today is much more than
the wages offered to manual laborers and service industry employees. Even

DOI:10.4324/9781003325581-8

renting a home can be unaffordable for low-wage workers, regardless of how much effort they put forth.

Politicians and the media largely ignore the obstacles to the Dream because it is assumed that in a land of opportunity if someone fails, it is their fault.[3] Although when the economy is slow or natural disasters hit, the media might highlight the struggles of individuals, they typically frame the discussion in terms of people who have "almost run through their savings" or focus on rags-to-riches stories. Showing people who have "almost run through their savings" ignores the millions of U.S. citizens who have no savings to run through. Similarly, rags-to-riches stories overestimate the ability of ordinary people to get ahead when they run out of resources.

Although the cost of living in Myrtle Beach is low compared to much of the country, most of the service industry jobs that dominate Myrtle Beach's economy do not pay enough for a worker to afford even the least expensive apartment in the area. As discussed in Chapter 5, in 2020 a person needed to make at least $15.20 per hour at a full-time job to afford a one-bedroom apartment anywhere in the county.[4] Few service-centered and manual labor jobs offer employees $15.20 per hour, and the cost of rent is continuing to rise while wages have largely stagnated. Even if workers were paid $15.20 an hour, many employment opportunities are seasonal and temporary. It is difficult to qualify for housing with a seasonal or temporary job. Thirty percent of the people we interviewed are part of the "working homeless," people who don't earn enough to rent even the cheapest housing and find themselves living in shelters or on the street while working full-time or part-time jobs.

Most individuals who are homeless in Myrtle Beach understand that the odds of finding a job that pays a living wage are low. At the same time, most of these people continue to believe in the American Dream; U.S. culture leaves them few other options. If they give up on the Dream, they are likely to be stigmatized even further, so they convince themselves that if they work hard enough, they will be able to find housing or move somewhere else with more opportunities. In this chapter, we discuss how the American Dream ideology is promoted by caseworkers at Springhouse and the effects of the Dream on the attitudes and behaviors of people who are homeless in Myrtle Beach.

Work as the "Key to Success" in Springhouse

Although individuals who are poor are typically stereotyped as lazy and unwilling to work, research shows that the value of work as a pathway to earning respect, along with the economic benefits it (if sometimes only theoretically) provides, is pervasive in all social classes.[5] In the nineteenth and early twentieth centuries, wayfarer's lodges made lodgers show their worthiness through their work efforts.[6] Today, the idea of work as a demonstration of worthiness is alive and well in Springhouse. Caseworkers in Springhouse push all their clients to become employed, even those with physical or mental disabilities that render them ineligible for most jobs. As work is touted as the means to achieve housing, the caseworkers act as cheerleaders and celebrate when their clients become employed by posting their "success" stories on social media.

Springhouse focuses on work to "reform" people, so they recruit local organizations to offer Springhouse residents training and life skills courses. The men's shelter regularly brings in people to teach financial literacy, cooking, life skills, and other classes that they hope will help their clients secure jobs. The reality that most low-wage workers in Myrtle Beach are not paid enough to afford housing is typically ignored.

Although the Springhouse caseworkers highlight work as the means to achieve housing, the thrill of gaining employment is often short-lived for their clients. Many residents of Springhouse quickly realize, if they did not know beforehand, that having a job, particularly a low-wage or seasonal position, will not bring in enough money for them to house themselves. Full-time employment is insufficient without other social safety nets or affordable housing options. The caseworkers' laser focus on employment does not include what their clients should do when their minimum-wage job is inadequate to qualify for housing.

On some level, the caseworkers at Springhouse understand that pushing work as the only solution for their clients is not productive. According to one caseworker:

> We tell them (Springhouse residents) to get a job, and we celebrate them when they do, but at the same time, we know that an eight dollar an hour job is not going to be enough for them to rent any type of housing by themselves.[7]

The caseworkers know that there is almost no affordable housing in the city or surrounding county, and the available subsidized housing has wait lists that can take years. Most of them, however, do not see any other options for their clients than to continue to work in the hopes that housing will become affordable or that they can work their way up until they begin earning what they need to afford housing.

What about people experiencing homelessness who cannot work? Many people at Springhouse are over 65 or mentally or physically incapable of working. For these folks, the caseworkers often aim to get their clients a disability or Social Security check every month. Unfortunately, those checks are seldom enough to support the client's food and housing needs. So, what are service providers to do? If they tell their clients that they will not be able to afford housing while working a full-time job at $8.00 per hour or that their Social Security check will not be enough, the client may give up.

Giving up is not an option, even if it is more realistic than praying for affordable housing to become available.

Believing the Dream

Still Believing—I Can Still Do It

Notwithstanding the mismatch between wages and housing prices, many people who are either sheltered or sleeping rough feel confident that they will eventually be able to make their dreams come true. Jessica's story highlights how the belief in the American Dream keeps people persevering despite seemingly insurmountable odds. We interviewed Jessica, a thirty-seven-year-old White female, in the living room of Springhouse's shelter for women. The shelter is a large home in a working-class neighborhood. If there were not a small parking lot in what was once the front yard, there would be no way to know that this building is being used as a homeless shelter. It would just look like a typical working-class home. The front room, once the living room, serves as an office and a place for clients to relax and hang out.

Jessica has two children who are in foster care, numerous health problems, and poor credit. Undeterred by these obstacles, Jessica is looking forward to finding a job. She believes that once she finds stable employment, she will be able to find an apartment and get her children back. We asked Jessica where she would like to work, and she replied, "I think the only job I could do is retail, but they won't hire me anywhere. I got a shoplifting charge a while back."

Although when we began talking to Jessica, she stated that all she needs to do is get a job and she will be fine, she later acknowledges the difficulties she will have in becoming housed even if she were to find a job. On top of the shoplifting charge, she also has seizures that prevent her from getting a driver's license. Her credit has been ruined due to numerous trips to hospital emergency rooms to treat several illnesses. "It sucks, man. They have ruined my credit because I cannot pay them. It doesn't stop them from sending me bills, though."

Despite facing numerous obstacles, Jessica's attitude is anything but depressed. She maintains that the American Dream is within her reach and that if she keeps working at it, one day, she will succeed. "If you really want something, no matter how big or small, nothing is impossible. Even sitting here [in the shelter], I am farther in life than I ever have been before." When we asked her where she would be in five years, she sighed, "Not in Myrtle Beach. I will have a stable job somewhere and be able to drive a car. I will have a house but will probably have to rent it." Jessica understands that homeownership is one of the primary principles of today's American Dream and that she will probably not become a homeowner. On the other hand,

Jessica is optimistic and believes that with hard work, she will continue to move forward in her life.

All I Need Is a Little Help

Like Jessica, Kent and Jordan are optimistic about the future. Kent and Jordan are both Black males in their 40s who are experiencing chronic homelessness. Kent has not been housed for about 11 years, and Jordan has been sleeping in his car for three years.

Kent is an affable guy who loves watching people. When we asked him where he sleeps, he said, "Little nooks, out of people's way." He has spent the last 11 years traveling from one town to the next. He has a routine. Every morning he eats breakfast at the public kitchen, and every evening he eats dinner at Springhouse. Springhouse also has a shower and laundry facility open to non-clients several mornings a week. Once a week, Kent takes his bundle of clothes to Springhouse to take a shower and wash his clothes. Kent appears satisfied with his routine but notes that some things are tricky for him. He says he wants and needs to get a job but has not had one in a long time because:

> I lost my Social Security card somewhere along the way. It is hard to get a job without that card. I don't drive, so I don't have a license either. You can't get a job or anything else without ID.

Although Kent calls himself a "veteran of the streets," he plans to be living in a nice house in Hawaii in the next five years. He stated, "There are a lot of people out here [the street] who are damaged psychologically. They are the ones who need help." He does not think he falls into this group. He believes that he will be on his way once he can figure out how to get his Social Security card. "It's crazy. Even the day labor places want those cards now." He believes that he will be off to Hawaii once he gets his card and can save up some money by working.

Jordan is also optimistic about his future. He has been sleeping in his car for three years, but he has big dreams. "Soon, I'll be back in school and hosting a podcast. What this city needs is help for people to start businesses, kick-starters, you know?"

"What will you need to get there?" we asked.

"My problem is my mindset and motivation. Other than that, I need help with the IRS and getting my stimulus check. I don't have an address, so I didn't get mine when everyone else did."[8]

Both Kent's and Jordan's comments highlighted another pervasive issue. Many people who become homeless have solvable obstacles to getting their lives back on track. Lack of identification is a problem faced by about one in ten people who are homeless in Myrtle Beach. We heard people discuss paperwork problems related to not having a physical address every week.

Because Jordan had been living in a car for so long, he did not have an address for the government to send his Covid stimulus checks. A thousand-dollar check could go a long way toward helping someone become housed, even if temporarily.[9]

I Just Need Job Training

Shelly is a 60-year-old Black female staying in the woman's shelter and struggling to pay her bills. She has two daughters who are couch surfing until they figure out what to do. Shelly and her daughters were living in her (paid off) home until about a year ago, when Shelly started getting very ill and realized the mold in her home was making her sick. She, along with her two daughters, had to evacuate.

Shelly did not graduate from high school, but she wants to take the GED. She thinks there are adult education courses that could help her, but she needs to find a program close to the shelter since her only means of transportation is walking.

"I don't have an income," she said, "but when I do, I have to hide my money from myself. I am really not good at money." Shelly believes that not having a job is her biggest problem, but it has been hard for her to find one. She feels that having a GED would help her get a job but thinks that her age is problematic regarding what she can do:

> I worked at a church for sixteen years, but when the pastor changed, I was booted out. I need to find a job suitable for me. I don't think I can do hotel work. I want to get out of the valley and go to a mountain top. I want to work with old people eventually. Once I get the job training, I need to get back on my feet. I need direction. I hope the good master [God] will help me find it if I keep the faith.

Just a Temporary Setback

Arnold also believes that once a few obstacles are out of the way, he will be able to live the American Dream. Arnold is a 55-year-old White male, he has been bouncing between the street and motels for a year. He has a felony on his record and does not have a driver's license, but he believes his setbacks are only temporary. "Once I get a job," Arnold said, "I can start building my retirement and buy a house in the suburbs. I think I can be comfortable in suburbia."

Like Arnold, Frank believes in the American Dream. Frank, a White 43-year-old male, has psychological problems and a criminal record that prevents him from passing the background check necessary for housing. Still, he firmly believes everything will work out if he focuses on his goals. Like many people who end up in homeless shelters after incarceration,

Frank has slept at Springhouse since he left prison three months ago. Frank has a job at a restaurant and is concentrating on his future. We found that many people who are new to homelessness are optimistic and, like Frank, believe that everything will work out. Frank is hopeful that this experience will not last much longer. He wants to be in a house in the suburbs in five years. "I'm gonna find a girl and have some kids. Then we will get a dog."

Arnold and Frank's experiences are not unique. Almost 10 percent of the people we spoke with report that having a criminal record is a barrier when looking for housing or applying for a job.[10]

Selling Himself (Literally) for the Dream

We met many people who are unsheltered when we go to public kitchens around town. Often these conversations are informal, and we may talk to someone once and never see them again. Pele was one of those people. Although we only had one conversation with Pele, his positive attitude and creative ways of supporting himself made an impression on us.

Pele is a middle-aged Hispanic male who is sleeping rough. He said he usually sleeps wherever he can find a spot out of the way of other people and the police. He has found ways to support himself because he has a tough time getting legitimate employment. Despite his precarious sleeping arrangements, one would never know Pele was homeless. When we met him, he had a button-down shirt on, khaki pants, dress shoes, and a big smile. He said he goes to the Clothes Horse weekly. "I'm there when they open to get the best stuff." The Clothes Horse is a non-profit that provides free clothes, kitchen items, blankets and pillows, jackets, and anything else someone might need. Anyone can go there weekly and pick out things they need for free.

"Do you have enough money to get by?" we asked Pele.

"Yes. I donate plasma every week. If they knew I was homeless, I couldn't donate, so I give them an address that isn't mine. I eat here [at the public kitchen] and pay for everything else with my plasma money."

"Where do you think you will be in five years?"

"I'll be in a house. I guarantee it." He added, "I believe in the American Dream. You have to work for it. Nothing will fall on your lap. At some point, I will open a food truck."

Although our conversation with Pele was short, it was clear that he believes in the Dream and has creative ways of getting what he needs. He did not appear to have a plan of how he would become housed in five years, but he was sure that a home and a business were in his future.

If I Did It Once, I Can Do It Again

In some cases, people experiencing homelessness have already lived what they consider the American Dream, and they assume they can do it again because they have done it before. Most of these individuals believe they are in a slump and will come out on top once again. They try not to think about the new obstacles (e.g., health problems, issues with transportation, or criminal records) in their path that may stem from their current state of homelessness.

Durkie, a 58-year-old White male staying at Springhouse, said, "I used to have a business. I was an electrician. I had multiple houses and ten cars. Now I have a bum knee and heart problems." Durkie explained that a few years ago, his business fell apart, and two of his daughters were incarcerated. As his focus shifted to his health and helping his daughters, his business began losing clients. Eventually, he had so few clients that he started selling his cars and other valuables. His house was the last to go.

Even with Durkie's health problems, two daughters in prison, and his current living situation in a homeless shelter, he believes he will be fine in a few years. "In five years, I will be in my own house again. I am certain of it. Right now, I have everything I need here. I just have to wait for a chance to get money."

Jett (46-year-old White male), once a successful welder whose family issues led him to lose his job and eventually his house, also plans to be back in business in the next five years:

> Nothing is keeping me from working. My biggest problem is I can't get to where the work is. Most jobs are out of range for me. The bus routes are inadequate. Once I get some wheels, I'll be on my way.

A New Start and a Parrot to Boot

Felix is a 58-year-old White male. We met him in an encampment in the woods, where he was sleeping rough. After he showed us his tent and the fire he and his fellow campers kept burning, we asked him to tell us his story. Felix had quite a story to tell. "I had a huge house and a parrot. I loved that parrot. Then my daughter sold me out."

"What happened?" we asked, and he answered:

> I had four DUIs. I went to jail for three of them. After the first DUI, I lost my job. I went to jail for the second one, and my daughter sold my car. I went in again after the third one, and my daughter sold my house. The third time I went in, my daughter sold my parrot. That was the last straw. I don't talk to her anymore. I loved that parrot.

Felix had lived in the encampment for about a year when we spoke to him. "Do you have plans for the future?" we asked.

"Yeah. I am going to start another business and have it all again. Maybe I'll get another parrot."

Mental and Physical Health and the American Dream

"I need to find structure in my life," Sharon, a White forty-year-old female, told us while sitting in the common area of the women's shelter. Although Sharon attributes her lack of permanent housing to her mindset and motivation, she has numerous other health obstacles in her way. Sharon is blind, has asthma, and has been in and out of psychiatric institutions for several years.

When Sharon is released from the psychiatric institution, she is usually taken to a homeless shelter. She does not have any friends or family to take her in. "I don't have anywhere to go, so I sleep outside or in here [the shelter]. When I have money, I stay in hotels." Despite her poor physical and mental health, Sharon can navigate finding a place inside to stay on most nights. "I can't work because I am blind. Without work, it is hard to find a place to live. When I get my life together, I want to get married and have a house with a dog." Despite Sharon's seemingly insurmountable odds, she still believes in the American Dream. Her dream, like many others, includes a family and a dog.

I Want to Work: It's Just Hard

Hector, a fifty-year-old Hispanic male, has been without housing for four months, but this is not his first experience with homelessness. He said, "My main problem is work. I lost my house because I lost my job. I can't get a new house because I can't get a job." Hector wants a job but has numerous health problems standing in his way. "I want to work; it's just hard. There's a lot of work I can't do. I can't lift much. Sometimes I have a hard time catching my breath. You see, I'm dealing with arthritis, heart failure, diabetes, and leukemia."

Unfortunately, Hector's story is far too familiar. Many of the people we spoke with are working or looking for work while trying to manage numerous severe chronic ailments, such as cancer, heart disease, or problems with their back, knees, hips, or feet. Over forty percent of people we talked with identified their physical or mental health problems as barriers to finding and keeping a job. Hector believes that once he is working, he will be able to start saving money and start his own business. He plans to be self-employed as an electrician soon.

It's Not Worth It

It is not often that people who are experiencing homelessness give up. By the time someone gets to the point that they are just "done," they have usually been living on the street for years. They have tried every way they can find to get housed and have run into roadblocks at every turn. Despite their best efforts, housing is elusive. In his book *Sidewalk*, about people sleeping rough in New York City in the 1990s, Mitchell Dunier calls this the "Fuck it" mentality.[11]

Thirty years later, and 500 miles south of New York City, we found a similar mindset among a small proportion of the people experiencing homelessness in Myrtle Beach. People with this attitude have given up on the Dream and see no future for themselves. This feeling may be realistic. It may also be a way to protect themselves from disappointment because they have been let down so many times.

Kate's (a 30-year-old White female) comments show an awareness of the structural barriers she and others who are homeless face:

> What they don't understand is that they need people like me to do the dirty work. The rich won't do it, but how do they expect us to live on nine dollars an hour? People would work more if you treated them better. The cost of living is too high. It is too hard to get approved for housing.

She plans to use the income tax refund she is expecting to get her camper out of storage and retreat into the woods.

I'll Be Better Off or Dead

"It's not worth it," said Benji (50-year-old White man). "I tried working those day labor jobs that they sent me to, but after paying them $5.00 to get me there and back, each way, it is just not worth it." For many people who are homeless in Myrtle Beach, the only businesses that will hire them are day labor companies. The day labor businesses will hire just about anyone for daily or weekly jobs. They even provide transportation, but the ride is $5.00 each way. Although this option is helpful to some people, for many individuals the backbreaking work (e.g., laying carpet, building houses, roofing, or pouring concrete) is too difficult for the low wages offered to them.

Benji is frustrated. "I have bad writing, so it is hard to fill out applications. Some want you to do it [fill out applications] on a computer, but I do not have a computer." He also believes that employers don't want to hire him due to the stigma associated with homelessness, so when he becomes desperate for money, he gives in and takes a day job. "I've had 20 of these day jobs over the last six months, but my body is sore. These are not real jobs, anyway. I am not healthy enough for this."

"Have you gone to the Housing Association for help?"

"Hmph," Benji grunted. "I tried them. I'm on their list. They don't call me back." The "list" Benji referred to is an intake form that any organization using HMIS can see and use. The Housing Association is the only organization that applies for federal funding to house people without income or jobs. Still, too few low-income housing units are available, and the federal government's criteria for housing applicants is very stringent. The Housing Association is helping people become housed every day, but many people are left out in the cold. There is just not enough low-income housing available.

"What's going to happen?" we asked. "Where will you be a few years down the road?" Benji sighed. "Either right here or dead. I don't really care anymore."

Jail or Dead

Many respondents believed that there are two options for their future. They will either have a happy ending or end up dead. Nikolai (45-year old White male) has been sleeping in an abandoned van for over a year. Like many others, he does not have any means of identification and does not know how to get it. He has tried to work with organizations to help him with housing, but it is difficult because he does not have a phone. Unlike many other people experiencing homelessness in Myrtle Beach, he does not feel sad or depressed, nor does he have any health problems. "I am pretty healthy. I got vaccinated and haven't had Covid." Another difference between him and many of his peers is that he does have health insurance through the Veteran's Administration. Because of his good attitude and access to health care, we were surprised at his answer to our question about where he would be in five years. His response was, "Either dead or in a nice house. I'm just being realistic."

Tyler, a 43-year-old White male who is sleeping rough, said, "I don't work. I don't want to work. Screw them. In five years, I am either going to be in jail or dead. Hopefully dead. I did not want to be in the mess I am in."

"Dead" is a typical response for people who have given up on living the American Dream. It is as though if they are not going to fit into the expectations of American society, the only other avenue they see is death.

Happy Families

Another component of the American Dream for many of our respondents is being reunited with their families. Many folks indicated that they needed a job and a house so that they could live with their family (and often a dog). Harvey (51-year-old Black man) said, "The American Dream means having a family."

Kerry, a 24-year-old Black woman who has been homeless most of her life, was previously married to a man who was abusive to her and did not have any children. She explained her five-year plan:

> In five years, I am going to be in a better place mentally—a healthy state. I am going to be remarried and have a big family, with at least four kids. We are going to have a car, a house, and go to church.

Chasing the Dream

We see extraordinary acts of resilience and effort throughout our time in the field. Benny, a 50-year-old White male, rode his moped 10 miles through the heat, rain, and cold, on a major highway every day to get to work. The speed limit on the highway is 55, but Benny's scooter only went 40 mph. He worked 8- to 10-hour days as a chef at the university and then rode his moped back to the Springhouse. When he returned to Springhouse, he was often hot, sweaty, or wet from the rain.

We kept up with Benny for several years. During that time, Benny always had a smile on his face. When he began working at the university, he was incredibly proud to be working a full-time job. He purchased his moped with the income from his work because he had been spending several hours a day on the bus. Although he was excited to have a full-time job, it became clear soon that the pay he received would never be enough for him to afford housing without help. Fortunately, Benny is a veteran, and after three years in Springhouse, he was transferred to The Housing Association's transitional housing apartments for veterans. Before he moved and we lost track of him, we asked him where he saw himself in five years. He replied, "In five years, I want to be working and living in a house with my family."

Conclusion

The American Dream is alive and well in the United States, even for people at the bottom of the economic ladder. One significant component of the American Dream is that if people work hard, the Dream can be within their reach. With enough hard work and perseverance, anyone can achieve the American Dream. Homelessness, however, can make it very difficult to achieve the Dream. As evidenced by the stories of people we met who are homeless, being without permanent housing can result from, or contribute to, other barriers to employment and subsequently housing.

As we discuss in Chapter 3 and Chapter 9, having a criminal record can make finding employment difficult; a criminal record can contribute to homelessness or result from living on the street. Similarly, physical and mental health problems can make working difficult; both can be either a cause of homelessness or a consequence of being homeless (see Chapter 3 and Chapter 6). Not having identification was frequently mentioned as a barrier to employment; as discussed in Chapter 3 and Chapter 9, this can result from encampment sweeps, identification not being returned after an arrest, or not having a place to store one's belongings when they are sleeping rough. Finally, not having access to adequate transportation can contribute to homelessness and result from not having permanent housing.

Despite the seemingly insurmountable barriers, people experiencing homelessness in Myrtle Beach and elsewhere still hold on to the American Dream, for the most part. This belief is in stark contrast to the perceptions of homelessness of the housed population. People who have never been without a home often attribute homelessness to a lack of desire or poor decision-making. The predominant stereotype is that people who experience homelessness are lazy and do not want to work.

There is a widely held conviction that if people who are sleeping rough can find employment, they will be able to afford housing. The experiences of the individuals we meet every day indicate that the problem is not that straightforward. Thirty percent of the people we have formally interviewed are working, and sixty-seven percent reported significant employment barriers. The top reasons for not working are physical or mental health problems (41 percent), lack of transportation (13 percent), a criminal record excluded from most work (7 percent), or a lack of identification (7 percent).

Despite either working in a job that does not pay enough to afford housing or experiencing significant barriers to employment, most people we met believed in the American Dream. Moreover, the service providers and public officials also believe in and promote the Dream. This ideology is problematic because the American Dream firmly places the responsibility for success on the individual. Many people experiencing homelessness feel that if they could get their mindset and motivation on track, they could work their way out of homelessness. While the lack of social safety nets, affordable housing, and living-wage jobs are sometimes acknowledged, neither the service providers nor people experiencing homelessness take this to the level of advocating for political and structural change.

Notes

1 United States Interagency Council on Homelessness. (2015). *Opening doors: Federal strategic plan to prevent and end homelessness*. www.usich.gov/resources/uploads/asset_library/USICH_OpeningDoors_Amendment2015_FINAL.pdf.
2 Adams, J. T. (1959). *The epic of America*. Little, Brown, and Company.
3 Anderson, M., & Tsikalas, S. (2021, May 17). Homelessness and the American Dream: An inconvenient truth. *Research Outreach*. https://researchoutreach.org/publication/.
4 South Carolina Interagency Council on Homelessness. (2020). *2020 South Carolina state of homelessness report*. www.schomeless.org/media/1172/final-edits-actual-final-scich-state-of-homelessness_final.pdf.
5 Sennett, R. (2003). *Respect: The formation of character in a world of inequality*. Allen Lane; Chamberlayne, P., Rustin, M., & Wengraf, T. (2002). *Biography and social exclusion in Europe: Experiences and life journeys*. Policy Press; Shildrick, T., & MacDonald, R. (2013). Poverty talk: How people experiencing poverty deny their poverty and why they blame 'the poor.' *Sociological Review*, *61*(2), 285–303.
6 See discussion of workhouses and wayfarers lodges in Chapter 1.
7 Interview with shelter caseworker 2019.

8 We spoke to Jordan during the 2020–2022 pandemic. The stimulus check he was waiting for was one of three checks sent out by the federal government.

9 Jordan wanted to rent a motel room for a few weeks with his stimulus check so he could spend time focusing on what to do next. It is hard to focus while living in a car.

10 See Chapter 9 for a further discussion on the effect of the criminal justice system on the prevalence of homelessness.

11 Dunier, M. (2000). *Sidewalk*. Farrar, Straus, and Giroux.

Chapter 7

Health and Perceptions of Health

"These last 15 days at the shelter have been shit. I want to work. But it's hard. I need to take medicine for my schizophrenia. I can't get it. I don't have insurance."

Fred (40-year-old White male)

Introduction

When we first began this study, we were surprised by the number of people who would tell us that they felt 'fine' even though they reported having severe disabilities and chronic illnesses. We were not necessarily surprised by the number of people who were homeless and ill, but we were floored by how nonchalant most individuals we met were about their disabilities. We soon realized that severe mental and physical illnesses are the norm rather than the exception in the homeless community, and that being 'nonchalant' is the only option for some individuals who are homeless in Myrtle Beach. Sixty percent of the people we interviewed indicated that they have problems with their mental or physical health. Of this sixty percent, only three percent mentioned minor health problems such as colds or coughs, while the other ninety-seven percent reported (often multiple) chronic health conditions. The most frequently reported health issues are heart problems (heart disease and high blood pressure), diabetes, back problems, chronic pain due to an injury, and mental health issues (including depression, anxiety, bipolar disorder, and personality disorder).

In this chapter, we discuss the relationship between homelessness and health. We begin by outlining what previous research has found about the extent of health conditions in the homeless community, and we describe what we heard from individuals in Myrtle Beach. We also explore the availability of health care for people experiencing homelessness.

DOI:10.4324/9781003325581-9

The Relationship Between Health and Homelessness

The average life expectancy for someone who experiences chronic home-lessness is about fifty years, thirty years earlier than the life expectancy of someone who is securely housed.[1] Women who are housed tend to live longer than men, but the life expectancy between men and women who are homeless is about the same.[2] The lower life expectancy of people experienc-ing homelessness pertains to both people who are sleeping in shelters and those who are sleeping rough. Any episode of homelessness can be a risk fac-tor for trauma, violence, mental illness, and infectious diseases. Experiencing any of these can be obstacles to becoming housed, result in lower life expec-tancies, and increase the risk of a person becoming chronically homeless.[3]

A 2010 national survey of individuals who were homeless found that most respondents had several health incidents in the prior year and did not have access to regular health care.[4] In this study, individuals who worked while experiencing homelessness were at a higher risk of severe health episodes, as they were more likely to feel a need to work to get paid rather than take care of their health. People who have insurance are not much more likely to access health care due to the prohibitive costs of copays and deductibles.[5] Individuals who experience homelessness are less likely to seek preventative care such as health screenings, dental cleanings, and vaccines than a person who is housed, even if they are insured.[6]

The lack of health care for individuals who are homeless between the ages of 50–64 is particularly problematic, because this is the age range when peo-ple generally start having more severe health events but are not yet eligible for Medicare. People who experience homelessness when they are over 50 are more likely to develop respiratory problems, chronic illnesses, and skin diseases. Due to the high cost of U.S. health care, individuals who become ill while homeless, particularly those who are over 50, often seek help from crisis-driven agencies such as emergency rooms and psychiatric hospitals.[7] Most housed people do not use emergency rooms for routine health care. However, over a third of people who experience homelessness do not have options other than emergency rooms for their primary medical care.[8]

Understanding the extent of illness and the resources available for mental and physical health is essential because poor health can affect people's abil-ity to work, save money, qualify for housing, or just get through each day. A person cannot work their way into housing if their health renders them incapable of doing any kind of work. Because there are few housing options available for individuals without an income, a mental or physical illness can lengthen a person's time without a home or result in chronic homelessness. We find that most of the people we met experiencing homelessness were either employed, despite their illnesses or health conditions, or would work if their mental or physical health were better.

The lack of access to affordable mental and physical health care has con-tributed to the marked rise in homelessness since the 1980s and the persis-tence of homelessness today. Today, poor mental and physical health can be either a cause or consequence of homelessness.[9]

Health as a Cause of Homelessness

Health problems can cause homelessness, particularly for the service sec-tor, seasonal, or manual labor workers, who are not likely to have health insurance or paid time off. When an individual who works in a low-wage job takes time off because they are sick, it often becomes challenging to pay their bills. If people cannot work due to their health, they may risk not paying their rent and being evicted. If they continue to work but have more medical bills than they can afford, they are at risk of homelessness as well. Additionally, if a person does not treat their illness or injury, it can lead to a much more severe ailment and homelessness.[10] One injury or illness can quickly snowball from time off work to missed bills, eviction, and a loss of housing.

Mental Illness Causing Homelessness

Chapters 2 and 3 discussed the shift from institutionalizing individuals with mental illness to leaving their care to states and communities through pub-licly funded community mental health centers. However, these proposed community health centers were largely theoretical, as proper funding for them has not been available from the start. We acknowledge that institution-alizing people is not the ideal solution, but neither are unfunded mandates that expect communities to care for individuals' mental health without the means to do so.

Although many of the individuals we spoke to can get some mental health care, the treatment they receive can be compared to putting a band-aid on a gunshot wound. The hospital typically treats the acute problem and then releases the person. This does not treat the underlying medical problems of the individual, or the structural problems that created the mental health crisis in the homeless community.

Baker is a 50-year-old White veteran; he has been living on the street since his wife died over a year ago. He suffers from severe depression, brought on by his wife's death. Baker currently sleeps on a concrete wall outside of the library. It was important to him that we make it clear that he sleeps on concrete, never on dirt. Recently Baker's belongings, including his ID, were stolen while he was sleeping. When we spoke with him in a public kitchen, he was despondent. "I tried to commit suicide, so I was in the hospital for a day. I'm struggling. I am hurt and broken up." When we asked him why the hospital only kept him for a day, he just shrugged.

Like Baker, Jace (a 41-year-old White male) struggles with his mental health. It was apparent when we met Jace that he was not in the right place. He should have been in the hospital for his mental health, but he was staying at Springhouse. The caseworkers at Springhouse are not trained to treat mental health issues like those experienced by Jace.

Jace goes to a counselor for his mental health but feels he needs more help. He rates his health as a five due to his mental state. He looked frustrated when he said, "I was recently hospitalized because I tried to kill myself. I was depressed and just couldn't see a way out." After one day, the hospital released him and transported him back to the men's shelter. We asked Jace what his plans were. "I have no idea," he said. "I think I should be in a mental ward somewhere, but they won't take me because I can't pay."

The system is failing Jace and Baker. They both know they need help and are willing to get treatment, but they have very few options. When health care is only available for individuals who can pay for it, people like Baker and Jace are left out in the cold to struggle alone. Most hospitals are profit-seekers, so they do not want to treat people who cannot pay. It is just not profitable.

From Riches to Rags

One day we were sitting at a table in the Neighborhood Kitchen when Jenny walked by. "I want to talk to you! Wait until I get done in the bathroom!"

When Jenny came out of the bathroom and sat with us, she said, "I think I'm pregnant. I always have to pee. You know how it is. Now, what do you want to know?"

Jenny was well-spoken and smartly dressed. She had a strand of pearls around her neck, and while they were beginning to look worn, her clothes were expensive. Jenny was happy to tell us her life story while waiting for lunch to be served. Jenny is 58-year-old White woman with bipolar disorder. Until recently, Jenny had it all. She has a master's degree, was married to a politician, and was a teacher in the school system for many years.[11] When she retired, all the local newspapers wrote stories about her. Jenny said, "Everything was fine, then my husband got arrested for seeing a prostitute, and I got divorced." Jenny goes to Big Lake Medical Center and the Mental Health Center. She is working with a lawyer to apply for SSI due to her mental status.

Although she is homeless, she still appears to have much of her social capital. She had nothing but good things to say about the mayor and the police in Myrtle Beach. She also has several family members, including two grown children, living in the area. "I have two children. They both have good jobs. One of them works for a state senator. Another manages a restaurant."

When we asked her where she sleeps at night, she replied:

> I sleep with men in hotels. I don't have sex with them. They just let me stay there to be nice. I don't want to have sex with them. Right now, all my stuff is on the Boardwalk. Someone is watching it for me while I eat here.

Jenny's story is just one example of how a cumulation of life events, and a decline in a person's mental health, can quickly snowball into homelessness.

Physical Health Causing Homelessness

Drake, a 58-year-old White male, saw firsthand how quickly one health event can escalate into homelessness. Sitting across the table from us at the Neighborhood Kitchen, with his walker nearby, Drake relayed that until recently, he felt like he was living the American Dream. "I made custom cars and competed in car shows. I won 23 Best in Shows," he said. He smiled and shook his head as though to clear his memories.

"I had a heart attack, and everything fell apart. I got blood clots in my arms and lungs from it." Drake now needs his walker to get around, and his health problems make it impossible for him to work at any job, much less build custom cars. "I can't get a house. I can't work anymore because of my health. The only place I'm headed is six feet under."

Like Drake, Nolan, a 51-year-old White male, also wonders how long he will be alive. Nolan was in a motorcycle accident that left him hospitalized for six months. When he was finally released from the hospital, he found that he had lost his job. He was also evicted from his apartment because he did not pay his rent while he was hospitalized. This was the first time he had been homeless. Nolan had slept in the woods, behind a building, and on the beach. Although he had only been sleeping rough for a week, Nolan said, "Being homeless is already getting old. I'm starting to get depressed and have been drinking a lot." Nolan explained that he is an alcoholic. When he was housed, he used Alcoholics Anonymous to help control his drinking, but sleeping outside had sapped all his willpower from him, "I should probably go back to A.A., but right now I am just overwhelmed."

In addition to his depression and self-medicating with alcohol, Nolan still feels the effects of his accident, including a brain injury and problems with breathing and walking. "I should be taking medicine for my brain, but I don't trust the doctors. The medicine may make me worse." When we asked him where he thinks he will be in five years, he said, "I hope I will be alive."

Gramps also became homeless after an accident. Gramps is a 60-year-old Black male who can be found in the men's shelter most days, rolling through the halls in his motorized wheelchair. Gramps says he is healthy, but he became homeless after he was in a car accident and lost the use of his legs. After his accident, he moved to Myrtle Beach. He has four daughters in the area and he thought they would help take care of him. When he arrived, however, he found that none of his daughters would take him. When we met Gramps, he had lived at Springhouse for over a year.

Despite his claim of being in good health, the month before we talked with Gramps, the caseworkers at Springhouse called an ambulance to take him to the hospital three times. In addition to his legs being hurt, Gramps also has a pacemaker and trouble breathing. Although Medicaid pays for most of his medication, he has trouble getting any pain medicine paid for through them.

Gramps' physical health and becoming homeless have led to a decline in his mental health. Although he usually appears in high spirits, Gramps says he worries daily:

> I just want a place to live. I just want a house. There are too many rules here, and the rules change quickly. In five years, I would like to be in China. I've always loved traveling, and I have always dreamed of going there.

Self-Employment

Tommy (46-year-old White man) was also in a car accident where he fractured his back. Like Nolan, Tommy had to spend a long time recovering from his injuries and could not work. For Tommy, the consequence of not working was swift and devastating as he had his own house-painting business. Before the accident, his business was going well, and he could afford health insurance. When he was in the hospital and unable to work, he could not pay the insurance premiums and his policy lapsed. "I couldn't paint houses with a broken back," he said. Eventually, he lost his house as well. When we met him, Tommy was staying at Springhouse. "In one year," he said, "I went from having a home and a business to this [living in the shelter]."

Despite all the problems Tommy has faced, he is healing, and he recently found a job working in construction, making $16.00 per hour. He is saving money for the down payment on an apartment. Unfortunately, even though the cost of living is low in South Carolina, Tommy may find it challenging to find an apartment that he can qualify for or afford. Construction jobs in Myrtle Beach are often temporary or seasonal, making getting approved for an apartment difficult, even if the applicant can afford it. Although Tommy's accident was not too long ago, he rated his health a ten out of ten. "I don't go to the doctor," he told us. "I never get sick."

Tommy's story resonates with many other stories we hear. Thirty-six per-cent of the people we interview are unable to work due to an injury or ill-ness, and over sixty percent of our interview participants do not have health insurance. These numbers contrast sharply with statistics for the housed population, in which only nine percent are uninsured.[12] Thirty-five percent of our respondents say they do not go to the doctor when they get sick, yet over half (fifty-four percent) report being hospitalized in the past year.

All in the Family

Sometimes health problems can lead to homelessness not just for the indi-vidual but also for their family members. We spoke to some people who became homeless while caring for a sick family member. Janelle, a 28-year-old Black woman, moved to Myrtle Beach to help her diabetic father. Janelle has a college degree and previously had a career in Virginia. When Janelle's father, Floyd, told her he was on the verge of homelessness, she dropped everything to come down and help him out. She did not think she would have trouble finding a job in Myrtle Beach. Shortly after she arrived to help her dad, the Covid pandemic hit, and she could not find a job anywhere. Now they are both homeless and are looking for a place to stay. "We are waiting for my father's disability to kick in," Janelle said.

Janelle's father, who already had diabetes and several other health issues, did not want the additional burden of Covid, so he got vaccinated and pres-sured Janelle to do the same. Janelle said, "I wouldn't have gotten it [the vaccination], but after all we have been through, the last thing I wanted was to get sick and give it to him."

Billy (a 60-year-old White man) moved from Phoenix to Myrtle Beach to care for his mother, who has dementia. He told us, "I got here, and she doesn't remember me. I've never been homeless before. I gave up everything to help her, and now I'm stuck at this shelter. They aren't even really help-ing me."

Health Problems as a Consequence of Homelessness

Severe and chronic health conditions can also be a *consequence* of homeless-ness. The National Health Care for the Homeless Council states, "Simply being without a home is a dangerous health condition."[13] Homelessness can not only exacerbate chronic health conditions, but it can also lead to new health problems or disabilities. Untreated health conditions are one of the factors in the low life expectancy of people who are sleeping rough. For example, people who are homeless are twice as likely to suffer from diabetes as those who are housed.[14] A person who experiences homelessness is also more likely to be exposed to infectious diseases and violence, suffer from sleep deprivation, and have illnesses related to weather exposure.[15] Additionally, being without a home is a risk factor for drug or alcohol use disorder. Almost half of the individuals with drugs or alcohol use disorders who are sleeping rough became addicted *after* they became homeless. Often, these individuals will turn to drugs or alcohol to self-medicate if they become depressed or develop an illness.

There is a widespread belief that the closure of state-funded psychiatric institutions caused the homeless epidemic we see today. Although deinstitutionalization (as discussed in Chapter 3) is one factor in the prevalence of homelessness, it is not (as some believe) that all formerly institutionalized patients have become homeless. Instead, the problem is that people who become mentally ill, either before or after becoming homeless, *no longer have an affordable recourse to meet their mental health care needs.* Mental health care is almost always either inadequate or unobtainable for people with low or no income. If the community health centers envisioned by policymakers in the mid-1900s were funded and implemented as planned, the correlation between mental health and homelessness might not be as strong.

I'm Better Off Than Him

Surprisingly, people in Myrtle Beach who are sleeping rough regularly describe their health as good before they list numerous significant health issues. On average, the people we spoke to rated their health a·seven on a ten-point scale. It is a conundrum. People say that they are healthy while at the same time listing numerous serious health conditions that render them unable to find and keep jobs. If any of these health issues were to happen to us, we would consider our health relatively poor. However, most people we talked to shrug off their health concerns. It is likely that their health is not their biggest concern or that they do not think there is anything that can be done. They may also be comparing themselves to their peers whom they perceive to be worse off than themselves.

Brock, a 51-year-old man who has been living on the street for sixteen years, told us his health is a solid eight, although he has severe heart problems, was recently hit by a car, and has been shot three times. "I'm an eight. Definitely an eight. At least I'm not pissing blood." He then nodded toward another person in the room. We assume Brock is comparing himself to that person.

Shared Spaces Affecting Health

Often, people who experience homelessness lack safe and sanitary places to eat, sleep, and bathe, making it difficult to meet basic health needs, along with the increased prevalence of health conditions they would not experience if they had secure housing.[16] Additionally, not having stable housing, whether the person is sleeping rough or in a shelter, can increase depression, suicidal tendencies, and anxiety.[17, 18]

We met George well into the Covid-19 pandemic. The county had opened up enough that we could start going back into the community to work with and talk with people. One of the questions we began asking is whether people have been sick with Covid. We spoke to George, a 35-year-old Black male, at a community kitchen. "Have you ever gotten Covid?" we asked.

George laughed. "Oh, man. I think I did. I think I did before they even knew what it was."

"What do you mean?"

He answered:

> In December. Before Covid began. I was sick. Everyone around me was sick. So sick. It was the strangest thing. We were smoking . . . something . . . we were all smoking it. Then everyone who was smoking got really sick. We coughed so hard we couldn't breathe. We were all staying together in the woods. It took so long to get over that shit. I think it was Covid. I really do. We were so sick it was scary.

We asked, "So you think you got Covid because you were sharing a pipe?"

"Yes. It was crazy. Then when Covid became a thing, we knew what it was . . . or we think we know. It had to be that. I have never been sick like that before."

"Did you get vaccinated?"

"Oh yes. They did it right here [in the public kitchen]. Everyone got the shot. No one wants to go through that again."

It seems like George was right about "everyone getting a shot." We have not spoken to any unvaccinated individuals who are sleeping rough. Big Lake Medical Center has had a massive public outreach to vaccinate low-income and homeless individuals. It is easy to get vaccinated at the public kitchen because BLMC is there when the people are there. People like easy.

The risk of health events for individuals living in a shelter can be as high or higher than for people sleeping rough. It is much easier for infectious diseases like tuberculosis to spread when people live closely together. We spoke with Harry, a 41-year-old Pacific Islander, in the common room at the men's shelter, where he sleeps on the floor because a bed is unavailable for him:[19]

> I am sick from being in the shelter. We need better air. It is not clean here. It's worse than the streets. And don't get me started on the mats. They won't even give them to us. I have been sleeping on the concrete floor for four weeks. I have been begging for a bed. People are getting sick from sleeping on the floor.

Harry claims his health has gone downhill since becoming homeless. He believes that the ventilation at Springhouse is inadequate and has worsened his asthma. Sleeping on the floor has increased his arthritis pain.

Health as Both a Cause of Homelessness and a Detriment to Finding Housing

The stories of people experiencing homelessness demonstrate that health and housing are inextricably linked.[20] It is not just temporary setbacks caused by accidents or injuries that can cause health-based homelessness. Sometimes there are more long-term health issues from which it is difficult to bounce back. Karen, a 53-year-old Black female, discovered she had cancer eighteen months ago. Karen moved to Myrtle Beach so her daughter could help care for her while she was getting cancer treatment. Soon after Karen arrived in Myrtle Beach, the apartment her daughter had lined up for them fell through, and they moved into a motel. When they ran out of money, Karen's daughter moved in with her boyfriend, and Karen went to the women's shelter.

Although she has never been homeless before, Karen does not feel like she has many options. In addition to her cancer, Karen should be taking medication for nerve damage, and she was recently in the hospital for a kidney infection. She is not currently taking the medicine she needs because she cannot afford it. Karen said, "All these bills that come with cancer treatment are haunting me."

Like many other people we talk with, Karen's health is both the cause of her becoming homeless and the reason she is currently homeless. She has few housing options unless she can work with The Housing Group to get into a subsidized apartment. Regardless, Karen does not mind staying in the shelter. "It's like family here. People are so nice." She continues, "I sometimes have anxiety and depression. It is easier to be happy at the shelter." Fortunately for Karen, the shelter allows people to stay there for up to two years. She has a little more time before being forced to be on her own again. Karen is fortunate that her health care needs have not completely handicapped her. The women's shelter is not handicap-accessible. The showers are upstairs, so to stay there, a resident must be able to climb the stairs. Luckily for Karen, she can still do that.

Tanner (a 32-year-old White male) is depressed, has ADHD, and is bipolar. He talks to the caseworkers at Springhouse about his problems. Although none of the caseworkers have psychiatric training, Tanner says talking to them helps him feel better. Tanner works at an asphalt company when he can, but he recently tore his labrum while on the job. A torn labrum is painful and makes any lifting or arm movement difficult. In addition to his other problems, Tanner was recently assaulted. The assault was so severe that it sent him to the hospital. When asked if he goes to the doctor when he gets sick, Tanner responded, "No. I just drink a bunch of Nyquil and go to sleep."

Tanner's mental and physical health makes working difficult and it's even more challenging to qualify for housing because he does not have a regular paycheck. Tanner's plight also highlights the danger of being homeless. In addition to the medical issues complicated or caused by homelessness, homelessness increases the risk of being assaulted on the street. Tanner found this out the hard way when his assault led to a hospital stay. Tanner's health problems increased his risk of becoming chronically homeless. Like many other folks we interview, Tanner became homeless due to one medical condition, and other medical conditions keep him from being able to qualify for housing or to pay for it.

When we were first introduced to Amelia, a 64-year-old Asian female, she had been staying at the women's shelter for three days. Amelia looked thin, frail, and much older than her age, sitting on a couch in the public sitting room. As she warmed her hands with a mug of coffee, Amelia discussed her life with us. She relayed that she only had a fourth-grade education but felt her life had been great until recently. She said, "I had two husbands in the military. I have traveled all over the country with my husbands." Amelia battles with addiction. Until recently, she had been clean for 12 years.

Amelia's son and her husband passed away within a few months of each other, and Amelia is having a tough time coping with the loss of the two people closest to her. Several months ago, she relapsed and turned to drugs to relieve her sadness and depression. As well as losing her son and her husband, she recently had a heart attack, and her addiction led to her losing her job and housing. "I'm here to sober up," she said. She was not looking for a place to rent at the time of our conversation because she wanted to "get back on track."

Amelia is having a difficult time staying healthy. She knows she needs to take heart medicine but cannot afford it. Although she gets some financial benefits as a military widow, she does not have health insurance. Amelia said, "I am still sad and depressed. I know I need to go to N.A. [Narcotics Anonymous], but I am just taking it one day at a time." Despite all of Amelia's physical and mental health issues, when we asked her to rate her health, she said, "Oh, I am probably an eight out of ten." Amelia works as hard as she knows how to keep her spirits up and does not see the need to dwell on her health concerns. Her mental and physical health caused her to become homeless and keep her from being housed.

Marshall provides another example of how a person's health can compound the difficulties for someone sleeping rough to become housed. Marshall is a 43-year-old Black male with untreated mental and physical health problems. As a child, Marshall was mentally and physically abused by his parents. Marshall said, "I left home when I was fourteen because life was too difficult with my parents. . . . I am currently living in an eight-person tent in the woods." Marshall is proud of his tent. He feels like he has come a long way. "At least I don't have to keep walking all night to keep the cops from hassling me."

"I was diagnosed with PTSD [Post-Traumatic Stress Disorder], bipolar, anxiety, and epilepsy. I don't take medicine for it anymore." Despite these issues, Marshall tries to minimize his health issues. "I'm pretty good, but I have some health problems. I'd rate my health as a 9 out of 10."

Marshall was already chronically homeless when we met him. Although his physical and mental disabilities are problematic, his criminal record renders him ineligible for subsidies. "I had a felony a few years back and don't qualify for Medicaid or food stamps because of it." When we asked Marshall about his goals for the future, he replied, "Goals? Stayin' alive. But I will probably be in heaven by then."

On the one hand, Marshall depicts his health as reasonably good, while at the same time he acknowledges that he should be getting help with his health care needs and does not feel as though he has long to live. The limited ability of agencies to help him due to his criminal record is one of the factors in Marshall's chronic homelessness. People can only try to get help for so long before they start giving up.

Veteran's Benefits

In contrast to Marshall, Christian, a 51-year-old Navy veteran, may be able to find some help in becoming housed. He became homeless the day before we met him at Springhouse. He said he became homeless after his girlfriend had kicked him out of their apartment. Although Christian said this was his first time being without housing, he also said that he had been staying in a motel for a couple of months and ended up at the shelter because he ran out of money for his room. It is unclear how long it had been since his girlfriend kicked him out or how long he had stayed in the motel before we met him at the shelter.

Christian's story got more complicated from there. At first, Christian looked as though he was healthy, and he rated his health as a seven out of ten. He later revealed, however, that he was on disability from the Navy, so if he did work, he would lose his disability benefits. "I also shouldn't work with this blood clot in my leg," he said, pointing at his thigh.

"Have you gone to the doctor for the blood clot?" we asked.

Christian shook his head and smiled a little. "The blood clot is because I have pins in my leg." The pins were put in his leg after he fell from the top of a three-story building a few years ago. "Last year, I had to have the pins replaced. The leg still hurts, so walking is hard sometimes." Shortly after this hospital stay and surgery, Christian was severely burned and had to stay in the hospital again. He was there for three weeks:

> I have Medicaid, so I can go to the doctor if I want to. I go to Big Lake Med. The insurance takes care of it. I just have to pay for my medicine. That's hard, though, when I have bills to pay.

"That sounds rough," we said. "Do you get depressed about all these health problems?"

Christian sighed. "I get depressed often."

"Do you have anyone to talk to about your depression?"

"No. I could use someone, though."

Christian's situation sounds rough, but because he is a veteran and is receiving veteran benefits, he may be able to find housing support. Several housing programs specifically target veterans. If he contacts the right people about housing, he has a chance of securing housing. Christian's situation also highlights the importance of talking with people about their health concerns. If we had merely given Christian a survey and asked him to check a few boxes, we would have made different inferences about what was happening with him.

Health and Outreach Efforts

Cara is a White woman who is about 25-years-old and weighs less than 100 pounds. She sleeps on the street, in abandoned buildings, or under bridges. Cara heard about an outreach event we held in a park and was waiting for us when we arrived. She was eager to help us set up. Once we got everything ready, we gave Cara a sandwich and sat down to talk to her. "I can't get help. Nobody will help me." Cara had six children, but two of them died. "I am depressed and think I am pregnant again, but I'm not sure." Cara picked at her sandwich. "I need to eat, but I have Crohn's disease, so eating really hurts my stomach. I try to eat rice at least once a day."

"I shouldn't be like this," Cara said. "I have a bachelor's degree in engineering, but I made a mistake and got involved in a robbery. I was in prison for a while. Oh! And I also have seizures." Despite of Cara's health and her poor criminal record, she did not sound angry. She was just sad. Later in the conversation, she relayed that she was also addicted to crack cocaine. "Nobody will help me. There needs to be more people to help out."

Big Lake Medical Center was at the outreach event, so after she was done eating, we sent Cara over to talk to the BLMC representatives. "Thank you so much," she said as she gathered up the remains of her sandwich. "Thank you for doing what you do and listening." We have not seen Cara since.

Despite public perception, almost all the people we encounter who are experiencing homelessness will take any help they are offered. During the Covid-19 pandemic, BLMC traveled around the county to provide Covid-19 testing and vaccinations. BLMC went to public kitchens and shelters and participated in outreach events we organized in public parks. People experiencing homelessness lined up to be vaccinated.

What Can We Do?

Part of the 1987 McKinney-Vento Homeless Assistance Act was to provide funding for community health centers for people who are experiencing homelessness. In Myrtle Beach, BLMC is an indispensable non-profit organization that provides a traveling dentist, vaccinations, HIV/STD testing, and free or affordable health care for anyone who needs it. However, there are still far too few resources for individuals needing mental health care. Most individuals living on the street or in shelters need more long-term care than BLMC and other mental health facilities in the area are equipped to provide.

So, what can be done to address the health care needs of people experiencing homelessness?

1) Affordable housing. Many problems associated with homelessness would not be problems if affordable housing were available. We need a different model than we have currently. Dramatically expanding Section 8 vouchers would be a start. If there were more government-funded vouchers where residents would pay no more than a quarter of their income in rent, fewer people would become homeless in the first place. The current Section 8 Housing available is not sufficient to meet the need. In Myrtle Beach, there is typically a waiting list that is years long. The government expenditure on policing, incarceration, and medical care for people experiencing homelessness would be better spent on subsidized housing for low-wage workers. When people are housed, there will be less need for other services.

2) Full funding of community clinics and long-term care for people experiencing mental illness. The McKinney-Vento Act and the deinstitutionalization of people with mental health conditions would be much more efficient if health services were fully funded and available. There is a shortage of mental health care providers around the country for both people experiencing homelessness and for people who are housed.

3) The U.S. health care system is the most expensive in the world and is less efficient than other post-industrial countries. One cause of this is that the pharmaceutical industry can donate large sums of money to politicians. The pharmaceutical industry should be prohibited from influencing politics. Because the pharmaceutical industry is profit-seeking and contributes to politicians, there is no incentive to change the current structure. Hospitals must be incentivized to treat all patients, not only those who can afford it. This expansion of treatment could be a reality with an expansion of Medicare for All.[21] This expansion would not only provide better treatment for both people who are housed and those who are homeless, but it could also prevent people from becoming homeless due to their health.

4) Increase funding for free or low-cost lawyers to work with individuals to get disability benefits, fight evictions and discriminatory housing policies, and help with paperwork.

5) Meet people where they are. Increase funding for more mobile medical clinics, psychiatrists, psychologists, showers, syringe exchange, and dentists. Getting to know people who are experiencing homelessness

increases trust between service providers and individuals. This approach includes going to public kitchens and shelters and housing-based health clinics where physicians could set up weekly clinics in lower-income neighborhoods. It would reduce funding needed for emergency departments.

Notes

1 National Coalition for the Homeless. (2018, December 21). *Remembering those lost to homelessness*. https://nationalhomeless.org/remembering-those-lost-to-homelessness/.

2 National Coalition for the Homeless. (2009, July). *Health care and the homeless*. www.nationalhomeless.org/factsheets/health.html.

3 Kushel, M. (2011). Older homeless adults: Can we do more? *Journal of General Internal Medicine, 27*(1), 5–6. https://doi.org/10.1007/s11606-011-1925-0.

4 Baggett, T. P., O'Connell, J. J., Singer, D. E., & Rigotti, N. A. (2010). The unmet needs of homeless adults: A national study. *American Journal of Public Health, 100*(7), 1326–1333. https://doi.org/10.2105/AJPH.2009.180109. The unmet needs of homeless adults: A national study. *American Journal of Public Health, 100*(7), 1326–1333. https://doi.org/10.2105/AJPH.2009.180109.

5 Brubaker, M. D., Amatea, E. A., Torres-Rivera, E., Miller, M. D., & Nabors, L. (2013). Barriers and supports to substance abuse service among homeless adults. *Journal of Addictions & Offender Counseling, 34*(2), 81–98. https://doi.org/10.1002/j.2161-1874.2013.00017.x.

6 Maness, D. L., & Khan, M. (2014). Care of the homeless: An overview. *American Family Physician, 89*(8), 634–640.

7 United States Interagency Council on Homelessness. (2015, June). *Opening doors: Federal strategic plan to prevent and end homelessness*. www.usich.gov/resources/uploads/asset_library/USICH_OpeningDoors_Amendment2015_FINAL.pdf.

8 Schanzer, B., Boanerges, D., Shrout, P. E., & Caton, C. L. M. (2007). Homelessness, health status, and health care use. *American Journal of Public Health, 97*(3), 464–469. https://doi.org/10.2105/AJPH.2005.076190.

9 Johnson, G., & Chamberlain, C. (2008). Homelessness and substance abuse: Which comes first? *Australian Social Work, 61*(4), 342–356. https://doi.org/10.1080/03124070802428191.

10 National Health Care for the Homeless Council. (2019, February). *Homelessness and health: What's the connection?* https://nhchc.org/wp-content/uploads/2019/08/homelessness-and-health.pdf.

11 We are not confident that Jenny could have been pregnant at 58. All of the other information Jenny told us could be verified by examining public records.

12 Keisler-Starky, K., & Bunch, L. N. (2021). *Health insurance coverage in the United States: 2020. Report P60–274.* www.census.gov/library/publications/2021/demo/p60-274.html.

13 National Health Care for the Homeless Council. (2019, February). *Homelessness and health: What's the connection?* https://nhchc.org/wp-content/uploads/2019/08/homelessness-and-health.pdf.

14 Ibid.

15 Ibid.

16 Parpouchi, M., Moniruzzaman, A., Russolilo, A., & Somers, J. M. (2016). Food insecurity among homeless adults with mental illness. *PLos One, 7*(11), 1–14. https://

doi.org/10.1371/journal.pone.0159334; Chang, F. H., Helfrich, C. A., Coster, W. J., & Rogers, E. S. (2015). Factors associated with community participation among individuals who have experienced homelessness. *International Journal of Environmental Research and Public Health*, *12*(9), 11364–11378. https://doi.org/10.3390/ijerph120911364.

17 Burgard, S. A., Seefeldt, K. S., & Zelner, S. (2012). Housing instability and health: Findings from the Michigan recession and recovery study. *Social Science & Medicine (1982)*, *75*(12), 2215–2224. https://doi.org/10.1016/j.socscimed.2012.08.020.

18 Tsai, J., & Coa, X. (2019). Association between suicide attempts and homelessness in a population-based sample of US veterans and non-veterans. *Journal of Epidemiological Community Health*, *73*, 346–352. https://doi.org/10.1136/jech-2018-211065.

19 This was before Springhouse stopped allowing overflow clients to sleep on the floor.

20 Thomson, H., & Thomas, S. (2015). Developing empirically supported theories of change for housing investment and health. *Social Science and Medicine*, *124*, 205–214.

21 National Health Care for the Homeless Council. (2019, May). *Medicare for all & the HCH community*. medicare-for-all-and-the-hch-community.pdf (nhchc.org)

Chapter 8

Stigma for All

"People do not like the homeless because they don't think we are people."
(Jake, a 47-year-old White male)

Introduction

When we spoke with Walter (a 41-year-old White male) at a public kitchen, he had been unhoused for 13 months. Two years ago, he lost his job when the retail store he was working at closed. Once he lost his job, he could not pay his rent and was evicted from his home. He now has a job at the recycling center, but he does not make enough money to afford an apartment's security deposit and first month's rent. When we ask him where he pictured himself in five years, he said, "I want to be working a good job and living in a house. I want to be normal."

We ask him what he means by 'normal.' "You know," he replies, "not looked at like I'm bad."

Jake (a 47-year-old White male) chatted with us in the common room at Springhouse. He had just arrived, having spent the last month sleeping in an abandoned house. He has been homeless on and off for the last 13 years. He's not working because he does not have reliable transportation, and not having a job keeps him from getting his own place. Moreover, he feels employers discriminate against people who are experiencing homelessness; he told us, "People do not like the homeless because they don't think we are people."

The sentiments Jake and Walter expressed exemplify one of our research's significant themes—being 'homeless' is a stigmatized identity. According to sociologist Erving Goffman, a stigmatized individual is one who is different from others in a deviant or less desirable way.[1] A stigma is a label that is difficult to remove. People who experience homelessness are often stigmatized because they are blamed for becoming homeless. The stigma associated with people who are homeless implies that they are inherently flawed in some way and less valuable than those who are housed.[2]

DOI:10.4324/9781003325581-10

Poverty is one of the last acceptable stigmas in the United States. Because of the individualistic nature of U.S. culture, children are taught from a very young age that there are winners and losers in the game of life. They are fed the American Dream ideology that asserts that hard work and effort will produce success and that if someone does not become successful (at whatever level they define success), it is their fault. Since the 1940s, the middle-class American Dream has been typified by having a family and a house in the suburbs.

Because the idea of the American Dream is so prevalent in U.S. culture, it is easy to stigmatize people for not achieving the Dream, and all that comes with it, including the house in the suburbs with the picket fence, family, and of course a dog. This ideology is likely why so many studies pathologize people who are homeless. The work of practitioners and academics often, sometimes unconsciously, implies that there must be something inherently wrong with someone if they do not have a fixed residence. It is commonly assumed that a person becomes homeless due to problems with drugs or alcohol, mental illness, or that they choose to sleep rough. It is much easier to believe that a person can be 'fixed' than to understand that individuals live in an unequal and dysfunctional system.

Most of us have heard a story about someone who panhandles and uses the money they are given irresponsibly. However, we are far less likely to hear about the seemingly insurmountable structural barriers people face when trying to survive without a home. The notion that homelessness is a personal problem is so ingrained in our culture that even people who are homeless often stigmatize others who are also without a home. They may try to distance themselves from other people who are unhoused because they believe their problems are unique and that they are different from others in the same circumstances. Stigmatizing people who are poor appears to be a universal trait in U.S. culture. In this chapter, we will discuss the stigma faced by people experiencing homelessness in Myrtle Beach and how stigma and the toxic charity model are inextricably linked.

Stigma from Service Providers

Most service providers in Myrtle Beach appear to work hard to serve their clients and care about what they do and the people they serve. Unfortunately, even people who spend their careers working with people who are homeless can still be subject to their own implicit bias. Stereotypes of homelessness are so pervasive that even people who work with individuals who are unhoused make subjective and often unrealistic assumptions. Early in this study, it became clear that many service providers see their clients first as someone who is homeless and an individual with unique circumstances second. The fact that a person is unhoused is often the client's master status, the status that defines them above all others.

The predominant strategy Springhouse uses for addressing homelessness focuses on individual-level behaviors that need *fixing* and not the social and economic factors that contribute to homelessness.[3] Service providers and city officials often speak of individuals who are without a permanent residence as children who need decisions to be made on their behalf. This bias is consistent with the paternalization of people experiencing homelessness found in other studies.[4] One component of paternalization is that service providers believe they know what is best for their clients. Caseworkers at Springhouse often feel responsible for helping 'fix' their client's problems without involving the client in decision-making.[5]

The overemphasis on addressing the perceived deficiencies in the individual rather than the structural context can be distressing to people who are experiencing homelessness. Ava, a 48-year-old White woman, lost her housing when her abusive husband emptied their joint bank account and disappeared. She suffers from depression and anxiety and is currently staying at the women's shelter:

> The caseworker puts too much pressure on us. I don't know what to do. It makes me anxious. When I ask what to do, I feel like I'm bothering people. They just expect us to do what we are told without explaining anything to us.

Rather than talking to Ava about her needs, the caseworkers pressured her to do certain things, such as "get a job!" without understanding what Ava needed.

Toxic Charity

The staff at Springhouse and numerous city officials believe in the toxic charity model of social service. This ideology may contribute to the overemphasis on the individualistic causes of homelessness and the stigmatization of people who experience homelessness.

In 2012, a non-profit organization, along with the city of Myrtle Beach, invited Robert Lupton, the author of *Toxic Charity: How Churches and Charities Hurt and How to Reverse It*, to speak at an event. In his book and at the event, Lupton argued that non-profit organizations and churches create dependency when they give people who are homeless "handouts" without making them work for what they are offered. Like the wayfarer's lodges discussed in Chapter 1, the toxic charity model assumes that some people are more "deserving" of aid than others. People are forced to work for things like food or a bed to show they are "worthy" of being helped. Lupton asserts that if the handouts are unavailable, people will get jobs and find ways to provide for themselves.

A 2015 news article described the response from non-profit organizations after Lupton's speech. Several non-profit agencies began to charge people who were seeking services a fee or have them work for clothes, a bed, or other services. The article reported the city's spokesperson saying, "Anecdotally, I'd say we've seen enormous changes since the toxic charity discussion."[6] The spokesperson went on to say that the service agencies were helping people feel better about themselves and become better able to become housed. He added that the toxic charity model was saving the agencies money.[7] Subsequently, the city also banned churches from providing emergency beds for individuals who are homeless to sleep in, citing zoning ordinances.

In 2016, when we began surveying people, we did not know that Lupton had been advising the city or that some agencies were operating under this model. We wondered why Springhouse was charging people to stay there. After learning of Lupton's discussion, we realized that his talk was the rationale for the shelter's policy of requiring residents of the men's shelter to do laundry or work in the kitchen as payment for their beds.

Martha was instrumental in bringing Lupton to speak to city leaders and service providers. She had been working with organizations serving people experiencing homelessness for over a decade and had previously served on the city council. About two years into our study, she met with us to discuss a homeless task force the city was coordinating.[8] She said, "I really believe in the toxic charity model. Why should we just give these people handouts? You cannot make them dependent." Martha implied that *these people* were somehow different from people who were not homeless and that they needed to be pushed to help themselves so that they do not become even more of a burden on society than they already are.

A conversation with Jeffrey, the director of another organization, highlights the influence of Lupton's talk. We were discussing the evolution of homelessness. Jeffrey said, "The closing of the mental hospitals is the reason for the new wave."

We responded, "The reduction of direct support to individuals has also been a factor, among other things. The government gives money to organizations like yours instead of giving people housing vouchers or rent support."

Jeffery nodded. "Well, they are doing the right thing. You don't want to give money to *these people*. They would waste it."

The accepted stigma surrounding people who are unhoused is typified by how the public, the media, and service providers talk about people experiencing homelessness. An individual who is unhoused will be labeled as 'that homeless person' or 'the homeless.' A person or a group is not defined by their traits other than their current state of not having housing. This stigmatization dehumanizes them and allows housed individuals to see this group as somehow "other."

Stigma and Employment

Employment is an area in which there is a disjuncture between service providers' attitudes and individuals' lived experiences. As found in other studies, numerous service providers blamed homelessness on the individual's poor decision-making. They argued that once their clients became employed, it wouldn't be hard to house them.[9] City Council members and service providers often issue statements such as, "They're homeless because they don't want help," "They won't take the help offered," and "*The homeless* are troublemakers who want to be homeless."

Social service programming based on the idea that finding employment will lead to stable housing is problematic because it is not true for most people who are unhoused.[10] As discussed in previous chapters, a person working in low-wage or seasonal occupations does not make enough money in Myrtle Beach to afford even the smallest apartment, even if they could pass the background and credit checks. Most of the individuals we meet have some income, whether from disability, Social Security, or employment. This income is not typically enough to pay rent anywhere in the county. Ideally, staying in a shelter would allow the individual time to save up money for a deposit and a few months' rent; however, the shelters in Myrtle Beach charge their clients to stay there, so even saving money can be difficult.[11]

Although we do not ask individuals how much they pay to stay at Springhouse, the men's shelter residents often complain about the "rent" they pay on their beds. If they bring it up, we ask them how much they pay, and we have been given varying amounts, from as little as $60.00 per month to $60.00 per week. Collecting "rent" on a bed is a way for the client to show the caseworkers that they are worthy of help and put effort into becoming housed.

As in previous generations' wayfarer's lodges, residents of the men's shelter are encouraged to work in the kitchen or do laundry if they cannot pay rent. Several Springhouse residents have also been given full-time employment at the shelter in exchange for a better room or one of the small apartments that Springhouse manages. They are no longer considered "homeless" because they work at Springhouse, but they can also become trapped. As the cost of their housing is tied to their pay, it becomes challenging for them to leave their "job" at the shelter for other employment. If they choose to quit their work at Springhouse, they immediately lose their housing. Thus, this situation creates a dependency on Springhouse, exactly what the toxic charity model opposes.

The people we encounter who are experiencing homelessness (sheltered or unsheltered) are typically far from lazy, and most try not to be dependent. Over a third of the 250 homeless individuals we have formally interviewed are employed in one or more jobs. Ten percent are looking for work, forty-three percent report mental or physical ailments that prevent them from working, and five percent are past retirement age. Many workers are employed in the service industry as day laborers or are paid under the table for odd jobs. Most of those who work are not paid enough to save money for an apartment of their own

Many folks we talk with express that the stigma attached to homelessness prevents them from gaining employment and eventually exiting homelessness. Jake stated that he had trouble finding a job. "No one will hire me because I am homeless." Craig (a 32-year-old White man), who is sleeping rough and does not want to stay in the shelter, believes he is having trouble getting hired because of his status as 'homeless.' "The label follows me wherever I go, especially because I don't have an address. They find out right away."

Can I Get a Mat, Please?

After interviewing people who were staying in Springhouse for about a year, we met with the caseworkers to suggest some things we could do to help meet the needs expressed by the residents of the men's shelter. At the time of the meeting, Springhouse had been allowing men to sleep on the concrete floor of the common room if there were not enough beds available. Many men who had beds expressed concern about their peers sleeping on the concrete. John (a 73-year-old Hispanic male) said, "We need mats; these guys should not be sleeping on the floor. If I slept on the ground all night, I would not be able to get up in the morning."

The men sleeping on the floor were stressed about it as well. Rodger, a 50-year-old White male who has been staying at Springhouse for several months, told us, "Lack of bed space in the shelter is problematic. I am sleeping on the floor. There is no available space. A mat or mattress would be helpful."

Waylon, a 30-year-old White man who is sleeping rough, looked disgusted when we asked him why he did not get a bed at the shelter. "They [Springhouse] kicked me out because I came in late. They wanted me to sleep on the floor. The FLOOR! I am afraid of that place anyway. I don't want to go back. I won't go back."

We were excited about relaying these comments to the director of Springhouse and the caseworkers because buying mats for people sleeping on the floor was something we could do to make a few people's lives easier. We told the director and caseworkers, "We can raise money for mats so that your clients do not have to sleep on the floor."

Caitlyn, the director of Springhouse, shook her head. "No. We have mats. They don't get them because they don't take care of them. Maybe sleeping on the floor will help motivate them to get up and get a job." The mats were in the shelter's attic, and we never saw them used. Caitlyn would rather the mats stay unused in the attic than be misused by shelter clients.

Shortly after this conversation, Springhouse stopped allowing any over-flow clients to stay there. If no bed was available, overflow clients were not allowed in unless it was below freezing outside. We are not sure if the decision not to let any overflow clients into the shelter was a direct consequence of this meeting, but we felt terrible about the outcome. Surely sleeping on the floor was preferable to being on the street, especially in inclement weather.[12]

Stereotyping Each Other

Although it is typical for the dominant group to hold stereotypes of a non-dominant group, there can also be within-group stereotyping and stig-matization. It appears that stigmatizing people one views as inferior has a universal appeal, regardless of the individual's status. One stigma management strategy is social distancing.[13] Individuals often compare themselves to others they perceive to be worse off or less worthy of help than they are. This comparison may make the individuals feel better about themselves, reduce the stigma directed at them, or help them advocate for services they need without the threat of others getting help first.

In Myrtle Beach, there is a high level of stigmatization between people experiencing sheltered homelessness and those sleeping rough. We often saw this at the evening meals provided by Springhouse. Springhouse serves dinner to anyone who wants it in the parking lot of the men's shelter every night, whether they are staying at the shelter or not. Groups associated with schools and other community organizations go into the shelter kitchen each evening to cook large homemade meals such as spaghetti, chili, or fried chicken. These community groups first serve the people who are sleeping rough. A door to the kitchen leads to the parking lot in front of the build-ing. The non-shelter residents who come for dinner line up (most of those who come for dinner are homeless, but some are not), sign their names and pick up a plate of food. There are picnic tables in the parking lot for them to sit at while they eat. The shelter residents are served when the individu-als outside are finished eating. Each night up to 150 meals are cooked: 90 for the people inside the shelter and up to 60 people outside. This program usually runs smoothly and is essential for getting food to people who are without other means of receiving it.

During the evening meal, Springhouse keeps the outside and inside peo-ple separated by not letting anyone enter or exit the shelter while people outside are eating. This policy is due to the animosity between some of the inside and outside people. Resentment between the shelter residents and people who are sleeping rough is common. When we asked individuals who are sleeping rough why they do not try to secure a bed in the shelter, we were often met with frustration or hostility. We heard, "They won't let me in because I haven't lived in the county long enough," or "They have beds available, but they keep telling me they are full."

Other individuals who sleep rough do not even try to stay in the shelter. One day we sat down with several men who were eating meals outside. As we were talking, several of the men became agitated.

Kevin, a 30-year-old biracial male who had been sleeping on the beach and in the woods for several months, told us, "The people in the shelter are sellouts. They can't handle the street."

Max (64 year-old White male) spoke up, "I'd rather sleep in the grass than that shelter. That place is full of drugs. Everyone in there is dirty and steals all my stuff." He went on to say, "It is scary in there."

Both Kevin and Max asserted that there were a lot of drugs in Springhouse, despite the zero-tolerance drug policy. Kevin stated, "They sell drugs right out in the open. There are not enough people watching." It could be that Kevin and Max felt that sleeping outside showed that they were strong, or they really believed that the shelter was more uncomfortable or dangerous than the street. It is more likely that the system had let Kevin and Max down so often that they had lost their faith in the institutions that should have supported them.

Conversely, people living in the shelter often stigmatize those who are sleeping rough. Harvey (51-year-old Black man) told us, "Yeah, those guys sleeping outside are losers. They are all addicted to drugs. They aren't even trying. People need to want it, and they do not."

Chrissy is a petite and muscular fifty-year-old White woman we talked to one afternoon in a public kitchen. She spends most of her days volunteering to teach people the Bible. She lives in her car with her small dog, Mitzy. We asked Chrissy what is needed for people who are homeless. "Let me tell you," she said. "People need to earn their keep. You can't just give people things. They take advantage." She went on to say:

> These people who sleep outside, they are like varmints. They pile up all this trash and just leave it everywhere. Someone needs to take all their stuff away. You know, what we need is a big brick building with a concrete floor. People could sleep there at night, and then all their trash could be hosed out of it in the morning. People want a place that's nice so they can decorate it, but they are not willing to get a job and pay for it. We need someone to tell them that they can do better and to show them that life can be better, but it has to be someone who has been there. Someone to show them that things can get better. People need to stop asking for a handout and work for what they get.

Chrissy clearly saw living in her car as superior to living outside.

I Worked My Way Up

Residents of Springhouse can be resentful of each other as well. We, along with our students, frequently cooked meals at Springhouse. One evening while we were standing outside taking a break, we talked to James (53-year-old White male), a security guard who, until a month before, had been a Springhouse client. As we watched the folks outside line up in front of the kitchen door for their dinner, James said, out of the blue, "They'll spend $70,000 on drugs in a month." He paused. "And then they are right back here."

We found this difficult to believe. "How much are these drugs they are buying for $70,000, and where do they get that kind of money?" we asked.

James just shook his head:

> They buy it (drugs) for all their friends and then rent real nice hotel rooms for a month or two. Pretty soon, they run out of money and come crawling back. They get hit by cars. Sometimes they do it on purpose. I've seen them do it.

James waved his hand in the direction of the street, "That is a crazy intersection. People get hit all the time—or pretend to."

"Why would they get hit on purpose? Cars are going pretty fast out there," we replied. The road is a major thoroughfare, and there is a gas station on the other side of the street. Recently someone was hit by a car while riding their bike across the road to the gas station.

"They want the money from insurance." James shook his head, "Dumb fucks." He laughed. Because Springhouse now employed James, he felt like he had risen about the rest of the people staying there. Springhouse allowed him to live in one of the small apartments they owned. "I worked my way up," James said. "The rest of these guys are too lazy to do much of anything."

I'm More Worthy

We also see stigmatization among people that appear to have the same status within Springhouse. We were assigned a resident to help us in the kitchen when we cooked dinner. One night, the resident who was helping us, Jeremy (64-year-old White male), looked over at the Springhouse residents lining up for food. "Some of these guys, they don't want to work. They just sit around here all day and do nothing." Jeremy does not have a job, but because he volunteers in the kitchen, he believes he is trying harder than others.

Pete (41-year-old Black male), another resident working in the kitchen that night, said:

> The biggest problem here is that people want everything for free. They don't want to work. People sit around here all day and do nothing. Me? I find a way to get the things I want. I don't ask for help.

"Do you have a job?" we asked.

"No, but I get what I need. I have a bike. I sold my plasma to buy it. I don't ask for handouts. People need more drive like me," Pete replied with a sigh. We often see this pattern of distancing oneself from others who are experiencing homelessness. They separate themselves by emphasizing how they are different or better than others, seemingly trying to convince themselves or us that they are worthy.[14]

While some people do not work and stay at Springhouse during the day, most of the folks who do not have jobs have legitimate reasons for being out of work. Many residents, particularly those over fifty, are not physically able to work. Over half of the people who stay in Springhouse have serious health issues: brain damage, cancer, heart disease, and untreated diabetes, to name a few. Other people staying in Springhouse are waiting to get new paperwork (e.g., Social Security cards, driver's licenses), which is often quite challenging. Pete and Jeremy were able to excuse and understand their situations but were not able or willing to understand the obstacles that are faced by others.

Stigma as a Coping Mechanism

Some people we met appear to understand how they are stereotyped and try to separate themselves from other individuals who are homeless. "I am not like the others in here," said Franklin, an unemployed forty-year-old Black health care worker staying at Springhouse. "I just need to get recertified and get back on my feet, and I will be fine. These other guys some of them just don't have it together. There are services here, but people do not take advantage of them." Franklin recently moved to South Carolina from Maryland, seeking a fresh start. He lost his professional license in Maryland due to alcoholism and wanted to start over in a new place. Once he got to South Carolina, alcohol caused him trouble again.

When Franklin moved to South Carolina, he planned to sleep in his car for a few nights until he found a job. One night, he was drinking beer in his car in a Walmart parking lot when a police officer drove through and found him. Once the officer realized Franklin was drinking in his vehicle, he arrested Franklin for public intoxication, DWI, and an open container violation. The officer took Franklin to jail, and his truck was impounded. Another officer dropped Franklin off at Springhouse when he was released from jail. "I wasn't doing anything wrong. I wasn't planning to drive. Now it will be harder to get a job without my truck."

Franklin is adamant that he is different from the other residents of Springhouse, and in one way, he is. Unlike many people who are unhoused, Franklin has a family in Maryland. He says they care about him and support him. He is not estranged from them and thinks he can return to Maryland anytime. His family would take him in and help him get back on his feet.

"Why don't you go back home?" we asked one day when we were sitting in the common room at Springhouse. He answered:

> I don't need to. Like I said, I'm not like the people here. They all want something for free. They just sit around all day. They need more drive. I can make it on my own. I need to prove this to my parents.

Franklin felt like his situation was just bad luck, whereas he believed other people with similar circumstances were homeless due to their moral failings. Shortly after this exchange, Franklin was asked to leave Springhouse for drinking and fighting. Franklin's alcoholism had caused his life to spiral out of control. He lost his professional license and found himself hundreds of miles from home, struggling to start his life over. Disassociating himself from the others living at Springhouse may have allowed him to feel like there was some part of his life in which he still had some control over.

They're Crazy—I'm Not

Another coping mechanism applied by some Springhouse residents is questioning the sobriety or mental capacity of others. Jane, a middle-aged Black female staying in the woman's shelter, had a series of heart attacks and numerous other health concerns. Her main concern, however, is the mental stability of her housemates. "There are a lot of crazy people in here. It is very mentally stressful. I cannot wait to leave." Jane asserted that the people there would make her crazy if she did not find housing soon. "I don't belong here."

Randall (49-year-old White man) expressed similar sentiments about the residents of the men's shelter. "A lot of the people staying here are damaged psychologically. They need help."

We chatted with Jasper at the men's shelter. He is a 50-year-old White male who works full-time as a repair person. He told us, "I am not like the other guys here. I 'm, not nuts, and I don't drink or do drugs. People need to get off drugs in here. They should drug test them. They let drunks in here too. It sucks."

Stereotyping by Others

It sometimes seems as though everyone has a story about how they tried to help individuals who are homeless and did not feel the recipient of their help appreciated it. In class, our students are often eager to discuss the bottle of water a panhandler rejected when it was offered to them. When friends and coworkers hear of our work with homelessness, they are often quick to explain why we should not give money to anyone who is homeless. "They will just buy drugs" is one common refrain. Other stories may revolve around how unappreciative some individuals who are homeless can be when they are offered food or a buck. For people who offer gifts to individuals who are homeless, it appears that there is an expectation that they should be extraordinarily grateful for whatever they are offered, whether they need it or not.

Recently the city began to advertise the "harm" in giving to people who are experiencing homelessness with a "Say No to Panhandling" campaign. They placed signs along the boardwalk parallel to the beach with a QR code and a link to places people can donate. They assume that money will

Figure 8.1 Say No to Panhandling

be better used if it is donated to agencies the city supports rather than if it is given directly to individuals.

Potential donors are also often particular about who they consider "deserving." For some people, homelessness is not a social problem worthy of their time, effort, or money. If the person who is homeless is a veteran, however, they tend to garner more favorable attention. Each year our class has a fundraiser for the programs we started (see Chapter 10 for a discussion of some of the programs). One year, the money we were raising was going toward a bike-share program at a transitional housing complex. We initially had difficulty finding enough donations, but money began rolling in when we advertised that the residents who use the bikes are veterans. We also learned that if we emphasize that Springhouse residents use bikes to go to work or look for work, people are more willing to donate.

Internalizing the Stigma

Numerous people have internalized the belief that they are solely responsible for their plight. One of the common answers to the question "What is your biggest obstacle to meeting your daily needs?" is "myself." Vinny (51-year-old White man) told us, "I just need to be responsible, and then I can reach my goal of working in an enjoyable job that offers security."

Dane, a 46-year-old White male who has been unhoused for fourteen years, feels the same. Although he has emphysema and COPD, he works five afternoons a week. The job does not pay enough for him to afford an apartment, and Dane says he probably cannot pass the credit check required for housing. He feels lucky that BLMC helps him get his medication. When we ask Dane about his most significant obstacle in becoming housed, he does not mention his medical problems or work that does not pay a living wage. He responds, "My obstacle is me, myself, and I."

We also hear from folks who perceived their mental illness as an individual failing. Ava (48-year-old White female), who suffers from depression and anxiety, told us that her mind was her biggest obstacle. She said, "If I could only get my mind straight, I could start getting my life together. I just need to change my mindset and get motivated."

Kyle, a 24-year-old White male who had been homeless for two years following an injury that left him with brain damage, told us, "The homeless are just forgotten. I feel like such a loser. Maybe I could find a positive influence to help me. Then I wouldn't be such a loser."

Conclusion

Although we expect some stereotyping of people who are experiencing homelessness by a largely uninformed public, it still catches us off-guard when we hear people who work directly with, or make policies for, people who are homeless write them off as a homogeneous group who have created their own problems. At first, we were surprised that people who are staying in shelters or sleeping rough were so willing to talk to us. Charles, a caseworker at the Housing Group, said, "These people are so used to being ignored. Nobody will even look at them. They are happy to talk to you because they want to be seen."

Interestingly, in all our interactions with people in and out of shelters, we found that the beliefs of people experiencing homelessness were the opposite of what the toxic charity model would predict. During our interviews, people who were unhoused articulated that they wanted structural changes to help them gain independence. When we asked what could be done to help house them, the top responses were: improved mental health, medical and addiction services, affordable housing, help to find living-wage jobs, and better public transportation. Not once did anyone ask for a handout.

The toxic charity model would assert that individuals who are homeless are undeserving and unappreciative. We see the opposite. Every time we volunteer to serve food at Springhouse, ask someone to sit down for an interview or loan out a bike, people are grateful for our help. We do not want to be thanked, and sometimes it is not very comfortable. Although the things we are doing are for them, we benefit as well. We would not have been able to write this book without their help. Also, counter to the toxic charity narrative, we find that most of the people we encounter want to work—even those with such immense physical limitations that the amount of activity they engage in surprised us. In all the time we worked with individuals experiencing homelessness, we only encountered three people who did not want to find housing through the traditional routes. Two of those individuals had tried and failed so many times that they had given up, and the other called himself sovereign. He believed the government did not have the right to dictate where and how he lived.

What Can Be Done?

In order to initiate long-term change, public perceptions of and attitudes toward people experiencing homelessness must change. We can start by changing the way we refer to people experiencing homelessness. Using the terms "the homeless" or "homeless people" make homelessness their defining characteristic—their master status. Using the term "people experiencing homelessness" or "individuals who are homeless" focuses on the state of being homeless as a temporary circumstance.[15]

Acceptance of the stereotypes of people who are experiencing homelessness has profound implications. Viewing people as having shortcomings that result in homelessness justifies the social order and legitimizes the status quo.[16] Moreover, we need to recognize that the assumption that people have other places to go but choose to sleep outside is based on a false premise.[17]

This mindset has been linked with the criminalization of homelessness.[18] If service providers, city officials, and even the people experiencing homelessness view the existing social structure as legitimate, then there is no motivation to advocate for structural changes.

Education must start in institutions, schools, social service providers, and law enforcement must work to educate about the stigmatization of homelessness.[19] If people experiencing homelessness are faced with stigma by those who are supposed to be helping them, they may become service-resistant.[20] Only a small number of people are chronically homeless, and they do not become chronically homeless overnight. However, people tend to stigmatize all who experience homelessness as chronically homeless and service-resistant. Education and advocacy must include members of the homeless community. The Faces of Homelessness is an excellent example. People who are experiencing, or have experienced homelessness, share their experiences with community groups and schools. This program addresses the lack of interaction, communication, and understanding between the housed and houseless communities.[21] Seeing individuals as human first and homelessness as a temporary circumstance can reduce much of the stigma surrounding homelessness.

Notes

1 Goffman, E. (1963). *Stigma: Notes on a spoiled identity*. Prentice Hall.
2 Belcher, J. R., & Deforge, B. R. (2012). Social stigma and homelessness: The limits of social change. *Journal of Human Behavior, 22*(8), 929–946. https://doi.org/10.108 0/10911359.2012.707941.
3 Wilson, T. D. (2018). A note on capitalist commodification of the homeless. *Review of Radical Political Economics, 51*(2), 282–297. https://doi.org/10.1177/ 0486613417741308.
4 Hoffman, L., & Coffey, B. (2008). Dignity and indignation: How people experiencing homelessness view services and providers. *The Social Science Journal, 45*(2), 207–222. https://doi.org/10.1016/j.soscij.2008.03.001.
5 Wilson, T. D. (2018). A note on capitalist commodification of the homeless. *Review of Radical Political Economics, 51*(2), 282–297. https://doi.org/10.1177/ 0486613417741308.
6 Bailey, I. (2015, April 19). Some homeless in Myrtle Beach prefer the street to Street Reach. *Sun News*. www.myrtlebeachonline.com/news/local/news-columns-blogs/ issac-bailey/article18909549.html.
7 Ibid.
8 The task force did not form until 2021. Their first recommendation was to tell people not to give people who are homeless anything and instead direct them to the (usually full) shelter.
9 Cronley, C. (2010). Unraveling the social construction of homelessness. *Journal of Human Behavior in the Social Sciences, 20*(2), 319–333. https://doi.org/10.1080/ 10911350903269955.
10 Shier, M., Jones, M., & Graham, J. (2012). Employment difficulties experienced by employed homeless people: Labor market factors that contribute to and maintain homelessness. *Journal of Poverty, 16*(1), 27–47. https://doi.org/10.1080/10875549.2 012.640522.

11 They did stop charging people during the Covid-19 pandemic.

12 Since then, Springhouse has received more beds and allows a limited number of "emergency stays." Emergency clients can enter at 8:00 pm and leave early the next morning.

13 Rayburn, R., & Guittar, N. (2013). "This is where you are supposed to be:" How homeless individuals cope with stigma. *Sociological Spectrum*, *33*(2), 159–174. https://doi.org/10.1080/02732173.2013.732876.

14 Rayburn and Guittar (2013) also found this phenomenon.

15 Kamelhar, B. (2019, February 18). The stigma associated with homelessness and how it leads to ineffective solutions both in and out of the courtroom. *Georgetown Law Library*. www.law.georgetown.edu/poverty-journal/blog/the-stigma-associated-with-homelessness-and-how-it-leads-to-ineffective-solutions-both-in-and-out-of-the-courtroom.

16 Phelan, J., Link, B., Moore, R., & Stueve, A. (1997). The stigma of homelessness: The impact of the label of 'homeless' on attitudes toward poor persons. *Social Psychology Quarterly*, *60*(4), 323–337. https://doi.org/10.2307/2787093.

17 Kamelhar, B. (2019, February 18). The stigma associated with homelessness and how it leads to ineffective solutions both in and out of the courtroom. *Georgetown Journal on Poverty Law & Policy*. www.law.georgetown.edu/poverty-journal/blog/the-stigma-associated-with-homelessness-and-how-it-leads-to-ineffective-solutions-both-in-and-out-of-the-courtroom/.

18 Markowitz, F., & Syverson, J. (2021). Race, gender, and homelessness stigma: Effects of perceived blameworthiness and dangerousness. *Deviant Behavior*, *42*(7), 919–931.

19 Belcher, J. R., & Deforge, B. R. (2012). Social stigma and homelessness: The limits of social change. *Journal of Human Behavior*, *22*(8), 929–946. https://doi.org/10.1080/10911359.2012.707941.

20 Hoffman, L., & Coffey, B. (2008). Dignity and indignation: How people experiencing homelessness view services and providers. *The Social Science Journal*, *45*(2), 207–222. https://doi.org/10.1016/j.soscij.2008.03.001.

21 National Coalition for the Homeless. *Faces of the homeless speakers' bureau*. www.nationalhomeless.org/faces/index.html.

Chapter 9

The Police Made Me Homeless

Regulating Behavior

Introduction

> "I'm homeless because I was arrested on a bullshit charge. Sleeping in my car. The police made me homeless."
>
> Joe, a 35-year old Hispanic male

The criminal justice system plays an enormous part in the prevalence of homelessness across the country, and Myrtle Beach is no different. Incarceration can be a risk factor for becoming homeless, and homelessness can be a risk factor for becoming involved in the criminal justice system. Additionally, having a criminal record can make becoming housed more difficult. About fifteen percent of the eleven million people who are incarcerated each year in the United States have experienced homelessness. Almost 50,000 people go directly from incarceration to homeless shelters yearly because they have nowhere else to go upon their release.[1] Individuals incarcerated for extended periods are seldom provided with assistance with reintegration, and many are ill-prepared for life outside prison. Moreover, due to the lack of affordable housing and the background checks required by landlords, it is often challenging to place ex-offenders in permanent housing.

In Myrtle Beach, like many other cities with tourist-centered economies, there is an emphasis on legislating the behavior of people who are homeless so that they will be encouraged to move to different locations or, at a minimum, keep out of public view. These policies and laws regulate the performance of necessary human behaviors in public (e.g., sleeping, sitting, or camping in public) or impede the ability of individuals or groups of citizens to provide services for people experiencing homelessness (e.g., providing food).

The effect of anti-homelessness policies on the mental and physical health of the individual is so significant that in 2019 the American Medical Association (AMA) passed a resolution stating that laws should protect the civil

DOI:10.4324/9781003325581-11

and human rights of people experiencing homelessness and not criminalize necessary human behaviors.[2] In addition, they declare that criminal sanctions should be a last resort for behaviors associated with homelessness.[3] The AMA asserts that the government should prioritize affordable housing, particularly for those who are chronically homeless.

Criminalizing the behaviors of unhoused individuals is more expensive than providing shelter or addressing the root causes of homelessness. These costs are paid for by taxpayers, whether they know it or not.[4] Studies show that it costs more to jail people who are unhoused than to shelter them. On average, one day in jail costs $87, whereas a shelter bed costs $28. Not only is criminalizing homelessness expensive and ineffective, but it is contrary to international human rights laws.[5]

In this chapter, we discuss laws that target behaviors associated with homelessness in Myrtle Beach and the surrounding county. Using our interviews and experiences as evidence, we demonstrate how these laws and practices affect the lives of individuals who are unhoused in Myrtle Beach. We discuss how interactions with the criminal justice system (e.g., being ticketed, arrested, or imprisoned) can cause or prolong homelessness and how experiencing homelessness increases interactions with the criminal justice system. We discuss alternatives to criminalization that are less costly financially and psychologically to both individuals and the community.

The Crime of Homelessness

Cities will often use exclusionary zoning to regulate where people who are homeless can stand, sit, and sleep, as well as where services for people who are homeless can be located.[6] Table 9.1 lists the Myrtle Beach ordinances frequently used to regulate the behavior of people experiencing homelessness. Many of these laws sanction behaviors that may be illegal for people who are homeless but are ignored if the person is housed.[7] These laws include behaviors such as standing, sitting, loitering, and trespassing. For example, in Myrtle Beach, many piers have signs that state, "It is Illegal to Loiter Under Pier." Tourists often sit under the pier when the sun becomes too hot, and there are no legal consequences when they do. If law enforcement thinks a person may be homeless, they may question, cite, or arrest the person.[8] The fact that these no-loitering signs target individuals who are homeless and are not enforced for everyone is evidenced by the fact that the pier at the state park (which you must pay to enter) has no such sign. Typically, people who are homeless do not pay to get into a state park and thus will not be sitting under the pier.

Sandy's story highlights the way that the pier ordinance is enforced. Sandy is a well-spoken 28-year-old White woman who is sleeping rough. She sleeps here and there—anywhere that is available. When we met her at a

Table 9.1 Myrtle Beach Ordinances[1]

14–302	Prohibits sleeping in a vehicle at night.
14–301	Prohibits panhandling.
14–3	Prohibits changing clothes in a car.
14–313	Prohibits soliciting in exchange for contribution.
14–312	Prohibits public begging or panhandling.
14–303	Prohibits sitting or lying on public sidewalks.
5–19	Prohibits sleeping on a public beach between 9 pm and 8 am.
14–67	Gives police the right to arrest for trespassing without being called by a business.
14–66	Prohibits public intoxication/impairment.
14–314	Prohibits trespassing in public buildings.
2009–20	Prohibits feeding the homeless in public places.
14–81	Prohibits public urination or defecation (this is an offense against "morality and decency").
12–92	Prohibits standing on sidewalks and allows for signs prohibiting sitting and standing.
12–904	Prohibits camping, sleeping, lodging, or the taking of residence in any camper, van, bus, or other motor vehicle on the public streets or in any park or public place.
14–222	Prohibits the misuse of parking areas.
14–315	Prohibits sitting or sleeping on the boardwalk next to the beach.
14–316	Prohibits using a park after hours or without a permit. Prohibits sleeping, reclining, or providing food in public park.

[1] Code of Ordinances, Myrtle Beach, SC Municode Library. Mini TOC: Chapter 14 — OFFENSES AND MISCELLANEOUS PROVISIONS | Code of Ordinances | Myrtle Beach, SC | Municode Library

public kitchen, we asked about her experiences with the criminal justice system. She replied:

> One time, I was sitting under the pier in the evening, and two police came up and started asking me all these questions. One of the questions was, 'What are you doing?' They could see what I was doing. I was reading a book. I was sitting next to the pier. I don't even think I was under it, and they arrested me.

We asked Sandy why she was arrested, and she replied, "They knew I was homeless because it was night, and I had some of my stuff around me. I wasn't sleeping there, though. I was just reading my book. They said I was trespassing."

We asked Sandy if that was the only time she had been arrested. She said:

> Nope. Sometimes I just want to ask regular people if I can sit next to them so that I won't get hassled, but then they'd think I am crazy. One time I was arrested for loitering with harmful intent. I don't even know what that was all about. Another time I was sitting in the park,

organizing my stuff. They got me for public camping. They just arrest people because they are homeless. They'll find a way to arrest you if they know you have nowhere to go.

In Myrtle Beach, although sometimes they are given warnings, people experiencing homelessness are often arrested for crimes associated with survival.[9] There are fewer than 200 shelter beds for the over 1,000 people who are without a home in the county. There are few public bathrooms and not many places where a person who is experiencing homelessness can legally sit or sleep. If an individual does not have a criminal record when they become homeless, it is likely they will have one once they are on the street, often without committing any crime other than those crimes associated with survival. Myrtle Beach enforces laws against sleeping in public parks and beaches, loitering, camping, panhandling, and other nuisance laws. For example, Mark (55-year old White male) told us, "If you are on the boardwalk with a cup and look homeless, the police will ask to look in your cup. They don't ask to look in the cups of tourists. People go to jail for having cups."

Silas, a White male who looks younger than his 38 years, sat down to speak with us in a public kitchen. When we asked him if he had any experience with law enforcement in Myrtle Beach, he laughed. "I just got out." he said. We asked him why he was arrested. "Last night, I was riding my bike on the boardwalk, and I was going very fast. I decided to see if I could beat a golf cart, and I did! I beat that golf cart on my bike!" He thought it was hilarious that he outrode a golf cart.

"You got arrested for riding your bike?" we asked Silas.

"I did. I guess I wasn't supposed to ride my bike there. They said it was 'disorderly conduct,' but I beat the golf cart!" We looked up the arrest records from the night before, and sure enough, his arrest was listed.

We analyzed the arrest records for the Myrtle Beach Police Department from January 1, 2022 through April 20, 2022. In these four months, we found 729 arrests that were likely people experiencing homelessness. We used the location of the arrest and the type of arrest to estimate which arrests were associated with people experiencing homelessness. For example, if someone was arrested for public intoxication in an area with bars that cater to tourists or locals, we did not include those records in the count. Of the cases we did include, 104 individuals were arrested more than once and comprise 306 of the 729 arrests made for petty crimes such as loitering, sleeping, and public intoxication. Although we have been repeatedly told that it is not a priority for the Myrtle Beach police to arrest people for crimes associated with homelessness, at a public meeting, a city official said, "We just arrested someone the other day for loitering. We thought they were about to shoot up. We couldn't let them do that."

A person released after incarceration is typically put back onto the street without support. Silas describes how difficult it can be to be released after an arrest:

> It is so crazy out there. They create criminals. I was arrested because I was high. They took all my stuff. When I was let back out, they gave me a bus ticket. I had no clothes, no money, and they took my ID. What was I supposed to do? I was also sick because I am an addict. I was forced to steal food and do other things I didn't want to do. I could not find anywhere to get help. It is a really bad system.

It is very inefficient to dedicate resources to policing people experiencing homelessness. Money that could be spent on housing, rehab, or mental health care is instead spent on salaries for police officers traveling back and forth between the beach and the jail (20 miles away), the courts, and feeding and housing people at the jail.

Feeding People—Kindness or Criminal?

It is illegal to feed people who are experiencing homelessness in Myrtle Beach. In 2009, the city of Myrtle Beach passed an ordinance restricting people from providing food to people in parks and other public property. For nine years before the city passed this law, churches brought food to public parks each Saturday to feed anyone who was hungry. Most of the people who came to these public events were homeless. Although public kitchens and other places in the city offer food during the week, there are few options for people experiencing food insecurity on the weekends. The 2009 ordinance stopped the public food programs. The ordinance states that groups may apply for permits to feed people, but can only get a permit four times a year.[10]

In 2013, a Quaker, Richard Hopkins, violated the ordinance by feeding people in a park without a permit and was given a $1,092 fine. Not only did the city want him to have a permit, but they also required him to have a million-dollar insurance policy to use the permit.[11] Hopkins sued the city and lost. In 2014, the Circuit Court for Horry County found that Myrtle Beach had a constitutional right to outlaw feeding people in public because it protected the public from unsafe food.

For nearly a decade, church vans have been pulling up to a public park to take anyone who is hungry to one of a rotation of churches each Saturday for lunch. Other people go to the park with sandwiches on the weekends, even though it is against the law. They appear to get away with it as long as they do not advertise their actions. These services are essential for people experiencing homelessness as the only available weekend food is the dinner meals served at Springhouse.

Sophia, a 49-year-old Black woman who has been homeless on and off for over thirty years, is currently sleeping on her friend's couch. Her mother kicked her out when she became pregnant at age 15, and she has not had stable housing since then. When we asked her if she had trouble getting food, she told us, "Yeah, it's really hard on the weekends. There is a church that provides weekend food sometimes, but I don't have a way to get there. They really need weekend services around here."

Encampment Sweeps

Sometimes, people will return to volunteer at an organization that helped them when they were unhoused. We met Rowan (58-year-old Black man), a volunteer at a public kitchen, after he had been housed for a few months. After a while, our conversation turned to where people could sleep without getting in trouble when the shelters were full. Rowan had a stack of business cards in the pocket of his button-down shirt. He pulled one out. "There are some good ones out there." He handed us the card. "This guy."

We asked, "This guy? You mean this guy is a good officer?"

Rowan replied:

> Well, he was, but he retired. I don't know if there are any good ones left. Most of them just go into the woods, cut down the tents, and throw everything out. If there are people there, they take them to jail. They took so many people to jail that they had to stop that for a while. The city jail was full.

We asked, "So they don't cut the tents down anymore?"

Rowan responded, "When they have room, they do."

In Myrtle Beach city limits, homeless encampments were common in the past. As wooded areas in the city are cleared and encampments are destroyed, it drives people experiencing homelessness deeper into the woods, moving from place to place each night, or out of the city limits. Homeless advocates in Myrtle Beach assert that the primary purpose of encampment sweeps is to make people who are homeless less visible in downtown areas so that the tourists will not feel uncomfortable.[12] These sweeps push people further away from the jobs and services they need. The longer a person is homeless, the farther they go into the woods to stay out of sight, making service resistance and chronic homelessness an inevitable consequence of anti-homelessness policies.

Johnny (38-year-old White man) talked to us in a public kitchen. "I used to sleep around here, but I kept getting ticketed. I got arrested once. Now I am way out in the woods. No one can find me." We asked Johnny what he needed, and he replied, "A better tent to keep the possums and raccoons away."

In our examination of four months of arrest records, we found sixteen arrests for camping, thirteen arrests for sleeping in a location not meant for sleeping (a park, the beach, or a car), and 218 arrests for trespassing after 6:00 pm. When people are arrested for "crimes" such as these, typically, it is because they have nowhere else to go. Such arrests often mean that the person loses all their belongings, including their ID, making it difficult for them to access other necessary services. The public nature of arrests of people experiencing homelessness reinforces the public perception of them as a threat or a nuisance that needs to be controlled rather than human beings trying to survive.

Unfortunately, even when a business has room and allows individuals to sleep on their property, they are often met with resistance from city officials. Bob, the director of a community kitchen, allowed a few people to sleep on their lot while he sought to help them find a permanent place to stay. One day Bob called us, "We've got to get another shelter now! They made me kick my sleepers out." The "they" he was referring to were not the police, but the officials from the code enforcement department. If the 'sleepers' were not told to leave, both the sleepers and Bob could be in legal trouble.

A Revolving Door

Nash is a 19-year-old Black man. When he was 17, Nash was arrested for breaking into a house in his parent's neighborhood. He just got released from prison and this is his first time living on his own. He cannot return to his parent's neighborhood. He said, "There is no support for people leaving prison. No network. When I got released, I bounced around on the street for a while. I've been in the shelter for the last 30 days."

Cara, a 25-year-old White woman, went from prison to the street. When we spoke with her at a resource fair, she told us:

> I don't know how I got here. I have a degree in engineering. Things have been rough. I don't have any family to help me. I can't get any help from any of the agencies around here. I have been pregnant six times, but only four of them made it. I think I am pregnant again. I ended up on the street after I got out of prison. I was charged with robbery. I only met with my lawyer once, so I just took the charges.

Sam's story is one example of the revolving door between shelters, the street, and jails. Sam (41-year-old White man) was arrested shortly after becoming homeless. It was a rainy day when he was released, and he had nowhere to go. A police officer dropped him off at the door of Springhouse. Sam went inside, and the officer drove away. A short time later, we saw him come back out of Springhouse with his backpack slung over his shoulder, grumbling under his breath. He walked through the rainy parking lot and down the street with his head hanging low.

A few weeks later, we saw Sam again inside Springhouse and told him that we saw him being turned away a few weeks ago. We asked him what had happened.

"The whole situation is insane," he said. "I had a fine for driving with a suspended license. I didn't have the money for it, so I got arrested." Since he did not have the money for the fines and fees needed for his release, he was kept in jail until his court date. "When I got out, a cop brought me here [Springhouse], but they said I couldn't come in. They were full." After being turned away from Springhouse, he had nowhere to go. He had been staying in a motel before his arrest, trying to work and save money for a new apartment. After he was jailed, he lost his motel room with all his stuff in it, his job, and his car was impounded.

With his car impounded, his job gone, and Springhouse full, Sam began sleeping on the beach at night. After a few days, he was arrested again for sleeping in public. "I had nowhere to go. I am not sure what they wanted me to do," he said, referring to the police. Once again, he was back in jail for not having the money to pay the fines associated with his arrest.

When Sam was released the second time, he was again taken to Springhouse by another police officer. "I told them they had to come in with me. I knew they wouldn't let me in." This time the officer escorted Sam through the door. Springhouse was still full, but a caseworker allowed Sam to stay until he figured out where to go. Sam believed he could stay this time because the police officer brought him in. If the police had walked him inside Springhouse the first time he was released, the second arrest might have been avoided.

We met Priscilla outside a local social service agency. She is a slight, 40-year-old White female who lost her housing when she could not pay her rent. She has thyroid cancer and lost her job when she became too sick to work. She has been sleeping in an enclosed stairwell for the last few months. She said:

> There are shelters for men, but not so much for women. It's no wonder they turn to drugs and prostitution. They get taken [to jail], but when they get out, they are in the same boat. People do what they need to do to survive.

When we asked Priscilla if she had been arrested, she nodded. "Yeah. A few times."

Many folks we speak with tell us that having a criminal record is a significant barrier to obtaining employment or housing. Tanner, a 32-year-old

White man with a college degree, said, "Having a criminal record really hurts. A lot. They classify you as a group, even with my education. It really weighs on you."

Collateral Damage

Criminal and civil punishment for behaviors associated with being human is a waste of public resources and can make it more difficult for people experiencing homelessness to secure permanent housing.[13] A criminal record, even with a misdemeanor conviction, can make an individual ineligible for subsidized housing and may result in exclusion from employment. If individuals feel like the police are harassing them, they are often less likely to seek services they may need. The criminalization of homelessness is especially problematic for people with mental or physical disabilities that prevent them from working or obtaining housing for themselves.

Sometimes when people who are homeless get arrested (even when the arrests are legitimate), the arrest itself can cause subsequent problems. We heard numerous stories of people who were arrested and did not receive their ID or other paperwork back when they were released. Somewhere between the person being incarcerated and them being released, their documents disappear, and when they contact law enforcement to follow up, they are met with a shrug.

We sat down to talk with Joe (35-year old Hispanic male) and Jim (42-year-Black male) about a week after they arrived at Springhouse. They did not know each other previously, but they arrived at Springhouse at the same time, and their stories are remarkably similar. We asked Joe to tell us how he ended up at Springhouse. He looked around the common room where we were sitting. "I shouldn't be here," He said. "I came here [Myrtle Beach] for a job, and I was living with my girlfriend. When I got here, the job that was supposed to be mine had been given to someone else." Joe shook his head. "I don't know anyone here. A week after I came here, my girlfriend broke up with me and kicked me out."

"What did you do?" we asked.

"I had an interview for a new job the next day, so I decided to sleep in my car and figure out what to do after I had my interview." Joe explained that he drove into a Walmart parking lot because he heard that they didn't hassle people who slept in their cars overnight:

> I was in the passenger seat, not the driver's side, and I had a couple of beers. About an hour after I went to sleep, I woke up to a cop banging on my window. He woke me up and charged me with public intoxication and DUI, even though I was not intoxicated or driving. I missed my job interview because of the police. I wasn't doing anything but trying to sleep. Yeah. I had a few beers, but I wasn't driving. I was

sleeping. When I got out of jail, they [the police] dropped me off here [Springhouse], but they didn't give my license back.

South Carolina is one of only four states (Hawaii, Oklahoma, South Carolina, and South Dakota) that has a law against sleeping in vehicles.[14]

Jim's story was remarkably similar to Joe's. Jim had recently moved to Myrtle Beach for work and was staying in a pay-by-the-week motel while he waited for his first paycheck to come in. He was parked outside the door of his room, and he could not find his motel key. Since the office was closed, he decided to have a few beers and sleep in his car until the morning. Jim, like Joe, was found by a police officer and arrested. "I was parked! I was five feet from the door of my room!" He stressed that he had not been drinking anything until he was "home." Jim, like Joe, claimed that the police kept his ID when they released him from jail. Additionally, to make things worse, all Jim's personal belongings were gone when he went back to the motel after he was released from jail.

A caseworker at Springhouse called the police station for both Joe and Jim, asking how to get the licenses back. In both instances, the police told the caseworkers that the licenses had been returned. There was nothing left for Jim and Joe to do but start over and try to find a way to get new identification, housing, and jobs.

We are often told stories of people who are arrested for a relatively minor offense, have their cars towed, spend a few nights in jail, and are then dropped off by the police at Springhouse, minus their belongings and identification. Getting a job, housing, or even a motel for the night is almost impossible without a license. Many people do not have access to their birth certificates or other documents that would help verify their identity to restore their license.

An experience we had one cold January afternoon exemplifies how anti-homeless policies can affect the attitudes of people who are experiencing homelessness toward police as well as potentially affecting the willingness of outreach workers and citizens to get involved. We went to a park where we knew there would be many people experiencing homelessness. We had collected jackets, socks, and hygiene items to hand out to people who wanted them. Five men ran up as soon as we arrived to see what we were doing. One man wearing a t-shirt and jeans grabbed a jacket and a scarf. "OH! My girlfriend would love this! Can I take it for her?" We gave him the coat and scarf and asked him if he wanted anything for himself. It was only about forty degrees outside.

He picked up a couple of pairs of socks. "I could use these."

Another man standing back a little looked around and said, "You know you're not supposed to be here. They'll pick you up if they catch you."

We were still trying to give the first guy a jacket or something else to keep him warm, but we responded, "Who will pick us up?"

"The cops. They don't be liking people giving us stuff." The second man was eyeing the stuff we had laid out while also checking his surroundings.

"We will be okay. Thank you. Do you want a jacket?"

He came closer. "Yes. Can I have two? I have a friend I stay with." He took his two jackets and wandered off, looking pleased.

The first man who took the stuff for his girlfriend came back; bouncing on the balls of his feet, he asked for a bag. He had changed his mind about taking the clothes we brought. We gave him a bag, and he began filling it with the stuff we had put out. "That guy's right. They'll get you quick if they see you. I'm just going to take this stuff and leave some for the others." Once his bag was full, he rambled away, calling a big THANK YOU over his shoulder.

Attitudes Toward the Police

As we highlighted in Chapter 3, criminalizing unavoidable human behavior follows the broken windows model of policing. This model posits that if minor 'crimes' such as loitering are policed, people will be less likely to commit more serious crimes such as vandalism or theft. Lana highlighted the problem with this type of policing when we interviewed her at a public kitchen:

> Police are always watching people, harassing them. They follow people around. They belittle the homeless. They give them $300 tickets. If they don't pay, they get a warrant. They get arrested. Now they have a record and can't get a job.

Lana is a 29-year-old White female who is sleeping rough. She believes that the police can justify arresting people for crimes of survival because they do not view people experiencing homelessness as human. She said, "I try to stay clear of them. They are very disrespectful and treat us like garbage. People around here see us as dirty. We get harassed because of the way we look. It is degrading."

Lana might be right. During the Covid-19 epidemic, we went, along with some service organizations, to a public kitchen to hand out hygiene bags and Covid-19 information. At one point, one of the officers who was at the event got a call. He drove off but was back in five minutes. "That was an easy arrest. He was walking right towards us." A person who was homeless had missed a court case and had a warrant for his arrest. He was walking toward the kitchen for breakfast and was picked up. We saw Lana again later that day. "Yep. That's what they do. Any time there is an event here, the police are also here. They pick people up, take pictures of us, and follow us. They are just waiting for us to do something wrong."

The police department is trying to address homelessness using strategies other than criminalization. They have an outreach team that works with the homeless community. The chief of police is spearheading a coalition bringing together service providers to better coordinate services to people experiencing homelessness. The police department has recently created a program called Outreach Wednesday, in which service providers and police walk through the city to help people experiencing homelessness connect with service providers. Unfortunately, the history of criminalization of homelessness in Myrtle Beach has made people experiencing homelessness leery of the police. At the beginning of the police-organized outreach event, we chatted with a man experiencing homelessness. He pointed at a few police officers standing at a distance and told us, "They do not want you helping us. They hate the homeless."

Keep Moving

At another community outreach event, we met Jeff, a 57-year-old White male. Jeff seemed to be in a good mood. He was making a lot of jokes. "I did crack once—for six years," he laughed. Despite his outward joviality, a few minutes later he became more serious. "It is a crime to be homeless in Myrtle Beach," he said with a shrug:

> I sleep in abandoned buildings and benches until the police come by and tell me to move on. They won't let me sleep. Really, I just want a job, but no one is hiring right now because of Covid. I don't do crack anymore, but I do drink to self-medicate. I have bipolar, manic depression, and a hernia. I am on disability, but I need a job to supplement because there is no affordable housing here. If I sit in the park for ten minutes, someone will call the police on me. Myrtle Beach is the worst place to be homeless.

He continued, "It is illegal to panhandle, I can't work, and can't get housing . . . What do they expect us to do?" Although people who experience homelessness are more likely to be suicidal than individuals who are housed, and unhoused folks often tell us that they think they will be dead in five years, Jeff was optimistic. "I will have a good job and be home with my five children in five years."

Willy, a 61-year-old White male, has a similar perspective. One afternoon as he stood outside of the public kitchen smoking a cigarette, he told us, "I came to Myrtle Beach to help my mom. She has dementia. I came here to take care of her, but she doesn't recognize me anymore," he said, "so I am out here. I've never had to sleep outside before." He waved at the road. "It's tough out there."

We asked Willy whether he had interactions with the police, and he dropped his chin to his chest. He paused a second before he responded, "Police harass repeat offenders. So, the same people are going in and out of jail. It is a waste of time and money to keep arresting people." He asserted that the government does not work with people who are homeless. "They work against us. It is a waste of time to keep harassing us. It doesn't help them or us. They harass us when we are sleeping. They gave me 30 days [in jail] for loitering."

Tracy is a 28-year-old White female. She has a broken pelvis, stage four cancer, and is in a wheelchair. Tracy cannot stay in the women's shelter because it is not handicap-accessible. When we ask her about the police, she said:

> People here don't care if you live or die. Sometimes I sleep on a wooden bench on the boardwalk. If the police see me, they make me move. I have been in jail for panhandling before. I don't know what they want me to do. I can't work. I'm in a wheelchair, and I have cancer.

She also said that if people get caught giving money to individuals who are homeless, the person helping can get taken to jail.

Why Criminalize?

Part of the motivation for the criminalization of homelessness appears to be the idea that if you make people who are homeless too comfortable, it will attract more people who are homeless to the area. For example, the 2014 National Coalition for the Homeless food sharing report quotes a Key West City Commissioner saying, "What we've got to do is quit making it cozy. Let's not feed them anymore."[15]

People repeatedly say to us, "Other cities give people bus tickets to come here. They know we have services for people who are homeless." Although it is common for cities to give people who are experiencing homelessness bus tickets to other cities, Myrtle Beach does the same thing. It is not that other cities are shipping people to Myrtle Beach; many cities, including Myrtle Beach, are trying to move their homeless population out. Giving people bus tickets does not solve the problem; it just moves people around. One city resident said, "As long as we cater to them [people who are homeless], they won't go away. They're hurting the local people and the local economy, [and] they're nothing but leeches."[16]

Police as First Responders to Health Incidents

The criminal justice system is often called to address community problems that another agency would better serve.[17] When communities lack an established systematic response to assist with problems associated with homelessness, the criminal justice system becomes the de facto service provider, particularly for issues dealing with a mental health crisis.[18] We saw this firsthand when we met Frankie.

Frankie (55-year-old White male) is severely disabled and is currently sleeping rough. Until recently, he had been renting a room in a house, paying for it with his disability check. His landlord kicked him out when someone stole his rent money from where it was stored—under his mattress. When we met Frankie at a public kitchen, he had been on the street for a couple of weeks and was despondent. He told us that when he was a child, he pulled a pot of boiling water off a stove and burned 40 percent of his body. Because of this childhood incident, he is severely scarred. He pulled up his shorts and shirt and showed us all the burn scars. "Look! I can't do anything about this. I've looked like this since I was little."

He showed us the scars from where he has rods in both legs, making one leg shorter than the other, and started crying:

> My boss drowned last week. It's crazy. He saved me from drowning a few weeks ago, and now he has drowned. I have almost died five times, but the Lord won't take me. I want to die, but the Lord doesn't want me.

Although we typically give out information pamphlets and show individuals what agency they should call, we were genuinely concerned with Frankie's mental health, so we started calling around for him. Almost every place we called offered to put him on a list, but we could not do anything for him immediately. Several organizations told us that if Frankie was suicidal, we should call the police. Calling the police would not help Frankie. In the end, we gave him a backpack with hygiene items and told him who to contact for emergency housing. We never saw Frankie again.

What Can Be Done?

Instead of giving people who are experiencing homelessness bus tickets out of town or jailing them, we as a society must begin to think of people as human first and as people who are experiencing homelessness second. Once we humanize the individual, we can change the narrative surrounding homelessness. Breaking the link between homelessness and the criminal justice system cannot depend on trying to reform the person. You cannot reform a person who commits a crime associated with being human.

Affordable Housing

Increasing access to affordable housing is the best way to reduce homelessness before it occurs. Affordable housing also reduces crime victimization and can save municipalities money. Many individuals we speak with have an income from work or other sources, such as Social Security. The income they have is just not enough to afford housing. If individuals have access to housing they can afford (paying no more than 30 percent of their income), there will be fewer people on the street. Studies have shown that housing reduces calls to police for mental health incidents, trespass violations, crimes committed by people who are homeless, and crimes committed against people who are homeless. There will also be fewer emergency room visits for mental health and health incidents.

Permanent Supportive Housing with Intensive Case Management

Housing First has long been advocated as a solution for homelessness.[19] Although Housing First can be successful, many people who experience homelessness need more than a roof over their heads. Increasing access to housing and intensive case management has been shown to have numerous benefits for the individual and society. Case management can ensure that individuals keep up with their bills and pay their rent on time. It limits the number of calls to police, reduces incarceration rates, and can keep children out of foster care. Permanent supportive housing, along with intensive case management, reduces emergency room visits and helps people who are disabled receive more appropriate health care.[20]

Outreach

When permanent supportive housing is unavailable, or if a person is service resistant, psychiatric outreach teams available seven days a week, low-barrier 24-hour shelters, and public day centers have been shown to reduce calls to police. These solutions are more effective when trained professionals are on-site for case management.[21] Myrtle Beach has none of these. The available shelters have many requirements, including a no-tolerance policy for drugs and alcohol and a condition that clients are county residents. If one can get a bed at a shelter, the case managers do not have the training to help with the mental health issues that most clients need.

Public Restrooms and Monitored Campsites

Public restrooms and campsites for people experiencing homelessness will not eliminate homelessness, but they can keep people from being cited or arrested for crimes associated with human bodily functions. Everyone needs to sleep and use the bathroom. Having safe, monitored places for people to rest helps to reduce the burden on law enforcement and jails. Additionally, if individuals are sleeping in a campsite or public parking lot, it can reduce crime and provide a place for social service agencies to feed people, provide case management, and help with the next steps.

Prison Reentry Programs

The shortage of available, affordable housing means that ex-offenders compete for the same limited number of housing units as people with no criminal history. Research has demonstrated that housing assistance with wraparound services (social services, treatment for substance abuse and mental health problems, and community support) effectively reduces new convictions.[22]

Conclusion

We acknowledge that the police are being asked to fill in the gaps left by social service providers.[23] The legal and criminal justice systems are not equipped to deal with many of the problems that homeless individuals are experiencing, which may contribute to their homelessness, such as substance abuse, mental illness, or disabilities. Although we asked individuals about their positive and negative experiences with law enforcement, most of the people we talk to have only negative experiences with police. Most of the people we spoke to about issues of homelessness feel as if the police are going out of their way to hassle them because they are homeless. These negative perceptions of the police reduce the likelihood that homeless individuals will call the police in an emergency.

The criminalization of homelessness does not work at any level. It does not deter people from committing "crimes" associated with being human, nor does it promote community safety.[24] Being arrested can spiral someone into homelessness. If an individual is already homeless, an arrest can extend the time they spend on the street. Policing people who are homeless is also costly to society; a night in jail is three times more expensive than a night in a shelter. Enforcing ordinances aimed at controlling the behavior of individuals who are homeless takes time that the police could spend more productively, particularly if there is nowhere else the person can go. It would be more effective and humane to direct community resources toward affordable housing and social services.

Notes

1 United States Interagency Council on Homelessness. (2019). *Reduce criminal justice involvement.* www.usich.gov/solutions/criminal-justice/.
2 American Medical Association. (2019). *Opposition to measures that criminalize homelessness.* www.ama-assn.org/system/files/2019-04/a19-bot28.pdf.
3 Ibid. American Medical Association.

4 United States Interagency Council on Homelessness. (2015). *Opening doors: Federal strategic plan to prevent and end homelessness.* www.usich.gov/resources/uploads/asset_library/USICH_OpeningDoors_Amendment2015_FINAL.pdf.

5 National Law Center on Homelessness and Poverty. (2019). *Housing not handcuffs.* https://homelesslaw.org/wp-content/uploads/2019/12/HOUSING-NOT-HANDCUFFS-2019-FINAL.pdf.

6 Grainger, G. L. (2021). Punishment, support, or discipline? Taking stock of recent debates about homeless governance in neoliberal cities. *Sociology Compass, 15*(8), 1–16. https://doi.org/10.1111/soc4.12909.

7 National Coalition for the Homeless. (2014, October). *Share no more: The criminalization of efforts to feed people in need.* https://nationalhomeless.org/wp-content/uploads/2014/10/Food-Sharing2014.pdf.

8 Bailey, I. (2015, April 19). Some homeless in Myrtle Beach prefer the street to Street Reach. *Sun News.* www.myrtlebeachonline.com/news/local/news-columns-blogs/issac-bailey/article18909549.html.

9 United States Interagency Council on Homelessness. (2015). *Opening doors: Federal strategic plan to prevent and end homelessness.* www.usich.gov/resources/uploads/asset_library/USICH_OpeningDoors_Amendment2015_FINAL.pdf.

10 Myrtle Beach, South Carolina—Code of Ordinances, 79. § 14–317(f)(3) (2022). https://library.municode.com/sc/myrtle_beach/codes/code_of_ordinances?nodeId=COOR_CH14OFMIPR.

11 O'Dare, T. (2013, July 26). Myrtle Beach judge rules citizens can't feed homeless in a public park, appeal likely. *My Horry News.* www.myhorrynews.com/news/local/myrtle_beach/myrtle-beach-judge-rules-citizens-cant-feed-homeless-in-public-park-appeal-likely/article_ffd75928-f540-11e2-9236-001a4bcf6878.html.

12 Bailey, I. (2015, April 19). Some homeless in Myrtle Beach prefer the street to Street Reach. *Sun News.* www.myrtlebeachonline.com/news/local/news-columns-blogs/issac-bailey/article18909549.html; National Coalition for the Homeless. (2014). *Food sharing report.* nationalhomeless.org_wp-content_uploads_2014_10_Food-Sharing2014.pdf (d36iur3orme9ke.cloudfront.net)

13 National Law Center on Homelessness and Poverty. (2019). *Housing not handcuffs.* https://homelesslaw.org/wp-content/uploads/2019/12/HOUSING-NOT-HANDCUFFS-2019-FINAL.pdf.

14 National Homelessness Law Center. (2021). *Housing not handcuffs 2021: State law supplement.* https://homelesslaw.org/wp-content/uploads/2021/11/2021-HNH-State-Crim-Supplement.pdf.

15 National Coalition for the Homeless. (2014). *Food sharing report.* nationalhomeless.org_wp-content_uploads_2014_10_Food-Sharing2014.pdf (d36iur3orme9ke.cloudfront.net).

16 National Coalition for the Homeless. (2006). *A dream denied: The criminalization of homelessness in U.S. Cities.* www.nationalhomeless.org/publications/crimreport/report.pdf.

17 Simpson, J. (2015). Police and homeless outreach worker partnerships: Policing of homeless individuals with mental illness in Washington, D.C. *Human Organization, 74*(2), 125–134. www.jstor.org/stable/44127081.

18 National Coalition for the Homeless. (2014). *Food sharing report.* nationalhomeless.org_wp-content_uploads_2014_10_Food-Sharing2014.pdf (d36iur3orme9ke.cloudfront.net).

19 The Urban Institute. (2021). *Alternatives to arrest and police responses to homelessness evidence-based models and promising practices.* www.urban.org/sites/default/files/publication/103158/alternatives-to-arrests-and-police-responses-to-homelessness.pdf.

20 Dohler, E., Bailey, P., Rice, D., & Katch, H. (2016, May 31). Supportive housing helps vulnerable people live and thrive in the community. *Center on Budget and Policy Priorities.* www.cbpp.org/research/housing/supportive-housing-helps-vulnerable-people-live-and-thrive-in-the-community.

21 United States Interagency Council on Homelessness. (2012). *Searching out solutions: Constructive alternatives to the criminalization of homelessness.* https://www.usich.gov/resources/uploads/asset_library/RPT_SoS_March2012.pdf.

22 Lutze, F., Rosky, J., & Hamilton, Z. (2014). A multisite outcome evaluation of Washington State's reentry housing program for high risk offenders. *Criminal Justice and Behavior, 41*(4), 471–491.

23 Simpson, J. (2015). Police and homeless outreach worker partnerships: Policing of homeless individuals with mental illness in Washington, DC. *Human Organization, 74*(1), 125–134. www.jstor.org/stable/44127081.

24 National Homelessness Law Center. (2021, November 30). *Comment on US interagency council on homelessness federal strategic plan.* https://homelesslaw.org/get-involved/homelessness-federal-strategic-plan/.

Chapter 10

Making an Impact
The Poverty Project

"Someone needs to go to a city council meeting and speak for the homeless
since we cannot speak to them firsthand."
                    —Dennis (A 37-year-old White male and Springhouse client)

Introduction

The research project described in this book was designed to bring about
social change. It is what sociologist Michael Burawoy calls organic public
sociology.[1] Public sociology aims to "make visible the invisible." One of
the main goals of our study was to identify and address the unmet needs of
people experiencing homelessness in Myrtle Beach. After we spent several
hundred hours in the homeless community and conducted over a hundred
formal interviews, we began to assess our findings to see what immediate needs our interview participants had that we could address. As we discussed in previous chapters, our respondents identified structural obstacles
to becoming housed—they could not find jobs that paid enough to pay
rent, they could not find affordable housing, they suffered from physical and
mental health problems that prevented them from working, and they could
not get adequate health care.

After our initial assessment of our experiences and interviews, we decided
that our best strategy to address the needs expressed by interview participants was to establish a significant presence in the area and become advocates for people who are experiencing homelessness. Over the last six years,
we have sought to provide a voice for people we meet who may not be able
to advocate for themselves. We have met with the leadership of non-profit
agencies, numerous elected officials, law enforcement leadership, and the
transportation authority. We have been asked to speak at community groups
and churches and to serve on several task forces and boards of directors of
organizations that serve the homeless community. We have written articles
for local magazines and appeared on the news discussing our research and

DOI:10.4324/9781003325581-12

its implications. Our goal is to consistently frame the private troubles of the people experiencing homelessness as public issues. We want to show the public what homelessness is and who experiences it, and to dissuade the public from falling back on stereotypes. We seek to show the public how easily people become homeless and to advocate for structural solutions to this social problem.

We did not expect to have such a strong desire to do something. Over the years, however, we have grown increasingly passionate about the issue of homelessness and became frustrated with the inadequate response to homelessness in Myrtle Beach. In contrast, we have been overwhelmed by the strength and resiliency we see in the homeless community and are impressed by the willingness of people experiencing homelessness to answer every question we throw at them. We began to ask ourselves what we can do to create a positive impact on the lives of people who are experiencing homelessness. Although we advocate for affordable housing, health care, and alternatives to the criminal justice system, these things are not issues that two college professors can address alone. We knew, however, that we could do 'something.' Thus, we worked with several existing non-profits to find solutions to several of the more immediate needs we found in our interviews. This chapter will discuss The Poverty Project and our efforts to create programs for people who are experiencing homelessness while at the same time advocating for structural changes.

Transportation as a Structural Barrier

Finding reliable transportation is often difficult for people who cannot afford housing. When we analyzed our survey results for the first time, we found that over half (fifty-two percent) of the respondents reported that having access to adequate and reliable transportation was a problem for them. People kept telling us that they could not get where they needed to go—medical appointments, social service appointments, recovery groups, school, church, work, looking for work, or the library (which provides computers individuals can access for free). While many individuals use the only public transportation available in Myrtle Beach (the bus), our respondents reported that the buses only run during certain hours and only go to specific places. Getting rides at night was problematic. Women, especially, said that walking at night was scary. Although some people staying in Springhouse and sleeping rough have a moped, car, or bike, most do not have a reliable method of transportation. A number of people had trouble getting or renewing their driver's licenses, while others did not have the money for the bus or taxis or could not get from the bus line to their job or other locations.

Forty-four percent of our respondents indicated that they used the bus to get from one place to another. There is one main thoroughfare in and out of the city, and the public bus system mostly rides in a T formation: up and down the highway leading to the beach and along the highway parallel to the beach. This can be an enormous disadvantage to people who depend on the bus to get them to work, school, and other places they need to go. Most of those places are miles away from where the buses stop. Dana (a 55-year-old White woman) explained the problem with the bus: "I use it [the bus] to go to work, but it stops two miles from my job. I have to get off the bus and walk two miles. I am tired before I get there." Dana is staying at Springhouse. She leaves early in the morning and comes home late, spending hours on a bus and then walking to work at a job that is a twenty-minute car ride from Springhouse.

Half of our respondents reported that they walk to most places, but it is difficult for many of them because of their health issues. Cody (a 51-year-old White male) has nerve damage and back problems, making it difficult to breathe and walk; he said, "I walk where I need to go, but it is painful." Although Myrtle Beach is a tourist destination, it is not pedestrian-friendly. It is difficult to get anywhere on foot, pedestrians are hit by cars regularly, and walking with health problems can make it even more challenging.

The weather can further complicate people's ability to get to their location. The weather in Myrtle Beach is hot and humid almost year-round, and in the summer, it will sometimes rain every day. This can cause additional stress on people who rely on public transportation to get to work. Most individuals who experience homelessness in Myrtle Beach already have many strikes against them, and transportation issues can become one more strike keeping them from being hired at a job. For example, they may have an arrest record or be missing paperwork such as an ID, birth certificate, or Social Security card. These constraints and not having a permanent address can make finding and keeping a job challenging. The last thing they want to tell an employer is that they do not have reliable transportation. Employers want to know that their employees can get to work, even on days when the weather is bad.

Jonas (a 32-year-old Black male) wants to work but is having difficulties getting hired. He is frustrated about his lack of transportation options. One day we were sitting in the communal area of the shelter. We asked him about a job interview from which he had just returned. Jonas sighed and stated:

> If I apply for a job and give this address [Springhouse], they won't hire me. If they ask how I am getting to work and I tell them I am walking, they *really* won't hire me. They don't want me coming in all sweaty before I even get to work.

When we first began going to Springhouse's men's shelter, a shelter resident used one of the Springhouse vehicles to drive other residents where they needed to go. There was a condition for getting rides, however. The men needed a specific place to go at a fixed time. For example, they could be driven to a job interview but not to the mall to apply for jobs.[2] This further inhibited Jonas' ability to get a job. "I can get a ride from here sometimes, but only if I know in advance. They won't take me unless I already have a job or a job interview." There were times when Jonas wanted to go to several places to pick up job applications, but he could not get a ride from Springhouse. "How am I going to get a job if I can't look for one?" he questioned. Although the shelter transportation system was useful for many residents who had places, such as the doctor, that they went to regularly, this did not help someone like Jonas.

The Rolling Forward Project

In 2017, we decided to start a bike-share program at Springhouse's men's shelter. Although the people at the women's and family shelters, and individuals who were sleeping rough, also needed rides, we chose the men's shelter because we could access the largest number of people there. Working with the caseworkers at Springhouse, we designed a program where the residents could borrow a bike for a day or a week to get them where they needed to go. We called the bike-share program "The Rolling Forward Project." We applied for grants and had our students conduct fundraisers for bikes, locks, helmets, and bike racks.

In the spring of 2018, we received a grant that helped us purchase helmets, t-shirts, and a bike rack. That same semester, our students held a fundraiser and raised enough money to purchase another bike rack. A church group donated several new bikes to us, but we still needed more. A Public Safety officer at our university stepped up and offered to give us the bikes left on campus after school let out for the summer. Students who go home after the school year is over often do not have the means to take their bikes home, whether in a car or on a plane. Public Safety officers go around campus, collect all the bikes left behind, and sell or donate them. In 2018, the bikes were donated to The Rolling Forward Project.

Outcomes of the Rolling Forward Project

In many ways, the bike program was very successful. We had up to fifty bikes being borrowed at a time, and some of the men at Springhouse began depending on the bikes as their primary means of transportation. We kept records of how the bikes were used. The most common reason for borrowing a bike was to either go to work (38 percent) or to look for work (10 percent). This is not surprising, as almost half of the residents at Springhouse are either working or looking for a job. Other uses of the bikes included going to medical or social service appointments, visiting family, going to church, going to the store, going to the beach, or going to the library.

Figure 10.1 Rolling Forward Bike

When we spoke with Zeke, a 29-year-old White male, he had been living at Springhouse for two weeks. Zeke became homeless after he was released from jail. He told us:

> Finding transportation is a big problem for me. I use the Rolling Forward program every day. I ride to work at 4:30 every morning. I also ride to the store. I use the program every day and haven't seen any problems with the program. It is pretty awesome and helps me a lot. Not many people would take the time to help people like us. I really appreciate it.

Reid, a 55-year-old White male, had been staying at the shelter for five months when we spoke to him. Before that, he had been staying with friends. He lost his housing when his business failed. He told us:

> Transportation is not a problem for me. I bike or walk from one place to another. I use the Rolling Forward program every day. I go to the store, gas station, and the soup kitchen. The program is very helpful because this old fat guy can't walk everywhere. The only problem with the program is that the bikes get stolen.

Individuals also told us that they used the Rolling Forward bikes to help their mental health. Mitchell, a 30-year-old White male, said:

> Bike number 49 saved my life. I have problems with rules. This is probably why I ended up here. When I get frustrated, I just rent a bike and ride out. I feel so much better after I ride around for a while and clear my head.

Managing Rolling Forward

At the beginning of the program, we did not have any policies regarding how it would be run. We knew that the shelter was perpetually short-staffed, but we failed to have a plan in place to implement the program. After the bike-share program was in place for a month, we met with the team of caseworkers at the shelter to see how it was going. There was a gentleman at the meeting whom we did not recognize. "This is Sammy. He runs the program." We were excited that the shelter had hired someone to run the bike program. It took a while, but later in the meeting, we realized that Sammy was a Springhouse resident. Sammy was a 30-year-old Black man; he was well-liked among the other residents. He did a good job managing the logs, recording when bikes were checked in and out, what needed to be fixed, and where the bikes were going.

On the one hand, we were excited that Sammy was running the program and doing so well. He seemed to be proud of the work he was doing. On the other hand, however, we were concerned about using Sammy as unpaid labor for our program. We asked ourselves whether this was ethical. Were we using Sammy for our needs when he could be doing something else? Was he spending time on the bike program when he could be working toward leaving Springhouse? We asked the director if we could apply for a grant to pay Sammy for his work. The director told us, "We do not pay clients." We were surprised by this statement. It seemed that if Sammy were paid for his work, he could save money to get out of Springhouse. As we studied the history of homelessness, we realized that (as we have explained in previous chapters) free labor is a common strategy to get people to 'show' that they are worthy of being 'helped.'

The next time we checked in at the shelter, Oliver greeted us. Oliver is a soft-spoken Hispanic man who was about 50 years old. He had only been at the shelter for about a month. Oliver became homeless after he was divorced. After he lost his housing, Oliver became seriously depressed and lost his job. Although he was initially reserved, managing the bike program seemed to pull him out of his shell. As time passed, Oliver showed that he cared about the bike program's success. He took a leadership role in running the program and went out of his way to share his story and discuss the bike program with our students who came to volunteer at Springhouse. In the end-of-semester reflection papers on their work in the shelter, quite a few students mentioned that Oliver had helped make them feel comfortable in an unfamiliar environment. Oliver also spent about 30 hours a week working in the communal kitchen, helping serve breakfast, lunch, and dinner to the 90 or more Springhouse residents. When he obtained a job as a chef at the university, the caseworkers replaced him in the Rolling Forward program.

Over the next several years, Springhouse had one resident or another running the Rolling Forward program, but they refused to hire anyone to run it. On the one hand, this was good for some of the shelter residents who felt that running the bike program gave them a reason to get up in the morning or gave them a feeling of control over something in their lives. On the other hand, it did not seem fair to have shelter clients work on our program for free when we wanted to pay them for their time. For example, Lucas (59-year-old White man), who ran the program while working two paid jobs outside of Springhouse, told a caseworker that he felt overwhelmed and that if he were paid for his work, he could quit one of his other jobs. When Springhouse refused to pay him, he quit the bike program and left the shelter.

Divergent Goals

The Rolling Forward program at Springhouse is an example of the way in which trying to 'help' people through an organization, rather than directly supporting individuals, can become difficult. One of the significant problems with the Rolling Forward program is that we had different goals for the program than the Springhouse staff did. While we shared the goal of increasing the ability of shelter residents to transport themselves, some of our other goals did not align.

As researchers, we were interested in demonstrating the program's effectiveness. To that end, we asked that the shelter staff keep logs of how often the bikes were borrowed and where the resident rode the bikes. Our goal was to use this information as we wrote grants to expand the program. It was challenging to have different people manage the program, each with their unique methods for operating it and record-keeping. It was not easy to keep track of supplies and to maintain clear records of who was using the bikes and where they were going. At one point, Springhouse stopped keeping records altogether.

Funding for the program also became problematic. We had secured a grant to purchase supplies for the bike program. The staff at the shelter seemed to view the grant money as endless and made excessive requests for supplies. The more money we provided, the more they requested. We met with the shelter's director and assistant director just over a year into the Rolling Forward program. They had exciting news for us: the shelter was willing to invest significant money into the program. There was a caveat, however. The shelter previously had cars and a van that would help get people to doctor's appointments, school, and work when they did not have rides. The shelter would eliminate most of the cars they owned and stop providing transportation for their residents. The idea was that people could use bikes to get where they needed to go.

Although we wanted to increase the mobility of individuals and their ability to get around, many Springhouse residents are incapable of riding a bike. Rolling Forward was intended to complement the transportation options already in place at Springhouse, not replace them. Thus, by not having a way to implement the program ourselves we found that there were unintended consequences. We did not foresee that Springhouse would eliminate the other transportation options because there were now bikes available.

Today, there are several bike-share programs for people who are experiencing homelessness in Horry County. We helped to organize the rideshare projects and we still collect bikes to donate to the programs, but we no longer fundraise or monitor them.

The Giving Wall

Another issue we discovered in our interviews was that many people experiencing homelessness need hygiene items but are reluctant to ask for them. During the Covid-19 pandemic, we realized that many people had responded to the question "What do you need right now?" with comments such as, "I really need deodorant. It seems stupid to ask someone for that." Alternatively, "I hate having to ask for things like lotion or tampons."

We read about other cities that had public distributions of hygiene kits for people experiencing homelessness. In these cities, hygiene kits are left in public spaces, often hung on a wall, and could be retrieved by those who need them without the indignity of begging for items such as soap and deodorant and other hygiene items that are necessary for essential self-care.

We emailed numerous organizations, including the mayor's office, about creating a public wall where we could hang up bags containing toiletries near areas where people experiencing homelessness congregate. The answer was a resounding "No!" A representative for the mayor's office said, "The mayor feels like this is not a good idea. It would attract too many homeless people to the area." Another non-profit caseworker said, "I wish I could, but the city owns this building. I don't think they would approve." Fortunately, one public kitchen agreed to host our wall. We decided to call it the Giving Wall. With donations from community groups, other non-profits (we received donations of menstrual products from the Period Project and condoms from a local non-profit health organization), and churches, we have been able to keep our Giving Wall well-stocked for over two years.

Figure 10.2 Giving Wall

Figure 10.3 Sara finds a recipient for a donated mat

The Giving Wall is beneficial for the people who use the public kitchen. Because each item is individually bagged, clients of the kitchen can 'shop' the wall to get what they need and leave what they do not. The Giving Wall is also part of our advocacy. When we post updates online about the wall or ask for donations, we can speak to the public about the issues associated with homelessness. When housed citizens donate to most organizations, they cannot see how their donation is used. However, with the Giving Wall, donors can see where their donations are going.

Latent Consequences of the Giving Wall

One positive latent consequence of the Giving Wall is that numerous community groups and countless Horry County residents donate items that we need. Our social media pages highlight items we need for the Giving Wall, such as sunscreen in summer and gloves in winter, and the community steps up. Other community members ask us about other needs we may have. One group of retirees makes mats out of plastic trash bags for people who are sleeping rough. We never would have thought of this on our own. We find that when people understand homelessness and the needs of people who are experiencing homelessness, the more empathetic they become.

Figure 10.4 Sara holds a sleeping mat made out of plastic bags that was donated by a community group

Advocacy and Free Buses

Throughout this book, we have been arguing that structural changes need to be made to address the needs of the homeless community. During the Covid-19 pandemic, we spoke to the director of the bus line about the need for reliable, free public transportation. We were also interviewed about the Rolling Forward Project's bike program for a news story about transportation. Shortly after these conversations, the bus system stopped collecting fares and added more routes. This change positively affected the ability of people experiencing homelessness in Horry County to meet their travel needs.

The impact of free transportation can be seen in our interview responses. In interviews conducted from 2017 through 2020, sixty-seven percent of people we spoke to said transportation was a problem. In 2021 however, only thirty percent of the folks we spoke with identified transportation as a problem. Kim, a 39-year-old White female who has been homeless for two years, told us, "One upside of the pandemic is that the buses are free. That's helped me a lot."

Conclusion

The initiatives we started now fall under an umbrella we call the Poverty Project. The Poverty Project is an example of public sociology.[3] We used the results of our research to address community needs, to speak with organizations about homelessness, and to start programs based on our survey responses. One of the unique aspects of our projects is that they addressed gaps in services, as identified by people experiencing homelessness. Too often programs are initiated by social service providers or politicians without input from the homeless community. This project has allowed us to help address some of the immediate needs of the homeless community and allows us a voice to advocate for people who sometimes cannot advocate for themselves. It also serves to call attention to the dire need for structural change locally and nationally.

Although we cannot change laws or policies on our own, our advocacy efforts today focus on educating the housed population about homelessness. As we discussed in Chapter 4, it is critical to consider the impact of social structure on the lived experiences of individuals. It is also critical to continually assess the needs of the target population. It is important to continually assess what it means to be a "success." Because we are not a non-profit organization ourselves, "success" would mean not having people who need our help.

Our plans for the future include working with city officials and service agencies in a town outside of Myrtle Beach to create a resource center for people experiencing homelessness. At the resource center, we could address other immediate needs that we have identified through our research, including helping individuals make connections to local service providers, providing help securing identification, and providing lockers for storage. One of the advantages of us starting the center, rather than supporting a center run by another organization, is that we will be able to better monitor what is available and how it is administered. We will do this by continually interviewing people in the community about their needs and whether or not the resource center is meeting those needs. We plan for our work and advocacy to end when homelessness is no longer a social problem.

Notes

1 Burawoy, M. (2005). For public sociology. *American Sociological Review*, 70(1), 4–28. https://doi.org/10.1177/000312240507000102.
2 Later in this chapter, we will discuss the elimination of rides offered at the shelter.
3 Nyden, G., Hossfeld, L. H., & Nyden, P. W. (2011). *Public sociology: Research, action, and change*. SAGE Publications. https://doi.org/10.4135/9781483349510.

Conclusion

The New American Dream

In Conclusion

As we stated in the introduction, when we started interviewing people experiencing homelessness, we thought our study would last one semester. Six years later, we feel like the characters in "Gilligan's Island" who thought we were going on a one-semester tour and ended up staying on the island for years. Over the past six years, we have met people experiencing homelessness through no fault of their own. We have also met people who became homeless after making a mistake, or a series of mistakes. We met people struggling to house themselves and those who have given up. Regardless of the point at which we meet them, everyone we included in this study has two things in common: they are without housing, and they are human.

Basic Human Rights

The Universal Declaration of Human Rights identifies housing as a basic right. The presence of homelessness violates this right along with other human rights, including the right to life, non-discrimination, health, clean water and sanitation, security of the person, and freedom from cruel, degrading, and inhumane treatment.[1] Throughout this book, we have highlighted how the social, economic, and political structure of the United States creates an environment in which some individuals are at higher risk of becoming homeless than others. Individuals born into poverty, who have mental or physical health issues, or who have interacted with the legal system, are at a higher risk of becoming homeless than those who do not have these traits. These risk factors exist regardless of the time and effort a person puts into getting ahead or what personal problems they may have.

Seeing the Truth in the Familiar

C. Wright Mills proposed the concept of the sociological imagination.[2] The sociological imagination allows us to see the connection between personal

DOI:10.4324/9781003325581-13

troubles and public issues. It encourages us to contextualize individual-level outcomes (personal troubles) as being influenced by structural factors. In earlier chapters, we argue that the social and political structure of the United States has changed over the last half-century, resulting in changes in the prevalence of homelessness over time. For all the folks experiencing homelessness, it is clear their situation was caused, or at least exacerbated, by structural factors. Many of our survey respondents identified a lack of affordable housing, lack of living-wage jobs, lack of adequate mental and physical health care, and lack of adequate and accessible public transportation as directly contributing to their becoming homeless and the difficulties they face when trying to become rehoused. The structural environment that creates an unequal and dysfunctional system makes homelessness a public issue or social problem.

The lack of government-supported safety nets contributes to homelessness among almost all of our survey respondents. Many respondents had an event that led to homelessness (loss of job, house fire, rent increase, death of spouse, divorce, injury, or sickness). A 30-year-old White male, Stuart, stated, "I was struggling before the fire. I am disabled; I can't work. But now I'm wrecked. That's how I ended up here [the shelter]." Noah, a 63-year-old mixed-race male, lost his housing following the death of his wife. As we sat outside the shelter, he told us, "I was doing okay before my wife died. She took care of me. I had a stroke, so it is hard for me to get around. I can't work. When she died, I couldn't pay the rent." Their stories highlight how many economically fragile Americans live one unexpected bill or crisis away from homelessness.[3] It is likely that with appropriate support, homelessness could be avoided for Stuart, Noah, and many others whom we meet every day.

Moreover, the inadequate support systems in place are difficult to access. Many people we meet need help navigating the system or are met with bureaucratic obstacles in their search for housing. Most people who are sleeping rough are unaware of many of the services offered in Myrtle Beach for people who are experiencing homelessness. We frequently hear people say they are sick but cannot go to the doctor because they do not have insurance or that they use the emergency room as their primary health care provider. They often do not realize that BLMC is nearby.

Some individuals living in the shelter, or sleeping rough, feel stuck because they have trouble working with Social Security, the Department of Motor Vehicles, or vital records to secure their identification. It is close to impossible to secure housing or employment without identification. Others have difficulty applying for or receiving benefits such as disability, food stamps, Medicaid or Medicare, or unemployment benefits.

It's My (Their) Own Fault

While homelessness is a social problem with structural causes, most of the people we meet, and many of the service providers who work with them, perceive homelessness as a personal problem. People experiencing homelessness are stigmatized by government officials, service providers, and each other. Moreover, factors that increase one's risk of homelessness, such as mental and physical illness or interactions with the criminal justice system, are often attributed solely to personal causes, while ignoring that they have structural roots. For example, we are often told that 'these people' would not be arrested if they did not break the law. City officials are referring to laws that include camping and loitering, but do not take into account that many individuals do not have anywhere else to go. With an inadequate shelter system that seldom has room for new clients, people who are homeless in Myrtle Beach have no other choice but to break the law. Humans need to sit and sleep to survive.

Most of our respondents, and those working with the homeless community, believe that the American Dream of a house, secure employment, and a happy family is possible for anyone who works hard enough. This ideology places all the responsibility on the individual and does nothing to encourage the social and political change needed to end homelessness. It is difficult for people with limited education and occupational skills to get a job and buy a house (no matter how hard they work) when few jobs pay living wages and there are too few affordable homes. Furthermore, the ability to pursue the American Dream is based on the assumption that you are physically and mentally healthy enough to work. More than half of the 250 people experiencing homelessness who we interviewed are not physically or mentally capable of working a full-time job.

As we demonstrate in the first three chapters of this book, policy decisions can exacerbate or mitigate social problems. The dramatic increase in neoliberal policies during the Reagan administration, and the presidential administrations that followed, has contributed to the current level of homelessness. Neoliberalism argues that the market is fair, and those who are economically unsuccessful are so because of their lack of effort. This viewpoint emphasizes that government should have a limited role; therefore, the provisions of safety nets and services are not on the neoliberal agenda. Services have been privatized to the extent that the non-profit industrial complex depends on the existence of homelessness for non-profit organizations to survive.

Neoliberal ideology purports the notion of an undeserving poor and the idea that people should work for any benefits they receive. We saw this in Myrtle Beach when the non-profits embraced the toxic charity model. Many organizations created to "help" people also stigmatize them. Throughout this book, we highlight how the current configuration of social institutions, specifically health care, welfare, and housing subsidies, and the criminal justice system, can cause and prolong experiences of homelessness.

Going Upstream

As Kim Hopper[4] wisely reports, we need to start looking "upstream" to end the homelessness crisis. The call to look upstream is based on a story attributed to numerous people, including Saul Alinsky and Irving Zola. The story goes like this:

Once upon a time, there was a small village on the edge of a river. Life in the village was busy. People grew food, taught the children to make blankets, and made meals.

One day a villager took a break from harvesting food and noticed a baby floating down the river toward the village. She could not believe her eyes! She heard crying in the distance and looked downstream to see that two babies had already floated by the village. She looked around at the other villagers working nearby. "Does anyone else see that baby?" she asked.

One villager heard the woman but continued working. "Yes!" yelled a man who had been making soup.

"Oh, this is terrible!" A woman who had been building a campfire shouted, "Look, there are even more upstream!" Indeed, three more babies were coming around the bend.

"How long have these babies been floating by?" asked another villager. No one knew for sure, but some people thought they might have seen something in the river earlier. They were busy at the time and did not have time to investigate.

They quickly organized themselves to rescue the babies. Watchtowers were built on both sides of the shore, and swimmers were coordinated to maintain shifts of rescue teams that maintained 24-hour surveillance of the river. Ziplines with attached baskets were stretched across the river to quickly get even more babies to safety.

The number of babies floating down the river only seemed to increase. The villagers built orphanages, taught even more children to make blankets, and increased the food they grew to keep the babies housed, warm, and fed. Life in the village carried on.

Then one day, at a meeting of the Village Council, a villager asked, "But where are all these babies coming from?"

"No one knows," said another villager. "But I say we organize a team to go upstream and find who is throwing these babies in the river."

What Can We Do?

We know what is upstream when we talk about homelessness. One of the significant conclusions we have drawn from our research is that there needs to be a societal shift in how we view and respond to homelessness. We need to move from perceiving homelessness as an individual failing to acknowledging the structural factors that contribute to homelessness, including low-paying employment, the high cost of housing, and lack of physical and mental health care. We also need to respond to the social problem of homelessness by creating safety nets so that people do not become homeless in the first place, and to not use the criminal justice system as a band-aid approach.

We need universal and affordable health care so that health crises do not result in homelessness.

One of the most effective ways to end homelessness is to prevent it.[5] Rental assistance programs and affordable housing options are effective means of preventing homelessness.[6] The lack of affordable housing is a key contributor to homelessness.[7] When housing subsidies are scarce, homelessness increases. For twenty percent of the people we interviewed, a lack of affordable housing was either the cause of their becoming homeless or their primary barrier to exiting homelessness. Additionally, the debate over homelessness needs to be reassessed. The discourse should focus on about social safety nets rather than about the 'deficiencies' of individuals. People do not become homeless overnight. If adequate safety nets, affordable housing, and health care are in place, much of the homeless epidemic could be relieved.

Research has demonstrated that when long-term housing assistance is provided to people experiencing homelessness, they can obtain and maintain stable housing.[8] There needs to be a concerted effort at all levels of government to:

1. Create and preserve dedicated affordable housing units.[9] Contrary to popular belief, most people who are unhoused are not chronically homeless. If housing were more affordable, fewer people would need to depend on services related to homelessness. We need a massive commitment from all levels of government to work for the common good by creating affordable housing. The Horry County 2040 plan acknowledges that the wages paid to most service workers are not enough to support their housing needs. This is true across the country as well. If the Housing Choice Voucher program (Section 8 housing) were expanded to meet the needs of the low-income population, there would be far fewer individuals who become homeless. Most people do not need (or necessarily want) 'free' housing. They need housing they can afford. The Housing Choice Vouchers require users to pay 30 percent of their income in rent.[10] This would be far preferable to the 80 or 90 percent of their income people are paying in the free market.

2. Invest in childcare, welfare, and other social supports so that people who can work can do so without losing financial support and the ability to care for their children.

3. Permanent Supportive Housing (PSH) has been shown to be effective in housing people with mental or physical illness. It also costs less than policing and hospitalizing individuals who are homeless. PSH must be offered with more flexibility in who qualifies. There must also be a dramatic increase in intensive case management by professionals who can treat the entire person, not just the part of the person who is homeless.[11]

4. A concerted effort toward immediate crisis response. Telling someone who is about to be evicted, or who is a victim of a natural disaster, to call a homeless shelter is not enough. To prevent chronic homelessness, incident-based homelessness must be addressed. This can take the form

of low-barrier emergency housing, apartments, or funding for short-term rentals in extended-stay motels.[12]

5. Increase the number of low-barrier shelters that are equipped with certified professionals who can meet the needs of the entire person so they can move toward transitional or permanent housing.

6. Increase funding for free or low-cost lawyers to work with individuals to get disability benefits, fight discriminatory housing policies and evictions, and help with paperwork.

Fifty percent of our respondents felt their criminal record contributed to their homelessness.

7. Reform the criminal justice system. Fund and support programs that assist ex-offenders in reentering the community after release; this may include mental health care, housing, jobs, health care, or all of the above.[13]

8. The criminalization of homelessness must be prevented and disincentivized. It does not help keep the streets safe and does not 'reform' people from crimes associated with being human.[14]

Fifty-seven percent of our respondents experience mental illness.

9. Fund community clinics and long-term care for people experiencing mental illness. Not enough places provide mental health care for individuals regardless of their insurance status.

10. Increase federal funding for these community mental health clinics so that people who need care can get it without being turned away for not having insurance

Sixty percent of the people we speak with have severe chronic health problems. For many, a health crisis contributed to their homelessness.

11. Health care reform is critical to addressing homelessness. Hospitals must be incentivized to treat all patients, not only those who can afford it. There must be incentives for hospitals that do treat patients who are without health insurance not to apply band-aids and kick them out for lack of payment. This expansion of treatment could be a reality with an expansion of Medicaid[15] and Medicare.[16]

12. Support and expand community-based health and social services that are easily accessible to anyone regardless of insurance status.

Conclusion

We have learned a tremendous amount in the past six years. This project has taken us "upstream" regarding the factors driving homelessness in our community. We have sat and talked with people who are too mentally or physically ill to work their way out of homelessness. We have visited with people who, because they lack viable alternatives, cycle in and out of jail, often arrested for engaging in survival acts (sleeping or sitting) in public. We have been shocked by the stigmatization people who are experiencing homelessness have encountered, sometimes by those serving the homeless community. Their stories have made us acutely aware of the extent to which homelessness is a structural problem that requires structural responses. This book is our call for others, especially those who serve and create policies affecting the homeless community, to go upstream and work to address the structural causes of homelessness.

Notes

1 UN Secretary General. (2015). Adequate housing as a component of the right to an adequate standard of living, and on the right to non-discrimination in this context. Special Rapporteur A/70/150, UN Secretary General. Assem. https://documents-dds-ny.un.org/doc/UNDOC/GEN/N15/242/95/PDF/N1524295.pdf?OpenElement.

2 Mills, C. W. (1959). *The sociological imagination.* Oxford University Press.

3 O'Flaherty, B. (2004). Wrong person and wrong place: For homelessness, the conjunction is what matters. *Journal of Housing Economics, 13*(1), 1–15. https://doi.org/10.1016/j.jhe.2003.12.001.

4 Hopper, K. (2022, March 29). Homelessness is only getting worse, but we know the solution: A right to housing. *America: The Jesuit Review.* www.americamagazine.org/politics-society/2022/03/29/homeless-housing-penny-lady-24215.

5 Fowler, P. J., Hovmand, P. S., Marcal, K. E., & Das, S. (2019). Solving homelessness from a complex systems perspective: Insights for prevention responses. *Annual Review of Public Health, 40,* 465–486. https://doi.org/10.1146/annurev-publhealth-040617-013553.

6 Coalition for the Homeless. *Proven solutions.* www.coalitionforthehomeless.org/proven-solutions/.

7 National Alliance to End Homelessness. *Affordable housing.* https://endhomelessness.org/ending-homelessness/policy/affordable-housing/.

8 Gubits, D., Shinn, M., Wood, M., Bell, S., Dastrup, S., Solari, C., Brown, S., McInnis, D., McCall, T., & Kattel, U. (2013). *Family options study: Short-term Impacts of housing services and urban development.* U.S. Department of Housing and Urban Development. www.huduser.gov/portal/sites/default/files/pdf/Family-Options-Study-Full-Report.pdf.

9 Coalition for the Homeless. *Proven solutions.* www.coalitionforthehomeless.org/proven-solutions/.

10 Ibid.

11 Bailey, P. (2020, January 27). Commentary: We need rental assistance and services, not punitive policies to end homelessness. *Center for Budget and Policy Priorities.* www.cbpp.org/research/housing/commentary-we-need-rental-assistance-and-services-not-punitive-policies-to-end.

12 Coalition for the Homeless. *Proven solutions.* www.coalitionforthehomeless.org/proven-solutions/; www.cbpp.org/research/housing/commentary-we-need-rental-assistance-and-services-not-punitive-policies-to-end.

13 Lutze, F., Rosky, J., & Hamilton, Z. (2014). A multisite outcome evaluation of Washington State's reentry housing program for high-risk offenders. *Criminal Justice and Behavior, 41*(4), 471–491.

14 National Homelessness Law Center. (2021, November 30). *Comment on US Interagency Council on Homelessness Federal Strategic plan.* https://homelesslaw.org/get-involved/homelessness-federal-strategic-plan/.

15 National Alliance to End Homelessness. *Policy priorities.* https://endhomelessness.org/ending-homelessness/policy/priorities/.

16 National Health Care for the Homeless Council. (2019, May). *Medicare for all & the HCH community.* medicare-for-all-and-the-hch-community.pdf (nhchc.org).

Methodology

In the Beginning

We[1] started this project for both personal and academic reasons. On a personal level, we recognized the extent to which people experiencing homelessness are underserved in our community and we wanted to do something about it. Academically, we saw an opportunity to engage our students in a project that could teach them about applied sociological research. We wanted our students to better understand poverty and homelessness's dynamic and complex nature. We did not realize how much we would learn along the way or that our one-semester project would be ongoing six years later. The data used in this book is derived from a six-year ethnographic study of individuals experiencing homelessness. The primary focus of our research was to identify the unmet needs of sheltered and unsheltered people experiencing homelessness.

Before this project began, we explored the literature on homelessness and how assessments of people experiencing homelessness have been conducted in other contexts. We found that there were (and still are) significant gaps in the literature on homelessness. Most importantly, almost no research asks people experiencing homelessness what services they want and could use. We were concerned about the absence of the voices of people experiencing homelessness in research about services provided to the homeless community. Most of the literature we found, whether written by policymakers, academics, or practitioners, focused on the evaluation of services offered to people experiencing homelessness, the pathological deficiencies of people who are unhoused, or the relationship between individuals and service providers. Some studies examine drug use and abuse, employment, HIV and AIDs, needle sharing, or physical and mental health in the homeless community. Others focus on the relationships between social service organization and their caseworkers with people experiencing homelessness. These micro-level topics typically center on "fixing" the individual and tend to lump all people who are unhoused together as one typology. Many of these studies sought to understand why individuals make the choices they make while at the same time ignoring the lived realities of people who have become unhoused.

Our Data

In 2016, we began by creating a survey that included questions about everything we thought might be of need in the day-to-day lives of the homeless population in Myrtle Beach, SC. We could not locate any previously published needs assessment surveys; therefore, we did not have a model to use for our survey. Consequently, the original survey was quite extensive. In addition to questions about the types of services that were useful or would be helpful if available, we included questions about a person's physical and mental health, education, job history, and other issues that might affect the individual's ability to house themselves now or in the future. We also asked them about practices or policies in the community that the participants felt were helpful or detrimental to them.

In addition to data from the surveys, we volunteered over 1000 hours at various organizations serving individuals experiencing homelessness. This allowed us to interact informally with people experiencing homelessness and the people working in the shelters, food pantries, community kitchens, and social service agencies. When we were volunteering, we paid attention to the social dynamics of what was being said and how clients and staff interact. We recorded our observations, resulting in over 400 pages of field notes regarding social service agencies and social service providers. We conducted eleven formal interviews with service providers. Additionally, we attended community meetings and met with community leaders (elected officials, the police chiefs in local communities, and directors of local agencies that serve the homeless community). If we did not write the notes in "real-time," we completed written reflections later, resulting in over 200 pages of field notes. These 600 pages of field notes, along with the formal interviews, are the basis for the ethnographic portions of this book.

Reflexivity

As we use grounded theory (see Chapter 4), we used a reflexive approach to data collection and analysis. We spent hundreds of hours coding our survey data and field notes to search for themes. We generated memos and created a narrative of our findings to develop linkages between our observations and the themes surfacing over time. We also modified, added, and removed questions from the formal survey to better address themes that we found or that did not generate useful data.

We were particularly interested in what frustrated the participants, the services they used, and the services they had trouble accessing. The questions we asked participants changed over time based on answers we received from previous respondents. We did not want to waste our participants' time, so early on, we began to cut out questions that were not useful. For example, in the first version of our questionnaire, we asked individuals whether they had problems with drugs or alcohol. After we had completed about fifty interviews, we realized that not one person admitted to having issues with either. After the question was taken off the questionnaire, many respondents referred to drug or alcohol abuse as an obstacle to becoming housed or something on which they needed to work. Sometimes we obtained more information by not asking about sensitive topics.

Over time, we also expanded some sections of the survey. When numerous respondents gave us similar answers to questions, we explored these topics in more detail by including follow-up questions related to these topics in new iterations of the surveys. For example, when transportation emerged as a significant barrier in early interviews, we added more questions about transportation to subsequent surveys.

We were also interested in information gaps. We wanted to know if there are available community services that are not widely known. For example, many of the folks we talk to respect BLMC, which is willing to treat patients who do not have much money on a sliding scale, sometimes seeing them for free. This resource is something we would not know without conducting these surveys. We are now able not only to ask participants about BLMC, but we can now refer people to this office if they do not know where to go for their health care.

Another good example is our question about whether the respondent believes in the American Dream. This line of questioning emerged a few years into our study when we observed a trend in respondents' answers to the question, "Where do you think you will be in five years?" We were surprised by the number of folks who said they would be working, living in their own house, with their family (and often a dog). Conducting research in this way has the potential to transform thinking and create new and unique solutions.[2]

Gaining Access to the Homeless Community

Our first interviews were conducted at the local men's and women's shelters. The men were sheltered in a large, run-down-looking brick building in a low-income neighborhood. The building housed up to ninety men. The women's shelter was in an actual house in a neighborhood. There were between twenty and twenty-five women staying at the home.

We soon came to two fundamental realizations. First, it was going to take some time to establish trust with the residents of the shelters. We underestimated the importance of establishing relationships with the people who were staying in the shelter. The residents met us with wariness and distrust the first couple of weeks we were in the men's shelter. One gentleman said, "What are you going to do for us? Are you going to talk to the mayor? We need representation!" We persevered. Twice a week, we, along with one or two of our students, went into the shelter and interviewed anyone who would allow us to talk to them. It took about a year before we gained the trust of some of the residents.

The more time we spent in the shelter, the more comfortable people felt talking to us. The comfort people felt with us was due to word of mouth. When shelter residents acknowledged us by name, other residents were less likely to hesitate before talking to us. They agreed to allow us, along with our students, to interview them formally. Starting the Rolling Forward Bike program also increased our credibility at the shelter. Residents could see we were genuinely trying to be advocates for them. We became known as the bike ladies. We would have never obtained the depth of information if we had just spent a semester surveying people about their needs.

Eventually, we became familiar to other organizations in the community as well and were able to gain access to people who were sleeping rough. We volunteered and conducted interviews at food pantries, community kitchens, and other social service agencies. We organized outreach events and participated in outreach events organized by other community organizations. We held three resource fairs in a park for people sleeping rough. These fairs aimed to give the unsheltered homeless information about area resources and conduct needs assessment surveys of those who attended. We served food, and numerous community organizations participated. BLMC performed HIV testing, the head of the CoC interviewed people to see if they qualified for housing, and representatives from a teen shelter were present. The resource fairs were held in public parks where many people experiencing homelessness hung out during the day.

Interviews

Between 2016 and 2022, we interviewed 250 men and women who did not have a permanent place to stay. Participants in the interviews had to meet two criteria: they must be over eighteen and homeless. We operationalized "homeless" as a person not having a permanent, habitable place to stay. For example, two people we interviewed stayed in sheds on someone else's property. Other participants stayed in motels (where they were billed by the night or the week) or in a homeless shelter. Although the individuals staying in motels or homeless shelters technically had a roof over their heads, they were considered homeless for this study. Participants were not paid, but we gave them small backpacks with hygiene items, socks, t-shirts, snacks, and other small tokens we could accumulate.[3]

Interviews of sheltered and unsheltered homeless were conducted using convenience sampling. We met participants in the locations where we were volunteering. The interviews we conducted at the community kitchens and outreach events primarily involved people sleeping rough. When we talked to people sleeping rough, even our "formal" interviews are often conducted in an informal, conversational manner. Often, we stood and talked with them while they waited to get in for lunch or dinner. We conducted numerous interviews with those sleeping rough while volunteering with the Point in Time Count (an explanation of the Point in Time count can be found in Chapter 5). The interviews we conducted inside the shelter were more formal. Because we also volunteered in the shelter, we were given a quiet space to sit down with our surveys and write the responses in real-time.

Before conducting each survey, we asked the potential respondent where they slept the night before and all the places they had slept in the prior month. We asked if they would agree to be interviewed if we ascertained that they were experiencing homelessness. We approached 276 individuals, and 250 agreed to participate in our study. Several people did not complete the entire interview, but respondents were mostly eager to talk to us. Twenty people were interviewed on more than one occasion. In these cases, their interviews were combined to create one case. Most interviews took between 15 and 30 minutes, but some took as long as an hour. If there was not enough time to complete the entire interview, or a participant grew tired of answering questions, some questions were not asked.

At the start of this project, we wanted to record the interviews, but most of the respondents were uncomfortable with being recorded. Thus, we relied on our handwritten responses and follow-up notes. To increase the reliability of taking written notes rather than recordings, we sought to have two people taking notes on each interview. The notes were then compared for accuracy.

Sample

Table 1 displays the demographic characteristics of the interview participants. Eighty percent of the respondents were male. Sixty-six percent of the people we interviewed stayed in a shelter, while forty-four percent slept on the street or other inhabitable locations. Sixty-two percent of respondents had a high school education or below, and six percent reported that they had graduated from college. The average age of our respondents was 44; the youngest person interviewed had just turned 19, and the oldest was 73. Table 2 indicates that the four biggest obstacles faced by our respondents were: not having enough money, physical or mental health problems, lack of affordable housing, and lack of adequate transportation. Tables 3 and 4 describe the self-reported health of our respondents. Over half of the respondents rate their health as seven or better on a ten-point scale, yet eighty percent of respondents indicated they had a serious health condition; heart disease, serious back, leg, or foot problems, and asthma, emphysema, and COPD were the most frequently named conditions.

Appendix Table 1 Demographic Characteristics of Survey Participants

(N = 250)	Characteristic	Responses (N)	Percent
Gender			
	Male	201	80.1%
	Female	49	19.9%
Race			
	White	156	62.4%
	Black	72	28.8%
	Other	22	8.8%
How long in Horry County?			
	Less than a year	75	30.0%
	Between One-Four Years	50	20.0%
	More than Four Years	125	50.0%
Marriage Status			
	Married	44	17.6%
	Not Married	206	82.4%
Education			
	Less than High School	62	24.8%
	High School Diploma	116	46.4%
	Some College	29	11.6%
	Community or Trade School Degree	27	10.8%
	Four-year degree or higher	16	6.4%
Interview Site			
	Men's Shelter	145	58.0%
	Women's Shelter	21	8.4%
	Public Kitchen	60	24.0%
	Street	24	9.6%

Appendix Table 2 Biggest Obstacles Reported by Survey Participants

Obstacle Now	Response (N = 250)	Percent
Having Enough Money	96	28.4%
Mental or Physical Health	41	16.4%
Affordable Housing	27	10.8%
Transportation	25	10.0%

Obstacle Now	Response (N = 250)	Percent
Few Work Opportunities/Low Pay	20	8.0%
Not Having ID/SSN	11	4.4%
Addiction	10	4.0%
Having Stable Sleeping Situation	7	2.8%
Criminal Record	5	2.0%
Motivation, Routine, etc.	5	2.0%
Other/Don't Know	3	1.2%

Appendix Table 3 Self-Reported Health

Health (Scale 10 = Most Healthy)	Response (N = 200)	Percent
1–3	25	12.5%
4–6	60	25.0%
7–9	75	37.5%
10	45	22.5%

Appendix Table 4 Health Conditions reported by Survey Participants

Health Condition	Response (N = 180) Actual numbers add up to more than 180 as some people reported more than one condition.)	Percent
Heart Disease/Heart Attack	31	13.7%
Asthma/Emphysema/COPD	18	8.0%
Serious Back/Leg/Foot Problems	45	20.0%
Arthritis (severe)	13	5.7%
Bipolar/Depression/Anxiety	17	5.7%
Drug/Alcohol Addiction	6	2.6%
Brain Tumor	4	1.7%
Diabetes	13	5.7%
Hepatitis/Cancer/HIV	13	5.7%
Severe Teeth, Hearing, or Eyesight problems	14	6.2%
Other Disabling Conditions (Includes unclear disabilities, accidents, addiction, etc.)	45	14.2%
None Reported	50	20.0%

Notes

1 We say "we" if it doesn't matter who was talking, and service provider can mean anyone at any of the agencies unless otherwise identified. We do this so that we can maintain the anonymity of speakers. Who said what precisely is not as important as

the themes. Everyone was given pseudonyms and comments were modified in the statement could be used to identify the participant. The same pseudonym is given to the same person if they are discussed more than once.

2 Wasserman, J. A., Clair, J. M., & Wilson, K. L. (2009). Problematics of grounded theory: Innovations for developing an increasingly rigorous qualitative method. *Qualitative Research, 9*(3), 355–381. https://doi.org/10.1177/1468794109106605.

3 Southworth, S., & Brallier, S. (2020). The American Dream: Using Robert Merton's strain theory to understand the beliefs and coping responses of homeless individuals. *Sociological Imagination, 56*(2), 61–81.

Definitions

Agency: Chapter 4
A person's willingness and ability to do something.
Aid to Families with Dependent Children (AFDC): Chapter 1, Chapter 2
Part of the 1935 Social Security Act. Authorized states to be reimbursed for providing financial aid to families with dependent children. The types of dependents who qualified for aid were expanded in subsequent reauthorizations of the bill until it was replaced by TANF in 1996.
American Dream: Chapter 4, Chapter 6
The ideology that is pervasive in the United States. The main tenet is that is a person is willing to work hard, they can get whatever they want. Historically the American Dream included a house, wealth, and family.
Anti-Homeless Laws (Anti-Homeless Policies): Chapter 3
Laws and/or policies that criminalize not having a permanent residence or seek to make being homeless so uncomfortable that people will 'choose' to relocate.
Ascribed Status: Chapter 2
Status given at birth. Ascribed status includes race and gender.
Biopolitics: Chapter 4
The state of creating social norms and enforcing those norms using sanctions.
Broken Windows Policing: Chapter 3, Chapter 8
A theory that if police target small crimes, it can keep larger crimes from occurring.
Class Consciousness: Chapter 4
When a person identifies with people who are in the same social class as they are. Marxists argue that when enough people exhibit class consciousness, they will be able to fight for their rights.
Common Good: Introduction, Chapter 1, and Chapter 2
Something that is done or practiced for the good of everyone in a community.

Community Mental Health Care Act of 1963: Chapter 3
Signed by President Kennedy. Called for the release of individuals from psychiatric institutions.

Comprehensive Employee and Training Act (CETA): Chapter 2
Under the Nixon administration, the government funded job programs that employed over 300,000 people.

Continuum of Care (CoC): Chapter 2, Chapter 5
The Continuum of Care is a way to coordinate services for people who are experiencing homelessness. Regions are separated into continuums so that there will be less duplication of services.

Deinstitutionalization: Chapter 3
The mass release of individuals from long-term psychiatric care. As state-funded psychiatric institutions were eliminated in the 1960s and 1970s, hundreds of thousands of psychiatric patients were released.

Department of Housing and Urban Development (HUD): Chapter 1, Chapter 2, Chapter 3
HUD is responsible for administering federal programs related to mortgage insurance, low-income housing, community development block grants, among other housing and urban development policies.

Dix, Dorothea: Chapter 3
Dix was an advocate for moral treatment. She believed that if mentally ill patients were treated with compassion, they could get better. Due to her advocacy, mental asylums were constructed across the U.S. to treat psychiatric patients with compassionate care.

Emergency Relief and Construction Act of 1932: Chapter 1
Provided loans for non-governmental agencies to build housing for low-income individuals and families.

Fair Housing Act: Chapter 1
Outlawed discrimination in housing.

False Consciousness: Chapter 4
Individuals exhibiting false consciousness typically think of themselves as being more like people who are above them in status than they are to people in a similar status. For example, someone who is working a minimum-wage job may not agree that the minimum wage should be increased because they believe that they will someday be the employer and wouldn't want to pay people more.

Federal Housing Administration (FHA): Chapter 1
Created by the Housing Act of 1949 to provide mortgage insurance so that banks could finance more home loans for the veterans returning from WWII. Over 95 percent of loans were given to Whites.

Federal Transient Service: Chapter 1
A 1935 New Deal program that set up shelters around the country to house people who were homeless. The FTS also provided food, job training, help with rent, and vouchers for rooms in boarding houses.

Grounded Theory: Chapter 4

A research method that uses inductive reasoning to develop theory. Rather than the research being guided by theory and hypothesis, the research creates the theory and hypothesis.

Habitus: Chapter 4

The internalization of values, language, behaviors, and beliefs. A person's habitus is collected via their social environment such as the values and beliefs, habits, language and behaviors of their peer group and family.

Homeless Emergency Assistance and Rapid Transition to Housing Act (HEARTH): Chapter 2

In 2009, President Obama signed this act which required the USICH to create a formal strategy to eliminate homelessness.

Homeless Management Information System (HMIS): Chapter 5

An information system used to collect data on housing and services provided to people who are homeless or at risk of becoming homeless.

Hooverville: Chapter 1

Makeshift campsites of groups of people who were homeless in the early 1900s. These were named after Herbert Hoover, the President at the time.

Housing Act of 1934: Chapter 1

Created the Federal Housing Administration

Housing Act of 1937: Chapter 1, Chapter 2

Authorized federal funding for low-income housing.

Housing Act of 1949: Chapter 1

This act authorized cities to clear their slums and replace them with public housing. Under this act, almost 800,000 units of public housing were created.

Housing Act of 1954: Chapter 1

This act called for more urban renewal and the destruction of most of the pay-by-the-night or -week lodging houses for the poor.

Housing and Community Development Act of 1974: Chapter 1

Created the Community Development Block Grant program. Money was allocated to states in the form of block grants rather than having the federal government give the money directly to people.

Housing and Urban Renewal Act of 1965: Chapter 1

Expanded Federal Housing Programs. Increased rental subsidies for low-income, elderly, or disabled individuals and families.

Housing Choice Voucher Program: Chapter 1

Housing vouchers for low-income individuals and families. After the tenant paid 30 percent of their income in rent, the federal government made up the difference between the value of the property and the amount for which the tenant was responsible.

Housing First: Chapter 2, Chapter 5

The belief and current housing policy that asserts that people need to be housed first without any preconditions. Once a person is housed, their other needs are easier to take care of.

Human Capital: Chapter 2

Capital that one invests in oneself, such as education or training.

Ideology: Chapter 2, Chapter 6

A belief system that guides action

Implicit Bias: Chapter 3, Chapter 7

A bias against a group of people that is unknown to the person holding the bias. Although the bias is unconscious, it can influence a person's actions or perceptions of specific groups.

Intersection Theories: Chapter 4

Focus on the intersection between structure and agency. Intersection theories examine how individual decisions are affected by social institutions.

Job Training Partnership Act of 1982: Chapter 2

Instead of having the federal government provide jobs to people directly, as had been done in the past, the Reagan administration allocated money to states to be used for job training.

Lake v. Cameron: Chapter 3

Court case that stated that people with mental illness should be cared for in settings that are the 'least restrictive.' Many individuals were released from psychiatric hospitals after this decision.

Martin vs. City of Boise: Chapter 3

2019. The final decision of the Ninth Circuit Court of Appeals concluded that the Eighth Amendment to the Constitution prohibits laws that criminalize sleeping, sitting, or lying down in public when there is no other alternative.

Marxist Theory: Chapter 3, Chapter 4

A structural theory that argues that capitalism causes poverty. People are exploited by landowners for their productive value.

Master Status: Chapter 7

The status trait that defines a person. The main trait that is associated with an individual.

McKinney-Vento Homeless Assistance Act: Chapter 2

The first legislation passed by the federal government that provided federal funding for emergency homeless shelters, food stamps, and job training for the homeless. In its initial investment, the federal government gave 350 million dollars to support programs, including supportive housing and emergency shelters.

Medicaid Act of 1965: Chapter 3

Authorized the implementation of government-subsidized health care to people who were disabled and/or retired.

Medicare: Chapter 1, Chapter 3
Government-subsidized health care program for people with disabilities or individuals over 65 years old.

Mental Health Services Act: Chapter 2
This act was passed by President Carter's administration. It provided funding for community centers that serve clients who have mental illness.

Mental Hygiene Movement: Chapter 3
After WWII, members of the Mental Hygiene Movement argued that psychiatric problems needed to be stopped before they started.

Micro Level Theory: Chapter 4
Theory that explains social phenomenon by examining the individual and interactions between individuals.

Moral Treatment: Chapter 3
Reformer Dorothea Dix advocated for psychiatric patients to be treated as though they were children—with care and compassion.

National Alliance to Prevent Homelessness: Chapter 3
A national non-profit organization that advocates for the rights of people experiencing homelessness.

National Homelessness Law Center: Chapter 3
A national non-profit organization that tracks anti-homeless laws and policies across the country.

National Industrial Recovery Act of 1933: Chapter 1
Used federal funds for the clearing of slums and the construction of close to 40,000 housing units through the Public Works Administration.

National Performance Review (NPR): Chapter 2
An interagency task force created by the Clinton administration to advise Clinton on ways to reduce government expenditures.

Neoliberalism: Chapter 1, Chapter 2, Chapter 3
Focuses on reducing government and promote policies that benefit the individual rather than the common good.

New Deal: Chapter 1
Legislation from 1933–1939 by President Roosevelt that included public works projects and legislation meant to help get Americans through the Great Depression.

Non-profit industrial complex: Chapter 2
A self-feeding loop between non-profit agencies and their funders. The non-profit must show they are 'succeeding' to get more funding. The more people they serve, the more funding they get. It is not in their best interests to eliminate their clients by serving them too well because they would lose their funding.

O'Connor v. Donaldson: Chapter 3
Outlined a limited number of cases where a person could be institutionalized against their will.

Omnibus Reconciliation Act of 1981: Chapter 2 Chapter 3
Reduced federal funding for AFDC, school lunch programs, psychiatric services, etc.
Panopticon: Chapter 4
Foucault uses this term to describe control mechanisms, such as surveillance, that keep people conforming to the rules of society.
Point in Time Count: Chapter 5
A yearly count of people who are homeless required by counties that receive federal financing for homeless programs.
Poor Work: Chapter 4
Work that does not pay enough to make a living wage. Poor work is typically reserved for individuals without formal education or training.
Political Elite: Chapter 5
A small number of people who hold the most political power and wealth in society.
Precariat: Chapter 4
Low-wage workers in a neoliberal economy.
Public Sociology: Chapter 10
A style of sociology that seeks to expand sociology so that it is relevant for the public and public policy by calling attention to social problems.
Safety Nets: Chapter 1, Chapter 2, Chapter 3. Chapter 4, Conclusion
Programs that protect vulnerable families or individuals from the impact of crises, such as natural disasters, loss of work, or other financial hardships.
Second Bill of Rights: Chapter 2
President Roosevelt argued that there needed to be a Second Bill of Rights that guaranteed that every citizen has a right to a safe and 'decent' place to live.
Section 8 Housing: Chapter 1, Chapter 2
Provides rental subsidies to landlords. Low-income renters pay 30 percent of their income and the federal government subsidizes the rest.
Single Room Occupancy Hotels: Chapter 1
Hotels where people pay by the night or the week.
Sleeping rough: Chapter 1, Chapter, 3, Chapter 5, Chapter 6, Chapter 7, Chapter, 9, Chapter 10
People who are homeless and not living in a homeless shelter or other uninhabitable structure.
Skid Row: Chapter 1
Areas of town where police and city officials push people who are without housing. These areas have cheap motels and bars, and people experiencing homelessness live on the street or in makeshift campsites.
Social Capital: Chapter 1
Who you know. Social capital includes a social network of people who can be used to help with information necessary to survive in any social environment.

Social Construct: Chapter 1

Social constructs are definitions created by people in power and accepted
by society. An example of this is the stereotypes of people who are
homeless today being categorized as lazy or deviant while in the past,
'hobos' were viewed in a more positive light. Social constructs can
change over time and from place to place.

Social Security Act of 1935: Chapter 1

Created a system to allocate pensions for people who are elderly and
welfare for mothers.

Social Security Disability Amendment of 1980: Chapter 3

Restricted the ability of individuals to qualify for housing subsidies and
vouchers for rooming houses from the federal government.

Stigma: Chapter 7

A negative label applied to an individual or a group.

Structural theories: Chapter 4

Focus on the effects of social structure on people's lives.

Structuration: Chapter 4

Anthony Giddens' theory argues that social structures reproduce social
systems and inequality.

Supplemental Food and Nutrition Program (SNAP): Chapter 2

Commonly known as food stamps, SNAP is a governmental program
that gives low-income Americans food vouchers each month. Currently, the government loads money onto a card each month for individuals to use at grocery stores or other places that sell food and accept
the vouchers.

Surplus Labor Force: Chapter 4

Extra people in society that can replace workers. As long as there is
someone willing to work for low wages, workers are replaceable. This
keeps workers working, and working hard, because they know they
are dispensable.

Temporary Aid to Needy Families (TANF): Chapter 3

Restructured AFDC. Created work requirements for welfare and reduced
the amount of time a person could receive welfare to five years.

Toxic Charity: Chapter 1, Chapter 5, Chapter 7

The toxic charity ideology promotes the idea that if you do not make
people work for what they are given, they will expect to be given a
handout and become dependent on charity.

War on Poverty: Chapter 1

A movement by President Johnson to eliminate poverty by expanding
social programs.

Wayfarers Lodges: Chapter 1, Chapter 7

Temporary housing for people who were poor in the nineteenth and
early twentieth centuries. Residents were often required to work for
the lodge in return for their housing.

Weak Ties: Chapter 1

People who may or may not be close to others but can help them succeed by giving them information about jobs or housing or giving one
a reference.

Welfare queen: Chapter 2

While running for president, Ronald Reagan stereotyped people who
were receiving welfare as a bunch of "welfare queens" out to scam
taxpayers out of their hard-earned money. This untrue characterization changed the public perception of welfare and supported reducing
welfare funding once he was in office.

Index